THE IVP NEW TESTAMENT COMMENTARY SERIES

Galatians

G. Walter Hansen

Grant R. Osborne
series editor

D. Stuart Briscoe
Haddon Robinson
consulting editors

INTERVARSITY PRESS
DOWNERS GROVE, ILLINOIS, USA
LEICESTER, ENGLAND

InterVarsity Press
P.O. Box 1400, Downers Grove, Illinois 60515, U.S.A.
38 De Montfort Street, Leicester LE1 7GP, England

InterVarsity Press, U.S.A., is the book-publishing division of InterVarsity Christian Fellowship, a
student movement active on campus at hundreds of universities, colleges and schools of nursing
in the United States of America, and a member movement of the International Fellowship of
Evangelical Students. For information about local and regional activities, write Public Relations
Dept., InterVarsity Christian Fellowship, 6400 Schroeder Rd., P.O. Box 7895, Madison, WI
53707-7895.

Inter-Varsity Press, England, is the book-publishing division of the Universities and Colleges Christian Fellowship (formerly the Inter-Varsity Fellowship), a student movement linking Christian
Unions in universities and colleges throughout the United Kingdom and the Republic of Ireland,
and a member movement of the International Fellowship of Evangelical Students. For information about local and national activities write to UCCF, 38 De Montfort Street, Leicester LE1 7GP.

USA ISBN 0-8308-1809-X
UK ISBN 0-85111-675-2

Printed in the United States of America ∞

Library of Congress Cataloging-in-Publication Data

Hansen, G. Walter, 1946-
    Galatians/G. Walter Hansen.
        p.   cm. — (The IVP New Testament commentary series)
    Includes bibliographical references.
    ISBN 0-8308-1809-X
    1. Bible.   N.T. Galatians—Commentaries.   I. Title.   II. Series.
BS2685.3.H36   1993
227'.407—dc20   93-38941
                                                                          CIP

British Library Cataloguing in Publication Data

A catalogue record for this book is available from the British Library.

17	16	15	14	13	12	11	10	9	8	7	6	5	4	3	2	1
08	07	06	05	04	03	02	01	00	99	98	97	96	95	94

*To my colleagues
at Trinity Theological College
in Singapore*

General Preface

In an age of proliferating commentary series, one might easily ask why add yet another to the seeming glut. The simplest answer is that no other series has yet achieved what we had in mind—a series to and from the church, that seeks to move from the text to its contemporary relevance and application.

No other series offers the unique combination of solid, biblical exposition and helpful explanatory notes in the same user-friendly format. No other series has tapped the unique blend of scholars and pastors who share both a passion for faithful exegesis and a deep concern for the church. Based on the New International Version of the Bible, one of the most widely used modern translations, the IVP New Testament Commentary Series builds on the NIV's reputation for clarity and accuracy. Individual commentators indicate clearly whenever they depart from the standard translation as required by their understanding of the original Greek text.

The series contributors represent a wide range of theological traditions, united by a common commitment to the authority of Scripture for

Christian faith and practice. Their efforts here are directed toward applying the unchanging message of the New Testament to the ever-changing world in which we live.

Readers will find in each volume not only traditional discussions of authorship and backgrounds, but useful summaries of principal themes and approaches to contemporary application. To bridge the gap between commentaries that stress the flow of an author's argument but skip over exegetical nettles and those that simply jump from one difficulty to another, we have developed our unique format that expounds the text in uninterrupted form on the upper portion of each page while dealing with other issues underneath in verse-keyed notes. To avoid clutter we have also adopted a social studies note system that keys references to the bibliography.

We offer the series in hope that pastors, students, Bible teachers and small group leaders of all sorts will find it a valuable aid—one that stretches the mind and moves the heart to ever-growing faithfulness and obedience to our Lord Jesus Christ.

Author's Preface

The warm welcome of churches in Singapore where I have served enables me to see how Paul's letter to the Galatians meets their needs. And as I have seen how the Holy Spirit can use that ancient document to set believers free to live for God and to heal painful divisions, my heart has burned with desire to communicate those insights so that others who long for a greater measure of freedom and unity in Christ Jesus will experience the "truth of the gospel" as they are "led by the Spirit." So I am indeed grateful for the opportunity given to me by IVP to provide a contemporary application of Paul's declaration of freedom in Christ.

I am well aware of the great number of excellent commentaries written on Galatians. My edition of John Bunyan's *Pilgrim's Progress* has a drawing of Bunyan seated by an open window, totally absorbed in his study of Martin Luther's commentary on Galatians. Bunyan wrote, "I do prefer this book of Martin Luther upon the Galatians (excepting the Holy Bible) before all the books that ever I have seen, as most fit for a wounded conscience." Like Bunyan, I also treasure Luther's commentary, and John Chrysostom's (written A.D. 395-398), and numerous commentaries written in my own time by many gifted scholars. The notes in this commentary cannot possibly express the wealth of insights gained from those who have gone before me. The major scholarly work of my own mentor, Richard Longenecker, deserves special mention. His direction of my doctoral dissertation on Abraham in Galatians and his recent commentary on Galatians established a solid foundation for this commentary.

At the same time that I have been writing this commentary, I have also been serving with my colleagues at Trinity Theological College in Singapore. They have often listened graciously to my efforts and responded with helpful suggestions. I joyfully dedicate this book to them.

G. Walter Hansen
Christmas 1993

Introduction

The first time I taught Paul's letter to the Galatians was during a church fight in Singapore. Ethnic rivalries endangered the unity of the church. The cross was being eclipsed by social competition: "We traditional Chinese are better than you westernized Chinese. You are like bananas: yellow on the outside, white on the inside!" "We Chinese are better than you Caucasian expatriates." These attitudes were not always expressed openly, but they were a turbulent undercurrent in the life of the church. Name-calling went in the other direction as well. When the American pastor's cultural stress reached the boiling point, he bitterly called the traditional Chinese elders a "bunch of hooligans." After they found *hooligans* in their Chinese-English dictionary, they were enraged by what seemed to them a terrible insult. It was especially tragic that this conflict occurred in Singapore, a society that was striving to find a basis for harmony in the midst of ethnic diversity. Instead of presenting a model for such harmony, the church expressed racial prejudice and exerted social pressure in ways that jeopardized the fabric of society.

In that context, our church desperately needed to hear and obey the central truths of Paul's letter to the Galatians. His letter addresses Christians whose preoccupation with keeping the law was splitting their churches along racial lines, separating Jews from Gentiles. Such splits could not be tolerated, because "there is neither Jew nor Greek, slave nor free, male nor female, for you are all one in Christ Jesus" (3:28). This new community which transcends all racial, social and gender barriers is based on the "truth of the gospel" (2:5, 14): Christ was crucified to set us free from the curse of the law so that we might receive his Spirit (3:1-2, 13-14). The Spirit, not the law, gives us our new identity as sons and daughters of God (4:6). Believers must defend their freedom in Christ from social pressures that promote ethnic divisions (5:1-6); they must also use their freedom to serve one another in love (5:13-14). We are no longer under the law that divides us; we are led by the Spirit who unites us (5:18).

Wherever ethnic rivalries are destroying societies, the book of Galatians calls Christians to express the truth of the gospel in communities where there are no ethnic or social or gender divisions. "For," as Paul says, "in Christ Jesus neither circumcision nor uncircumcision has any value. The only thing that counts is faith expressing itself through love" (5:6). When we understand that Paul's reference to circumcision actually encompassed all the Jewish customs that separated the Jewish race from all other ethnic groups in his day, we see that he is using the truth of the gospel to obliterate all ethnic divisions. As he emphasizes by repetition, "neither circumcision nor uncircumcision means anything; what counts is a new creation" (6:15). This "new creation" is a new community of all believers where the divisions and alienations of the world are overcome and healed in Christ. While there is freedom in Christ to maintain and respect ethnic, social and gender distinctives, these distinctives must not be allowed to cause divisions between believers in Christ.

The central focus of the entire letter is the equality and unity of all believers in Christ. Paul demonstrates that faith in Christ and the consequent presence of the Spirit establish the identity and guide the behavior of those who belong to the family of believers.

☐ The Crisis in Galatia

To appreciate Paul's letter to the Galatians we need to understand the crisis that provoked his response. Our understanding of the crisis and of the theology of Paul's opponents must be based on a careful reading of and between the lines of Paul's letters. While I acknowledge the dangers of "mirror reading" (see Barclay 1987:73-93), the basic picture I present here is, I think, plausible. Jewett (1971:198-212) and Martyn (1983:221-35) are especially helpful for understanding the crisis Paul was addressing.

When Paul first preached the gospel in Galatia, a number of Galatians accepted him and his message with open hearts (4:13-15). When they believed the gospel of Christ crucified, they received the Spirit of God (3:1-2). The presence of the Spirit, who did miracles among them (3:5) and led them in their worship of God as "*Abba,* Father" (4:6), confirmed the blessing of God on these new Gentile believers.

But not long after Paul planted the churches in Galatia, some Jewish Christians taught these new believers that it was necessary to belong to the Jewish people in order to receive the full blessing of God. Therefore they required the marks of identity peculiar to the Jewish people: circumcision, sabbath observance and kosher food (see 2:12-14; 4:10; 5:2-3; 6:12-13). No doubt they used the story of Abraham's willingness to be circumcised to persuade the Galatian believers that without membership in the Jewish people by circumcision they could not participate in the covenantal blessings promised to Abraham. Evidently they also preempted Paul's authority by claiming support from the higher authority of the original apostles in the Jerusalem church. They probably pointed out that the mother church in Jerusalem still faithfully followed Jewish customs.

The message of the rival teachers struck a responsive chord in the Galatian churches. The Galatian converts may have been feeling a loss of social identity, since their new faith in Christ excluded them from both the pagan temples and the Jewish synagogues. So they sought identification with the Jewish people—God's people—by observing the law. Apparently they were also convinced that if they came under the discipline of the Mosaic law, the law could empower them to overcome evil. Mesmerized by the message of the impressive teachers of the law, they became disenchanted with Paul.

Their focus shifted from union with Christ by faith and dependence

on the Spirit to identification with the Jewish nation and observance of
the law.

☐ Destination

The destination and date for Paul's letter to the Galatians have provided
a notorious and fascinating historical puzzle for scholars. But since the
outcome has little if any effect on the interpretation of the major themes
of the letter, those who are not especially interested in such puzzles may
want to skip this section and move on to read about the form of the
letter.

The Pauline authorship of this letter has never been seriously ques-
tioned, but there has been a long, arduous debate about the destination
and date of the letter. A survey of all the positions taken in this debate
would be impossibly lengthy and complicated; instead I simply set forth
the most basic points of the discussion.

Paul addressed his letter to the "churches in Galatia" (1:2) and rebuked the recipients for being "foolish Galatians" (3:1). Some scholars
(notably Lightfoot 1957:18-35 and Betz 1979:3-5; 1992:872), following
the majority of patristic, medieval and Reformation commentators, argue
that the letter was written to churches in or near Ancyra, Pessinus and
Tavium, three cities in northern Asia Minor (modern Turkey). This territory was originally conquered and settled by a distinct ethnic group of
Celtic (Gaulish) descent in the third century B.C. Those who hold to this
"North Galatia" hypothesis take Acts 16:6 ("the region of Phrygia and
Galatia") and Acts 18:23 ("the region of Galatia and Phrygia") as refer-
ences to Paul's missionary trips to "North Galatia." From their perspec-
tive "Galatia" in these two verses designates the northern region of Asia
Minor, not the southern Phrygian and Lyconian regions. The proponents
of the North Galatia hypothesis also believe Paul is referring to a particular racial group when he addresses the Galatians (Lightfoot 1957:19-21;
Luhrmann 1992:2). They consider it unlikely that Paul would refer to
Christians of Phrygia and Lyconia as Galatians when they were actually
not Galatians by race but by Roman rule. The true Galatians, descendants
of the Celtic tribes from Gaul, inhabited the area of the present Turkish
capital, Ankara.

Other scholars (notably W. Ramsay 1962:91-193; Burton 1921:xxi-xliv;

Bruce 1982:3-18; Longenecker 1990:lxi-lxxii; Mitchell 1992:871) argue that the "churches in Galatia" were planted by Paul, as recorded in Acts 13—14, in Pisidian Antioch, Iconium, Lystra and Derbe in southern Asia Minor and consisted of Gentiles from diverse ethnic origins (Phrygians, Pisidians and Lyconians). Those who hold to the "South Galatia" address for the letter take Acts 16:6 and Acts 18:23 as references to Paul's return trips to South Galatia.

The weight of evidence seems to be in favor of a South Galatian location (Hemer 1990:227-307 is the best recent defense of this view). In Paul's time Galatia was the name for the entire Roman province stretching from Pontus in the north to Pamphylia in the south. All the residents of this province were properly called Galatians, whatever their ethnic origin. By the third century A.D., the province of Galatia was reduced to approximately its ancient ethnological dimensions, the original northern territory of the Celtic invaders. It is not surprising that patristic commentators, followed by medieval and Reformation commentators, assumed that Paul had addressed his letter to churches in North Galatia, since that was the only Galatia that existed in patristic times.

Paul normally classified the churches that he founded according to Roman provinces: "churches in the province of Asia" (1 Cor 16:19), "Macedonian churches" (2 Cor 8:1), "you in Achaia" (2 Cor 9:2). So it would be natural for Paul to refer to churches in Iconium, Antioch of Pisidia, Lystra and Derbe (all cities within the Roman province of Galatia in his time) as "the churches in Galatia" and to refer to the members of those churches as Galatians. Indeed, no other single name would have been appropriate for them. Since there is no clear evidence that Paul founded churches in North Galatia, it seems best to take the account of Acts 13—14 as a record of the founding of the churches in Galatia that are addressed in Paul's letter to the Galatians. Acts 16:6 and 18:23 refer to subsequent visits by Paul to strengthen those same churches.

☐ Date
Paul begins his letter with a sketch of his life from the time of his conversion to the time of writing this letter. A comparison of this autobiography with material in his other letters and with the account of his life in Acts has led to a number of conflicting hypotheses regarding the

date of this letter. These hypotheses can be evaluated in the light of three lines of evidence: (1) Paul's Jerusalem visits, (2) the meaning of *first* in Galatians 4:13 and (3) the location of the churches in North or South Galatia.

The reliability of the narrative framework of Acts is accepted on other grounds in this discussion. While it is important to recognize that the letters of Paul are the primary source for building any Pauline chronology, his letters need to be related in some way to Acts if the trustworthiness of Acts is accepted. Some (like Knox) who reject the narrative framework of Acts construct an entirely different chronology on the basis of the letters alone (see Donfried 1992:1021-22).

Paul's Jerusalem Visits and the Date The basic point of dispute regarding the Jerusalem visits is how to match Paul's visits to Jerusalem described in this letter with his visits to Jerusalem described in Acts. Only two visits are mentioned in Galatians: the first postconversion visit, in 1:18, and the conference visit, in 2:1-10. If we accept the reliability of the overall narrative framework of Acts, then we have an account of five of Paul's visits to Jerusalem recorded in Acts: (1) first postconversion visit, Acts 9:26-30, (2) famine relief visit, Acts 11:30, (3) conference visit, Acts 15:1-30, (4) quick visit, Acts 18:22, and (5) arrest visit, Acts 21:15-17. Of the many attempts to relate the visits described in Galatians to those of Acts, two merit special attention: Galatians 2:1-10 = Acts 15:1-30 and Galatians 2:1-10 = Acts 11:30.

Galatians 2:1-10 = Acts 15:1-30 If we match the Galatians 1:18 (first postconversion) visit with the Acts 9:26-30 (first postconversion) visit and the Galatians 2:1-10 conference visit with the Acts 15:1-30 conference visit, then Galatians would be placed after the Jerusalem conference described in Acts 15:1-30 (= Gal 2:1-10). Such an equation seems reasonable, since the two accounts of the conference visit refer to the same issue (the obligation of Gentile converts to be circumcised and to keep the Jewish law), the same participants (Paul and Barnabas go to Jerusalem to confer with Peter and James and others) and the same decision (the requirement of circumcision is not imposed upon Gentile converts).

Major objections raised against this equation point to Paul's statement under oath in Galatians 1:15-24; in surveying his encounters with the Jerusalem church he makes no reference to the famine relief visit (Acts 11:27-30) or to the "apostolic decrees" of the conference (Acts 15:20, 29). Some scholars assert that holding to the equation Galatians 2:1-10 = Acts 15:1-20 in the light of these two omissions necessarily involves an attack on the truthfulness of Paul's account, or the account in Acts, or both. Yet such scholars as J. B. Lightfoot (1957:127-28), H. Ridderbos (1953:32-34) and R. A. Cole (1989:31-35), who certainly uphold the reliability of both accounts, argue that neither the famine relief visit (Acts 11:27-30) nor the "apostolic decrees" (Acts 15:20, 29) were relevant to his discussion in Galatians 1 and therefore he had no obligation to record them. The point of Paul's autobiography was to record his relationship with the original apostles in Jerusalem, not simply his visits to Jerusalem; it was not necessary for him to refer to the famine relief visit (Acts 11:27-30) since he did not meet with the apostles then. At least the Acts account of that visit makes no mention of such a meeting. And it makes sense that Paul would not refer to the apostolic decrees, since the Acts account does not present them as a negation of the major decision not to require circumcision. Therefore Paul's claim that "those who seemed to be important . . . added nothing to my message" (Gal 2:6) fits with the record of the conference visit in Acts 15. Since the Galatian Christians were all too eager to come under whatever decrees came from the Jerusalem church, Paul may have decided that any mention of the apostolic decrees would have been ill advised unless it was absolutely necessary. Since he never appealed to the apostolic decrees in any of his letters, we may conclude that he did not feel obligated to do so. After all, his authority was not based on decrees from Jerusalem but on "revelation from Jesus Christ" (1:12).

Another criticism of the Galatians 2:1-10 = Acts 15:1-20 equation is that it makes it difficult to explain the withdrawal of Peter and "even Barnabas" from table fellowship with Gentile Christians in Antioch (Gal 2:11-14) *after* guidelines for such fellowship had already been established at the Jerusalem conference, according to the Acts account. But even if the conflict in Antioch occurred before the Acts 15 conference, as some scholars suggest, it still is difficult to explain Peter's behavior. We still have to ask why he would withdraw from table fellowship with

Gentile Christians in Antioch after the Jerusalem conference described by Paul in Galatians 2:1-10. From Paul's perspective, Peter's conduct was indefensible because it violated the truth of the gospel which had been defended in the Jerusalem conference.

Galatians 2:1-10 = Acts 11:27-30 The criticisms of the Galatians 2:1-10 = Acts 15:1-20 equation have led some to suggest another equation: Galatians 2:1-10 = Acts 11:27-30. The benefit of this equation is that it avoids any suspicion that Paul has failed to report all of his post-conversion visits to Jerusalem. In this equation the first two visits in Acts equal the two visits listed in Galatians. And Paul did not refer to the apostolic decrees for the simple reason that this letter was written before the conference in which those decrees were set forth.

It is also easy to see similarities between Paul's account of the conflict in Antioch in Galatians 2:11-14 and Luke's Acts 15:1-2 description of the conflict in Antioch before the Jerusalem conference. Both refer to a conflict over the application of the Jewish law to Gentile converts, and both indicate that the conflict was stirred up by a delegation from Jerusalem. If these accounts refer to the same event, it would be reasonable to conclude that Paul wrote Galatians on the eve of the Jerusalem conference of Acts 15:1-20. And if so, we can identify the conference visit of Galatians 2:1-10 with the famine relief visit of Acts 11:27-30.

But this identification also faces problems. There is no record of a conference visit in Acts 11:27-30, or even any indication that Paul and Barnabas met with the apostles. Of course Acts is a selective account, but there is very little evidence in the text for matching the Galatians 2:1-10 visit with the Acts 11:27-30 visit. Even though there are minor differences between Galatians 2:1-10 and Acts 15:1-20, at least both passages seem to describe a conference in Jerusalem. Furthermore, if Galatians 2:1-10 = Acts 11:27-30, then there were two conferences in Jerusalem: first the Galatians 2:1-10 (= Acts 11:27-30) conference; second the Acts 15:1-30 conference. Many scholars have thought it highly unlikely that there were two conferences in quick succession in which the same people debated the same issue with the same outcome. This duplication of conferences is unnecessary if the Galatians 2:1-10 = Acts 15:1-20 equation stands. In my opinion, this equation is the least problematic. Therefore, it seems that the letter to the Galatians was written after Paul's

Jerusalem conference visit of Acts 15 (= Galatians 2:1-10).

The "First" Visit and the Date (4:13) Paul's reference to the time when he "first preached the gospel" in Galatia (4:13) has been taken as a clue for the date of the letter. Unfortunately, all sides of the debate claim this clue as support. Even if the term *first* should be taken as a true comparative (the former of two), it is by no means clear which visit it designates: it could refer to the Acts 16:6 visit as preceding the visit of Acts 18:23, or it could refer to the visit of Acts 13:14—14:23 as preceding the visit of Acts 16:6, or it could refer to the Acts 13:14—14:21 visit as preceding the return journey of Acts 14:21-23. So this term does not provide much help in dating the letter to the Galatians.

The Destination and the Date The question of the letter's date is related to the question of destination. But it must be admitted that a determination of the destination does not necessarily determine the date. If the framework of Acts is accepted, then a destination of North Galatia means that the letter was written sometime after the so-called first visit to North Galatia (after Acts 18:23), sometime after A.D. 53. If South Galatia was the destination (as seems more likely in light of the discussion above) and the equation of Galatians 2:1-10 = Acts 11:27-30 is accepted, then the letter could have been written immediately after the first missionary journey to South Galatia (Acts 13—14) and before the Jerusalem conference in A.D. 49. But if South Galatia was the destination and the equation of Galatians 2:1-10 = Acts 15:1-20 is correct (as I think it is), then the letter was written sometime after the Jerusalem conference, anytime after A.D. 50.

A comparison of Galatians with 2 Corinthians and Romans shows a similarity of tone and themes, especially in relation to the controversy over the role of the Mosaic law in Gentile churches. This similarity may indicate that these three letters were written during the same period, a time when Paul had to struggle fiercely for his Gentile churches' freedom from bondage to the Jewish way of life. Perhaps the absence of any of the language of the doctrine of "justification by faith, not by works of the law" in the Thessalonian correspondence indicates that Galatians was written after those early letters. If these observations are accepted as supportive evidence, then we may conclude (as I do) that the letter was written sometime between A.D. 54 and 56.

Of course we must admit that theological comparisons with other letters have been used to support both an early date (Longenecker 1990:lxxxiii) and a late date (Lightfoot 1957:43-56; Buck 1951:113-22; Cole 1989:32-34). The subjective nature of such comparisons and the occasional nature of Paul's letters (each letter responds to a specific occasion) mean that these attempts can be only secondary lines of support for theories in search of firmer ground.

☐ The Form of the Letter

Since my outline of Galatians depends on an understanding of the form of Paul's letter and the structure of his argument, I need to define those matters briefly here.

A detailed comparison of Galatians to Hellenistic letters of the same period indicates that Paul used a standard form of letter called the "rebuke-request" form (see Hansen 1989a:22-44 and Longenecker 1990:c-cix). Departing from his custom in all the rest of his letters, in Galatians Paul does not follow his salutation (1:1-5) with any form of thanksgiving. Instead he expresses astonishment and rebuke: "I am astonished that you are so quickly deserting the one who called you by the grace of Christ" (1:6). The expression "I am astonished" was often used in letters of that time to rebuke the reader for not meeting the expectations of the writer. The expression of rebuke was usually followed by reasons for the rebuke. Paul scolds his readers for their disloyalty to the gospel (1:6-10) and undergirds that rebuke with an autobiographical account of his loyalty to the truth of the gospel (1:11—2:21). Then he rebukes them for their foolishness regarding the gospel (3:1-5) and undergirds that rebuke by explaining the meaning of the gospel in the light of his exposition of the Scriptures (3:6—4:11).

Letters of rebuke also contained requests to set things right. Paul begins his request in 4:12 with a personal appeal to imitate him in his stand for the freedom of the gospel. This appeal is strengthened by an autobiographical account of his relationship with the Galatian believers (4:12-20) and an allegorical treatment of the Abraham story (4:21-31). The request to stand fast for freedom is then spelled out in a series of specific ethical instructions (5:1—6:10). Paul underlines the main themes of the letter in his own handwritten subscription (6:11-18).

☐ The Structure of the Argument

Recent rhetorical analyses have attempted to explain the methods and structures of Paul's argumentation in Galatians. They point to many similarities between the structure of Paul's argument in Galatians and the guidelines for rhetoric in classical rhetorical handbooks. H. D. Betz classifies Paul's argument as an example of forensic rhetoric, since he is viewed as adopting the tactics of persuasion used in law courts to address the judge or jury in order to defend or accuse someone regarding past actions (1979:14-15). Paul defends himself against accusations (1:10); at the same time he accuses his opponents of perverting the gospel (1:7). Using the categories of classical forensic rhetoric, Betz outlines Galatians as follows:

I. Epistolary Prescript (1:1-5)

II. Exordium (introduction, 1:6-11)

III. Narratio (narration, 1:12—2:14)

IV. Propositio (proposition, 2:15-21)

V. Probatio (confirmation, 3:1—4:31)

VI. Exhortatio (exhortation, 5:1—6:10)

VII. Epistolary Postscript/Peroratio (conclusion, 6:11-18)

But Betz has to admit that he is not able to cite parallels to the exhortation section (5:1—6:10) from the classical rhetorical handbooks. For this reason G. Kennedy argues that Galatians is best viewed as deliberative rhetoric, since it aims to exhort or dissuade the audience regarding future actions by demonstrating that those actions are expedient or harmful (1984:144-52). Paul seeks to dissuade the Galatian believers from following the false teachers by pointing to the harmful effects: severance from Christ and grace (5:4), exclusion from the kingdom of God (5:21) and a reaping of corruption (6:8). He underscores the expediency of the course of action he has exhorted them to follow by offering the promise of the harvest of eternal life (6:8) and granting a benediction on all those who walk according to "this rule" (6:16). (Betz's rhetorical analysis of Galatians has also been reviewed and refined by others, including Brinsmead [1982], Hall [1987] and Smit

[1989].)

It seems best to classify Paul's Galatians argument as a mixture of forensic and deliberative rhetoric (Hansen 1989a:55-71). The rebuke section of the letter (1:6—4:11) has the characteristics of forensic rhetoric, but at 4:12 a major shift to deliberative rhetoric occurs. Paul is no longer so much concerned to accuse or defend as he is to persuade the Galatian believers to adopt a certain course of action. He begins his appeal to this new course of action in 4:12: "Become like me." That exhortation is then supported by the command from the Abraham story to "get rid of the slave woman and her son" (4:30), clarified by authoritative instructions to stand in freedom (5:1-12) and defined in specific terms in the ethical exhortation to walk in the Spirit (5:13—6:10).

This study of the form of the letter and the structure of the argument produces the basic outline that is followed in this commentary.

☐ The Social Dimension of Justification by Faith

My interpretation of key issues in this commentary departs somewhat from many traditional interpretations. It is important, therefore, to clarify some of the perspectives that guide my interpretation.

Since the Reformation, most Protestants have viewed Galatians as an impassioned defense of the doctrine of justification by faith apart from the works of the law. I certainly agree wholeheartedly that Paul uses the verb *to justify* (2:16-17; 3:8, 11, 24; 5:4) to express his conviction that God has declared believers in Christ righteous on the basis of their faith in Christ, not on the basis of their observance of the law. There is no question in my mind that this letter undercuts any teaching that right standing before God depends on anything but faith in Christ.

But the Protestant preoccupation with the question "How can I, a sinner, be right before a just and holy God?" has resulted in an individualistic perspective on justification by grace through faith. The social implications of justification have been largely ignored. As a result the doctrine of justification by faith has been seriously misunderstood and misrepresented. In a book widely read in Singapore, Tu Wei-Ming, a Harvard Confucist scholar, asserts that the Protestant doctrine of justification has led to an excessive individualism: "The Protestant dispenses with all intermediaries between God and himself. He relates directly to

God from the secret recesses of his heart and in his inner separateness from his fellowmen. . . . The Protestant ethic has led to all kinds of problems such as excessive individualism and excessive rights-consciousness" (1984:74-75, 86). Perhaps Protestant doctrine would not have been subjected to such a devastating critique if the social implications of the doctrine of justification had received proper emphasis. (Note that the social dimension of justification has, however, been given special emphasis in the twentieth century by Barth [1968:241-67], Dahl [1977:95-120] and Cousar [1982:56-59].)

In Galatians Paul develops his argument for justification by faith in order to correct a social problem: Gentile believers have been excluded from fellowship with Jewish believers because they did not observe the law. Paul demonstrates that justification by faith means that Gentile believers are included within the people of God; on the basis of this doctrine Gentile believers have the right to eat at the same table with Jewish believers.

Paul uses the Old Testament story of Abraham's faith to show that faith in God is the mark of belonging to Abraham's family. The conclusion of his argument from Scripture in Galatians 3 declares the unity and equality of all in Christ: "There is neither Jew nor Greek, slave nor free, male nor female, for you are all one in Christ Jesus" (3:28).

If a church does not defend in practice the equality and unity of all in Christ, it implicitly communicates that justification is not by faith but by race, social status or some other standard. Faith must not be defined in individualistic terms; faith as Paul defines it in Galatians 5:6 is "faith expressing itself through love."

☐ Paul's Critique of Judaism
Paul's letter to the Galatians has been read as a direct attack on Jewish people for their legalism. But a careful analysis of his letter shows that his attack is directed against the Galatian Christians who had departed from the true gospel and against Jewish Christians who had perverted that gospel. There is no basis for interpreting his letter as a direct attack on Judaism. (See especially Siker 1991:28-50.)

Yet it is true that what Paul says about the fulfillment of the Abrahamic promise and the function of the Mosaic law has implications for Judaism.

Since the seed of Abraham is Christ (3:16), identification with Christ through faith, not identification with the Jewish people through the law, is the only way to be included in the seed of Abraham and to inherit the fulfillment of the promises to Abraham (3:29). The God-given function of the Mosaic law (see below) could not obstruct or negate the fulfillment of God's promise to bless all nations in Christ, the seed of Abraham (3:8, 15-19). Thus law-keeping Jews who were still relating to God on the basis of the Mosaic covenant needed to turn in faith to Christ and to find the fulfillment of God's promises in him.

Furthermore, it is not accurate to view Paul's letter to the Galatians as an attack on Jewish Christians for legalism in their own relationship with God. In 2:15-16 Paul expresses the common confession of Jewish Christians: that justification is by faith in Jesus Christ, not by the works of the law. Jewish Christians did not have a legalistic view of their own relationship to God; they knew that they had right standing with God not because of their observance of the law but because of their faith in Christ. Their problem was not legalism; it was ethnocentrism. They were convinced that the blessing of God was given to the people of God, and that only the Jewish people were the people of God. So they were insisting that all Gentile Christians had to become part of the Jewish nation before they could enjoy the full blessing of God.

This demand did require Gentile believers to take a legalistic approach to their relationship to God. The Gentile believers were led to think that their identification with the Jewish nation by observing the law was a necessary condition for a right relationship with God. But Paul rejects this legalistic approach for the Gentile believers precisely because it contradicts what the Jewish Christians knew to be true for themselves: "We who are Jews by birth and not 'Gentile sinners' know that a man is not justified by observing the law, but by faith in Jesus Christ" (2:15-16).

☐ The Social and Moral Functions of the Mosaic Law

The vast and growing literature on Paul and the law cannot possibly be summarized in this brief introduction. But it is important to indicate two perspectives on this subject which guide my interpretation of Galatians.

First, we need to keep in view "the social function of the law" in Paul's day if we are to understand Paul's statements about the law. The Mosaic law was used to draw a line between the Jewish people and all other racial-social groups. The vast system of Mosaic regulations "locked up" the Jewish people; they were "held prisoners by the law" (3:23), separated socially by the Mosaic law from all other ethnic groups. The Jewish people identified themselves as the people of God through their observance of the Mosaic law. Under the influence of the rival teachers, the Galatian converts were trying to keep the Mosaic law so that they could be identified with the Jewish people, the people of God. (Dunn has highlighted the social function of the law [1990:129-264]. See Watson for a sociological approach to Galatians [1986:49-72].)

Paul's arguments against that use of the Mosaic law as a line of social demarcation are based on the experience of the Spirit and the exposition of Scripture. The presence of the Spirit establishes the identity of the Gentile believers as sons and daughters of God. This experience of the Spirit is the fulfillment of God's promised blessing to Abraham that he would bless all nations in one family. Since the Galatian believers were already identified as the people of God by the presence of the Spirit in the fulfillment of God's promises to Abraham, it was "foolish" for them to seek to establish their social identity by observance of the Mosaic law.

Second, we need to understand Paul's view of the moral function of the Mosaic law. While all commentaries on Galatians (as far as I know) interpret Paul as rejecting any attempt to keep the Mosaic law in order to *earn* God's blessing, very few have the perspective that Paul also rejects attempting to keep the Mosaic law as an appropriate *response* to God's blessing. In other words, although everyone agrees that observance of the Mosaic law is not the way to *begin* the Christian life, many still maintain that observance of the Mosaic law is the way to *continue* in the Christian life. But it seems clear to me that Paul proclaims freedom from obligation to the Mosaic law (5:1-6) not only as the basis for beginning the Christian life but also as the basis for continuing the Christian life. (An excellent recent study of the moral function of the law is presented by Westerholm [1988:105-222].)

Paul teaches in this letter that the Mosaic law has a moral function, but only negatively: it points out transgressions and imprisons all under sin (3:10, 19, 22); it cannot impart life or produce righteousness (3:21). Therefore we cannot attain moral perfection by trying to observe the

Mosaic law (3:2-3), nor can we win moral victory over the sinful nature's desires by submitting to the guidance of the Mosaic law (5:13-18). But what the law cannot do God does by his grace: through the cross of Christ he removes the curse of the law (3:13); by the Spirit he reproduces the righteous character of his Son in us (5:22-23) so that the ultimate moral standard of the law is fulfilled (5:14; 6:2). Therefore if we are controlled by the Spirit, we are not under slavery to the Mosaic law (5:18). We are free from the curse of the law (3:13) and the supervision of the law (3:25) so that we can live for God (2:19) by serving one another in love (5:13).

Outline of Galatians

COMMENTARY

☐ Greetings (1:1-5)

One missionary friend always captures my attention by scrawling a special message to me in red ink across the top of his formally typed prayer letter and drawing red arrows to several paragraphs circled in red. The main points of the letter shout out at me. Once I see them, I know what the letter is all about; the rest expands and explains.

Paul grabs our attention in the introduction of his letter to the Galatians by filling the typical formal greetings with two strong emphases: his God-given authority and his Christ-centered message. Once you grasp these points, you have the gist of the whole letter.

God-Given Authority (1:1) In Paul's day, Greek letters began with a formal salutation: the writer's name, the recipient's name and a greeting. Paul introduces himself as *an apostle—sent not from men nor by man, but by Jesus Christ and God the Father, who raised him from the dead.* The title *apostle* designated one who was given authority to represent another. This title was used in the early church in a broad sense to designate missionary leaders (see Acts 14:14). The title was also used in a narrow sense for those who had been given unique authority from Christ to be his representatives and the founders of the church (see Acts

1:21-26). In Galatians 1 Paul claims the title for himself in the narrow sense. He recognizes that there were those who were apostles before him (1:17), but he does not see himself as subordinate to the original apostles. If the original apostles had been the source of his commission or the agents of his commission (as the false teachers in the Galatian church were probably suggesting), then he would have been subordinate to them. But his authority was not derived from a human source or even through a human agency; his authority was directly given to him *by Jesus Christ and God the Father, who raised him from the dead.* Note how this antithesis clearly places Jesus Christ on the side of God *(not from men nor by man, but by Jesus Christ).* The risen Lord had directly commissioned Paul. So those who challenged Paul's message were in fact challenging the Lord who had commissioned him.

Have you ever found yourself questioning, challenging or even rejecting any of Paul's statements? Paul's claim to apostolic authority should cause us to reconsider when our own opinions or "the general consensus of scholarly opinion" would lead us to disagree with him. It appears that the Galatian readers were in danger of turning from Paul's message and hence discrediting his authority. From Paul's time to our day, many have pointed to apparent contradictions and "hard sayings" in his letters and scolded him for his errant teachings. But if Paul has apostolic authority by virtue of his direct commission from the risen Christ, then we may not judge him on the basis of our opinions, for he is the apostolic representative of Christ. Our acceptance of Paul's authority should be guided by Jesus' own words to his apostles: "He who receives you receives me" (Mt 10:40).

Paul's affirmation of his divine appointment also encourages us to affirm our own divine appointments. We may not play the role of apostles, but we are given work to do by God's appointment. If we view our

Notes: **1:1** The office of the prophet in Israel's history is the background for Paul's understanding of his authority as an *apostle,* since he describes his apostolic appointment in language that echoes the prophetic call (see 1:15-16; compare Is 49:1-3; Jer 1:4-5). The rabbinic office of the *shaliach* also sheds some light on the meaning of the special office of the *apostle* established by Jesus. A *shaliach* was a legal representative who carried the delegated authority of the one who sent him. As the rabbis often said, "A man's *shaliach* is the man himself" (Rengstorf 1964:414-20).

Paul's double denial—*sent not from men nor by man*—is probably a reference to the

work as just another job to do for a difficult boss, we will soon become discouraged. But if by faith we can see that God has given us work to do for him, then we can overcome even the most difficult obstacles. All work is sacred if it has been given to us by God. Paul was able to endure through all the hardships he faced because he was convinced that his work was given to him by God.

Christ-Centered Message (1:2-5) After Paul introduces himself (v. 1) and identifies his readers (v. 2) in keeping with the conventions of Greek letters in his day, he greets his readers: *Grace and peace to you from God our Father and the Lord Jesus Christ. Grace and peace to you* is a combination of the typical Greek and Hebrew forms of greeting. But it is much more than that. These two words sum up the basis and the consequence, the root and the fruit, of the total work of salvation accomplished by God through Jesus Christ. Grace is God's unconditional, unearned acceptance of us accomplished through the love-gift of Christ. The experience of grace by faith results in peace, a sense of harmony and completeness in our relationship with God and with one another. To look for grace and peace from any person, organization or activity in the world is to forget that *God our Father and the Lord Jesus Christ* are the only source of these blessings.

The mention of the name of Christ sparks a declaration about the work of Christ. In three brief phrases Paul outlines the basic structure of his Christ-centered message. First, Christ *gave himself for our sins.* The sacrificial, self-giving work of Christ on the cross is the final answer to the problem of all our moral failure and guilt. For that reason the victory over sin accomplished by the cross of Christ is the main theme of this letter (2:20-21; 3:1, 13; 4:4; 5:1, 11, 24; 6:12, 14), which rebukes believers for substituting humanistic solutions for the cross of Christ.

Second, the purpose of the cross is expressed dramatically: *to rescue*

Jerusalem apostles and especially Peter, since they are featured so prominently in his autobiography (see 1:17—2:14). Paul denies that they are either the ultimate source *(ouk apo)* or the intermediate agency *(oude dia)* of his apostleship (so Longenecker 1990:4).

1:2 The *churches in Galatia* were those churches established by Paul and Barnabas in the southern part of the Roman province of Galatia, in Pisidian Antioch, Iconium, Lystra and Derbe (see Acts 13—14). See the discussion in the introduction regarding the North Galatia versus South Galatia address of the letter.

us from the present evil age. Paul had an apocalyptic view of history. The revelation (apocalypse—see 1:12, 16; 3:23) of God in Christ had already intersected and forever changed the nature of human history. The cross of Christ inaugurated God's new created order ("new creation"—6:15) in human history. All who believe in the cross are rescued from *the present evil age* and included in the "new creation." The present age is controlled by destructive, malignant forces, "the basic principles of the world" (4:3, 9). The works of the law do not offer a way of escape. Only the cross of Christ sets the prisoners (3:23) free.

Think of all the movies depicting heroic efforts to rescue prisoners of war. The terrible risk involved, the danger and sacrifice, the suspense and violence, the final emotional homecoming of the emaciated prisoner with his courageous deliverer—these are all elements of the most dramatic story of all, the story of the cross of Christ. And because this story is true, Christians can now enjoy the freedom of the new creation; we are no longer prisoners or slaves under the tyranny of this present, dehumanizing system. "It is for freedom that Christ has set us free" (5:1)!

Third, the plan for the cross is *according to the will of our God and Father.* The Father planned our rescue. At the right time he sent his Son to accomplish our rescue (4:4-5). And now the Father has sent the Spirit of his Son into our hearts to let us know that we are no longer slaves, but children of the Father (4:6-7). The accomplishment of the Father's plan in history is the expression of his grace and the basis our peace.

With the wonder of God's amazing grace in full view, it's time to sing a doxology to God (1:5)—*to whom be glory for ever and ever. Amen!*

□ REBUKE SECTION (1:6—4:11)
True love cares enough to confront.
> Better is open rebuke
> than hidden love.
> Wounds from a friend can be trusted,

1:4 According to Jewish expectations expressed in Jewish apocalyptic literature, *the present evil age* would be terminated when God inaugurated the "age to come," the Messianic age (see, for example, 4 Ezra 7:50; see also Longenecker 1990:8-9). But the perspective of the New Testament is that the "age to come" has already been inaugurated by Christ within *the present evil age.* Believers have already been rescued by Christ's death and resurrection

but an enemy multiplies kisses. (Prov 27:5-6)

Paul demonstrates true love for his Galatian friends by confronting them. In all of his other letters to churches, Paul follows his introductory greetings with a thanksgiving section ("I thank my God for you . . ."). But in Galatians there is no thanksgiving section. The absence of a thanksgiving indicates how extremely serious the problem in the Galatian churches was from Paul's perspective. Instead of offering a thanksgiving, Paul moves right into a lengthy rebuke. He begins the body of his letter with an expression of rebuke, a statement about the reason for his rebuke (1:6) and a reminder of previous instructions. He restates the rebuke in the form of rebuking questions in 3:1-5 and 4:8-10, which add rebukes for foolishness (3:1-3) and negligence in not following the knowledge they had (4:9). The first rebuke regarding a change of mind in 1:6 is restated in 3:3 and 4:9. An expression of distress in 4:11 communicates Paul's negative reaction to this change of mind. The tone of rebuke pervades the entire section of the letter from 1:6 to 4:12.

We know that this rebuke comes from a heart of love. Paul views his friends with affection as "brothers" (1:11; 3:15; 4:12, 28, 31; 5:11, 13; 6:1, 18) and even as "dear children" for whom, he says, "I am again in the pains of childbirth until Christ is formed in you" (4:19). His rebuke expresses strong, deep love. As a wise pastor, he knows that "the corrections of discipline are the way to life" (Prov 6:23).

A young Chinese pastor recently told me that the overriding concern to "save face" in his culture makes confrontation rare and difficult. I responded that in my Southern California home culture, the limitless tolerance for "doing your own thing" often means that confrontation is viewed as illegitimate, judgmental interference in someone's private affairs. Yet we agreed that when confrontation is necessary in certain circumstances because it best expresses our love for others and our commitment to the gospel, we must dare to rebuke with humility and gentleness (see 6:1), even if such a confrontation is countercultural.

from the evil power of the present age, and they already participate in the power of the age to come (1 Cor 10:11; Heb 6:5). But they have not yet been totally removed from the present evil age; hence they constantly need to guard against being conformed to the pattern of this age (Rom 12:2; NIV: "this world"). See also Martyn 1985:412-20.

□ Rebuke for Desertion (1:6-10)

The Galatian believers probably thought they were simply adding a few Jewish customs to the gospel in order to enhance the value of their faith in Christ. But this addition to the gospel actually negated the essence of the gospel. First Paul rebukes the Galatians for their desertion; next he blames the confusion on those who perverted the gospel; and then he pronounces a solemn condemnation of all who tamper with the truth of the gospel.

Desertion from the Gospel (1:6) Paul's expression of astonishment is actually a stinging rebuke: *I am astonished that you are so quickly deserting the one who called you by the grace of Christ and are turning to a different gospel.* The present tense of the verb *deserting* tells us that the Galatian Christians had not yet decisively carried out their desertion. They were just starting to turn around and leave. Paul's letter was designed to arrest them before they had gone too far. The one they were deserting was the one who had called them by the grace of Christ. While this may be read as a reference to Paul himself, similar references to God's call by his grace in Paul's life (1:15) and in the Galatians' experience (5:8) indicate that the reference is to God. Paul is stunned that people who had just recently experienced so much of God's miraculous power by his Spirit in their lives (3:1-5) would now turn away from him. They are turning their backs on God in order to follow a different gospel.

The content of this different gospel will become evident as we read the letter. But it is clear already that this gospel was not God-centered. It was drawing people away from God to focus on themselves. Preoccupation with racial identity, religious observance and ceremonial rituals was robbing them of their experience of God's grace expressed in Christ. The irony and tragedy of the situation was that in their pious pursuit of spiritual perfection (3:3) they were actually turning away from God.

Notes: 1:6 Paul's expression of amazement—*I am astonished (thaumazō)*—was a common expression of rebuke in Greek letters of his day. See the introduction and Hansen 1989a:33-44.

Paul's accusation that the Galatian converts were *so quickly deserting* does not necessarily indicate that only a brief amount of time passed between their conversion and their apostasy. This phrase may be an echo, a veiled allusion, to Israel's defection in the episode of the golden calf (Ex 32:8, "they have been quick to turn away") and in the era of the judges (Judg 2:17, "they quickly turned from the way"). See Longenecker 1990:14.

The Galatian tragedy is a warning for us that not every quest for spirituality is in reality a quest for God. The emphasis in our day on "spirituality" and "spiritual formation" may be a way of finding God. But it may also be a way of running and hiding from God. When we are enticed by provocative books on New Age spirituality, we must remember that the Galatian Christians were trapped by a message that promised spiritual perfection but turned them away from God.

Perversion of the Gospel (1:7) The fascinating, even spellbinding teaching of some people in the Galatian churches had turned the Galatian believers away from the true gospel. Paul boldly asserts that the different gospel which is so attractive to the Galatian Christians *is really no gospel at all*. It is a perversion of the gospel of Christ, perpetrated by some people who are trying to cause confusion in the Galatian churches.

Probably these people claimed that their message supplemented and completed Paul's message. They would not have viewed their version of the gospel as heretical. After all, they did not deny the deity of Christ, the cross of Christ or the resurrection of Christ. They subtracted nothing from Paul's message. They only added to it.

But Paul does not allow their gospel to stand as a legitimate option. He sets forth a radical antithesis. His gospel cannot be served alongside other gospels, buffet-style. There is only one true gospel of Christ. The rest of his letter defines the true gospel in antithesis to the false gospel, so that the readers will reject the false and embrace the true.

Condemnation of Perverters of the Gospel (1:8-10) Paul places all advocates of a gospel that differs from his gospel under condemnation. Adherence to the true gospel is the final test of true authority. Even the authority of a messenger from heaven or the authority of Paul himself must be tested by loyalty to the gospel. It is important to note that Paul holds himself accountable to this ultimate measure of authority. His

---

1:6-7 The Greek phrase here says that the gospel to which the Galatians were turning was "a different gospel which is not another gospel." In this context the word translated *different (heteron)* points to a qualitative difference (a gospel of a different kind); "another" *(allo)* means another of the same kind (another gospel of the same kind). Paul was obviously making a radical distinction between his gospel and the so-called gospel of the false teachers. The false teachers were not teaching the gospel; they were teaching heresy. Paul draws the same kind of distinction between the true gospel and heresy in 2 Corinthians 11:4.

apostolic authority is not arbitrary; it is valid only as long as he is faithful to the true gospel.

In the history of the church we can observe two extremes in the use of authority. Sometimes those who have leadership roles do not exercise their God-given authority; leaderless churches drift into compromise and divide into competing factions. This was the condition of the Corinthian church. But on the other hand, some persons in leadership roles attempt to exercise absolute control over the church and place themselves above any criticism; enslaved churches lack freedom to grow in faith and love. This was the condition of the Galatian churches. The intruders campaigned for the exclusive devotion of the Galatian Christians (4:17).

The extremes of anarchy and tyranny can be avoided in the church only when we implement Paul's combination of authority and accountability. Leaders in the church should lead with authority, because God is the ultimate source for their position; but they should also lead with humility, because God has set the final standard in the truth of the gospel, by which all are judged. Leaders must be held accountable to this final standard by those who are led.

In verse 9 Paul repeats his previous instruction, which eternally condemns anybody for preaching a gospel other than what the Galatian converts had originally accepted from Paul. Paul's double condemnation sounds terribly harsh and severe in our ears. It expresses an absolute intolerance for anyone who differs from his gospel. How can we seek to maintain harmony in a context of religious pluralism, we might respond, except by showing tolerance for all religious alternatives? Doesn't Paul himself argue for a tolerant acceptance of differences in other situations?

We need to understand that Paul was willing to accommodate himself to differences in matters such as what foods to eat or what days to celebrate (Rom 14—15; 1 Cor 8—10), but when the central truth of the gospel was at stake, he drew a clear line and refused to compromise. He was unyielding in his defense of "the truth of the gospel" (2:5, 14), because he wanted to protect the freedom of God's people. Paul did

---

1:8-9 Paul's pronouncement of eternal condemnation against all who preach a different, perverted gospel establishes the gospel he preaches as the ultimate standard of authority

teach that Christians should "live at peace with everyone" (Rom 12:18); but when anyone negated the core of the gospel, especially the significance of the cross, he did not hesitate to forcefully refute that person, as we see here in Galatians and in his other letters (see 2 Cor 11:13-15; Col 2:8). While we should seek to maintain harmony in a context of religious pluralism by showing tolerance and respect for people of other religious persuasions, this should not lead us to compromise in any way the exclusiveness of the true gospel of Christ.

Of course our unwillingness to compromise the truth of the gospel will sometimes make us quite unpopular. In verse 10 Paul recognizes that his double condemnation of all who preach a gospel different from his gospel will certainly not be seen as an attempt to please people. His rhetorical questions call for a negative answer: "No, Paul, you are obviously not trying to win human approval, but God's." Perhaps Paul had been accused of trying to please people by preaching a gospel that did not require Gentiles to follow Jewish customs. But now after pronouncing judgment on all who preach a perversion of his gospel, he considers himself to be cleared of any accusation that his ambition is to please people. Such an ambition would indicate that he was not a true servant of Christ. By his loyalty to the gospel despite opposition, Paul proves his complete submission to the lordship of Christ. As a faithful servant to Christ, he is a rebuke to the Galatian believers who are so quickly deserting the One who called them and turning to a different gospel (1:6).

True servants of Christ will not win popularity contests with people who "gather around them a great number of teachers to say what their itching ears want to hear" (2 Tim 4:3). But even when they are unpopular, true servants of Christ are marked by unswerving loyalty to Christ. We can still hear the clear gospel message today because courageous men and women suffered greatly for their uncompromising defense of it in years past. They resisted immense pressure to renounce their faith in Christ, and they boldly declared, as Martin Luther did, "Here I stand. I can do no other. God help me."

---

by which all are judged. "All figures in the historical transcript are subordinated to it. That includes Paul and the community" (Schütz 1975:123; see also Hansen 1990:45-46).

□ Paul's Autobiography (1:11—2:21)

At this point Paul turns from his rebuke for desertion to an autobiographical account. By clearly setting forth the story of his own loyalty to the gospel, Paul intensifies his rebuke for disloyalty. In contrast to the Galatian believers who turned from the gospel of Christ to follow Jewish customs, Paul tells how he was converted from Judaism and commissioned by God to preach the gospel of Christ and how he was faithful to his commission. His life stands as an eloquent witness to the truth of the gospel.

His autobiography begins with a thesis statement about the origin of the gospel, recounts his conversion and call, describes his first visit with Peter in Jerusalem and the conference with the apostles in Jerusalem, recalls his conflict with Peter in Antioch, and concludes with a personal affirmation of his commitment to live by the gospel.

Thesis Statement (1:11-12) You might expect that after Paul rebuked the Galatians for desertion he would challenge them to recommit themselves to Christ. Eventually he does command them to "stand firm" (5:1). But before he challenges them, he prepares the way for his imperatives by telling his own story. He does not call for his readers to do anything that he has not done himself. He does not simply point to the way; he has lived out the way of faithfulness to the gospel of Christ. We might do well to learn from Paul that the best way to challenge others to live for Christ is by our own example.

The key to understanding Paul's life story is his encounter with Christ. Paul gives us that key right at the beginning of his autobiography. He wants his dear brothers and sisters to know that the gospel he preached was not made up by human beings, received from human beings or taught to him by human beings; rather, it was received by revelation from Jesus Christ. Note how the *not . . . nor . . . rather* structure of this claim is parallel to the structure of his affirmation of his apostolic authority in verse 1. Just as he vigorously denied any human origin of his apostleship,

---

Notes: 1:12 The NIV translation *by revelation from Jesus Christ* implies that Jesus Christ was the source or agent of revelation. F. F. Bruce, however, along with most commentators, says the phrase means that Christ was the object of revelation, since that is the point of 1:15-16: "God . . . was pleased to reveal his Son in me" (Bruce 1982:89; so Burton 1921:43; Betz

so now he denies any human origin for the gospel he preached.

Perhaps these strong denials are Paul's refutation of accusations that he got his message secondhand from the original apostles. Perhaps the troublemakers in the Galatian churches were suggesting that they had a more complete version of the gospel from the original apostles and that the gospel Paul had preached was abbreviated or truncated. But we have little clear evidence to support any theory about the teaching of Paul's opponents. Whatever may have been said about him or his message, Paul wants to make sure that everyone will clearly understand the gospel he preaches. So he affirms in the strongest terms possible that the essential nature of the gospel is God-made, not man-made, because the origin of the gospel he preaches is the *revelation from Jesus Christ,* not human tradition. The rest of his autobiographical account is constructed to support his claim for the revelatory origin and nature of the gospel.

Before we continue our study of Paul's autobiography, however, we must address a question that is raised by his claim in this passage that he did not receive the gospel from any human being. This claim seems to be contradicted by his assertion in 1 Corinthians that he had received the gospel from others (1 Cor 15:3-11: "For what I received I passed on to you"). It is helpful to understand the different contexts for these statements. The Corinthians were in danger of subtracting from the central content of the gospel by denying the resurrection of Christ. They were probably influenced by Hellenistic philosophy, which affirmed the immortality of the soul but denied the resurrection of the body. In that context Paul emphasized that from the very beginning of the gospel tradition everyone agreed that the bodily resurrection of Christ was central to the gospel. Paul's gospel did not differ from the early Christian tradition in its basic content. Thus he was eager to affirm that the gospel he had passed on to the Corinthian church was the same as he himself had received from the early church.

The Galatians, however, were in danger of adding to the central content of the gospel by requiring Gentile Christians to maintain a Jewish

---

1979:63; Fung 1988:54; Guthrie 1973:66). On the other hand, Longenecker (1990:24) argues that just as Christ was the agent of Paul's apostleship (1:1), so he was the agent of the revelation of the gospel to Paul (1:11-12).

lifestyle. They may have been influenced by the law-observant Jerusalem church. In this context Paul could not appeal to early church tradition or practice for support. But he could and did appeal to his revelatory encounter with the risen Christ when he was commissioned to preach the gospel to the Gentiles. His mission to the Gentiles was part of his gospel; it was a gospel for Gentiles. Paul understood his Gentile mission to imply that Gentiles would be justified by faith in Christ apart from observance of the Mosaic law. So when he claims that his gospel was not received from any human being (1:12), his focus is not so much the central facts of the gospel as it is the meaning of those facts *for Gentiles* which was given to him by revelation from Jesus Christ. In fact, as we see in the rest of his autobiography, it is the gospel *for Gentiles* that is Paul's primary concern.

We may illustrate Paul's unique understanding of the gospel in the light of his Gentile mission by recognizing that every Christian is uniquely gifted by God for a special mission in life. This does not mean that every Christian can claim to have received special revelation as Paul did. But because each Christian is uniquely gifted by the Spirit and called to serve God in some special way, each Christian has a very personal understanding of the gospel message. For example, as I have attempted to contextualize the gospel for the Chinese people in Singapore, where I teach, I have developed a fresh understanding of the meaning of the gospel *for Singaporeans:* Buddhism's aim to set us free from destructive desires and Confucianism's aim to achieve harmony in our families are both fulfilled when Christ rules in our hearts and homes. All true Christians agree on the basic content of the gospel as Paul defines it in 1 Corinthians 15:3-11, but each Christian sees the gospel in a unique way through the lens of his or her distinctive God-given mission in life.

Conversion and Call (1:13-17) The best evidence for Paul's claim to have received his gospel by revelation from Jesus Christ is his conversion. The dramatic change in his life demands some explanation. How could such a fanatical opponent of the followers of Christ become such

---

1:13 *Church of God* was one of Paul's favorite titles for the church (1 Cor 1:2; 10:32; 11:16; 15:9; 2 Cor 1:1; 1 Thess 2:14; 2 Thess 1:4; 1 Tim 3:5). Its use here in the singular form and

a devoted preacher of the gospel of Christ? Paul explains that the cause of such a radical change was God's gracious revelation of his Son to him. To appreciate the impact of God's intervention in Paul's life we need to look more closely at three pictures Paul gives of himself: (1) the picture of himself before his conversion; (2) the picture of his encounter with Christ; (3) the picture of himself after God called him.

1. Paul reviews the record of his pre-Christian life in order to show the wonder of God's grace. Twice he refers to his past as his life *in Judaism*. Although he never ceased to identify himself as a Jew ("I am an Israelite myself, a descendant of Abraham, from the tribe of Benjamin"—Rom 11:1), he only used *in Judaism* as a way of describing his life before he became a new creation "in Christ." The term *Judaism* was used in Jewish literature for "the Jewish way of belief and life" as contrasted to the way of life in Hellenism. In other words, the distinctive Jewish beliefs and customs which established the boundaries between the Jewish people and the rest of the Hellenistic world were of supreme importance to Paul before his conversion, but they were of no importance after his conversion. Jewish identity markers such as circumcision, kosher food and sabbath observance were Paul's primary concern before his conversion; but they were no longer significant for Paul after he found his new identity in Christ. As he declares at the end of his letter: "Neither circumcision nor uncircumcision means anything; what counts is a new creation" (6:15).

The contrast between Paul and the Galatian believers stands out in bold relief here. As a Jew, he had turned from his preoccupation with the distinctive Jewish way of life to serve the risen Christ; as Gentiles, they were turning from their focus on Christ to a preoccupation with the distinctive Jewish way of life. No wonder Paul calls them "foolish Galatians" (3:1).

Paul draws attention to two characteristics of his previous way of life in Judaism: his intense persecution of the church (1:13) and his zealous devotion to Jewish traditions (1:14). The two are connected. The message of the church, that a crucified Messiah provides salvation for all,

in opposition to *Judaism* points to the unity of all local churches in one universal church.

contradicted the traditions of Judaism. Certainly a Messiah on a Roman cross contradicted the Jewish expectation of a Messiah on David's throne. And Jews believed that salvation was to be found only in the law-observant Jewish nation. No wonder then that Paul's zeal for the Jewish traditions made him a fanatical persecutor of the church.

This description of his former life has direct application in the development of his argument. The Galatian believers' preoccupation with Judaism is challenged by this alarming picture of the consequences of devotion to Judaism in his own life. And his point that the gospel he received was not from human beings but by revelation from Jesus Christ is confirmed by this picture of a fanatic who was so opposed to the gospel that no one could have changed his mind except God himself.

2. In his description of his former life, Paul himself is the subject of all the verbs: *I persecuted . . . tried to destroy . . . I was advancing . . . and was extremely zealous.* In contrast to Paul's ego-centered former life, God himself is the central subject in Paul's conversion. God is the subject of all the verbs: *God, who set me apart . . . called . . . was pleased to reveal.* God abruptly interrupted Paul's life and turned him around.

As we study Paul's account of his conversion, we can observe four dimensions of God's work in conversion. Of course, Paul's experience of conversion was unique and cannot be used as a model for all to follow. God works in unique ways with each individual. But Paul's account does shed light on the nature of God's gracious work in conversion.

First, God's choice precedes conversion. Like the prophets, Paul sees

---

1:14 When Paul says that he was *extremely zealous (perissoterōs zēlotēs),* he did not mean that he was one of the Zealots (so Lightfoot 1957:80-81) but that he was, as we might say today, "a radically conservative" type of Pharisee, a passionate observer of the Jewish laws and traditions. The Pharisaic movement had its roots in the Maccabean revolt (about 166 B.C.), and its driving passion was expressed in a deathbed appeal by Mattathias, the father of the Maccabean leaders, to be zealous for the law: "And now my children, be zealous for the Law, and give your lives for the covenant of your fathers. . . . Be strong and show yourselves men on behalf of the Law; for therein shall you obtain glory. . . . Take unto you all those who observe the Law, and avenge the wrong of your people" (1 Macc 2:50, 64). See Donaldson 1989:655-82.

A good understanding of what Paul refers to as *the traditions of my fathers (tōn patrikōn mou paradoseōn)* may be gained by reading in the Mishnah, a compilation of the oral law that had been developing and had been passed down from one generation to the next since the time of Ezra. The Mishnah was produced in its written form by leading rabbis at the

himself as set apart by God from his birth for his prophetic role (see Is 49:1 and Jer 1:4-5). Although he recognizes that his former life was lived in opposition to God's will, he still claims that his entire life is part of the sovereign plan of God. We may not be able to explain this apparent contradiction, but we can learn from Paul that the sovereignty of God is never an excuse for rebellion against God; it is a basis for trust in God's wisdom and love. As an old hymn puts it, "We'll praise Him for all that is past / And trust Him for all that's to come."

Second, God's decision to set Paul apart from birth led to the life-transforming event of God's gracious call. The two parallel phrases *(set me apart . . . called me)* teach us that conversion is based on God's loving initiative. Before Paul was born, God chose him. While Paul was trying to destroy the people of God, God called him. That is the meaning of grace: undeserved love. "Amazing grace, how sweet the sound that saved a wretch like me!"

Third, God's gracious call led to revelation: God *was pleased to reveal his Son in me.* The inwardness of God's revelation stressed here by the phrase *in me* should not be taken as a contradiction of Paul's claims elsewhere to have seen the risen Christ (1 Cor 9:1; 15:8; see also Acts 9:1-19; 22:3-16; 26:12-18). Paul strongly affirmed the external, objective nature of his encounter with Christ on the Damascus Road. But in that encounter, Paul says, God "made his light shine in our hearts to give us the light of the knowledge of the glory of God in the face of Christ" (2 Cor 4:6). God's revelation of his Son in Paul illuminated his mind and heart so that he saw and knew Jesus to be the Son of God. Paul's ex-

---

end of the second century A.D.

1:15-17 The complex sentence structure of 1:15-17 may be diagrammed as follows. Subordinated clauses are indented to the right.

But when God,
    who set me apart from birth
    and called me by his grace,
was pleased
    to reveal his Son in me
        so that I might preach him among the Gentiles,
I did not consult any man . . .

This diagram shows that the main point of the sentence is Paul's denial of any dependence on the original apostles for the gospel he preached to the Gentiles.

1:16 Paul uses the title *Son* or "Son of God" four times in this letter (1:16; 2:20; 4:4, 6) and fifteen times in all his letters. See Kim 1982:109-36.

clamation "Christ lives in me" (2:20) expresses the lasting result of this inward encounter with the living Christ. The danger of substituting external observance of the law for this intimate relationship with Christ is the central burden of Paul's message to the Galatian believers. His lengthy arguments lead to this point: "God sent the Spirit of his Son into our hearts" (4:6). His severe warnings alert them to this danger: "You who are trying to be justified by law have been alienated from Christ" (5:4).

Fourth, Paul says that revelation was given *so that I might preach him among the Gentiles* (1:16). Paul's conversion included his commission to preach the gospel. He did not have a two-stage experience: first conversion, sometime later a commission to preach. His mission to the Gentiles was given to him in the initial experience of conversion. Christ met him on the road to Damascus in order to send him on his mission to the world. As a result Paul interpreted the gospel itself in the light of his mission to the Gentiles. He called his gospel "the gospel to the Gentiles" (2:7).

God's revelation of his Son is a personal, inward experience of the heart, but it was not meant to be kept private. The purpose of revelation is evangelism. The fruit of true conversion is mission. Evangelism is not some optional extra, an elective course that may or may not be taken. It is the inevitable result of real conversion. There is a centrifugal force released in the experience of conversion which compels the truly converted to participate in God's mission to the world. Too often in testimonies the only results of conversion we hear about are the personal benefits: *my* peace, *my* fulfillment, *my* freedom. But we learn from Paul that God's primary purpose for our conversion is to send us out into the world with the good news about Christ. Our involvement in God's mission in the world is the best testimony to God's gracious work of conversion in our lives.

3. The conclusion of Paul's conversion story is that after his conversion he *did not consult any man.* The phrase *any man* in the NIV is a paraphrase for "flesh and blood." When Peter affirmed that Jesus was the Messiah, the Son of God, Jesus replied, "Blessed are you, Simon son of Jonah, for this was not revealed to you by flesh and blood [by man— NIV], but by my Father in heaven" (Mt 16:17). Now Paul claims that the

same thing is true for his revelation from God.

We can catch the flow of his argument so far by summarizing it this way. The thesis that I did not receive the gospel from any human being but by revelation from Jesus Christ (1:11-12) is demonstrated by the following facts: I was opposed to the church before my conversion (vv. 13-14); in my conversion, God himself revealed his Son in me; and I did not consult with the church after my conversion (vv. 15-17). Paul's argument is designed to show that he is not dependent on or subordinate to any other church leaders for his authority to preach his gospel to the Gentiles. His authority is derived from the gospel that had been revealed to him by God. Therefore when the Galatians turn away from the gospel preached by Paul, they are turning away from God.

Paul is especially concerned to prove that he was not dependent on the original apostles in Jerusalem. He denies that he visited them immediately after his conversion (v. 17). Perhaps Paul is responding here to an accusation that his failure to require circumcision was a departure from the true gospel that he had been commissioned to preach by the original apostles in Jerusalem. It's difficult to know what accusations, if any, Paul is responding to in this part of his argument. But we can be sure that whether Paul is on the defensive or on the offensive, he is determined to prove that his gospel was given by divine revelation, not human tradition, and that his commission to preach this gospel to the Gentiles was part of that divine revelation. He did not receive his commission from the original apostles. While he recognizes the original apostles' priority in time, he adamantly denies that they or their messengers have any authority to change his gospel to the Gentiles, since they are not the source of that gospel—God is.

Instead of visiting the original apostles in Jerusalem after his conversion, Paul *went immediately into Arabia and later returned to Damascus* (v. 17). It seems clear from the context that Paul is setting up a contrast between going to Jerusalem to receive teaching from the apostles and going to Arabia. Does this contrast imply that during his time in Arabia he received teaching from the Lord? Many commentators have thought so, and it seems a reasonable inference to draw from the context. But we must admit that Paul does not disclose what happened during the time in Arabia. Those were hidden years, at least hidden from any public, historical record.

In our day, when celebrities are converted, the religious media rush to publicize their conversions for the widest possible audience. Put them on TV; feature them in prime-time talk shows. But this immediate publicity can be dangerous to the spiritual health of new converts. Under the harsh, glaring lights of the media they have no space to think through the implications of their new faith, to work through their inconsistencies and to listen to the Lord. They sometimes feel used and abused. They need time, as we all do, to be hidden from the public eye in order to grow and deepen in their faith. Hidden years seem to be part of God's plan for his servants. Moses spent forty years in the desert before his day of fame in Pharaoh's court.

Paul's First Visit with Peter in Jerusalem (1:18-24) After establishing that he was totally independent from the apostles in his conversion experience, Paul now provides a sworn testimony regarding his first encounter with the apostles. His purpose in this account is to demonstrate that his gospel to the Gentiles came not from church tradition but from God, and that he was faithful to this gospel.

Paul is careful to number his years and even count his days: three years after his conversion he spent only fifteen days with Peter. The contrast he draws between the comparatively long time apart from any contact with the apostles and the brief time with Peter highlights his independence. His message must have already been formulated by the end of those three years between his conversion and his first encounter with Peter. And such a short visit with Peter did not alter his course. The purpose of his visit was not to be taught by Peter or to come under Peter's authority, but *to get acquainted with Peter* (v. 18). Of course they would not have wasted time on small talk. No doubt their conversation during those two weeks centered on Christ and the ministry of the church. Paul would have been deeply interested in Peter's accounts of

---

1:18 The basic meaning of the verb *to get acquainted with (historeō)* in classical Greek literature is "to inquire from," "to get information from" (Bauer 1979:383; Kilpatrick 1959:144-49). Dunn argues for the classical meaning here (1990:110-13), but most commentators say that the common Hellenistic usage of the verb, with the sense of "making someone's acquaintance," is what Paul has in mind here, since he is arguing that he did not receive his gospel by instruction from the original apostles (see Betz 1979:76; Bruce

Jesus' life and ministry. And his concern for the unity of the church would have compelled him to build a good relationship with Peter. But these understandable interests and concerns do not provide a basis for portraying Paul as a disciple or subordinate of Peter. It is just such a portrayal that Paul's account is designed to refute.

In Paul's record of appointments for that two-week visit, he insists that James, the Lord's brother, was the only other apostle he saw (v. 19). From Paul's references to James in chapter 2 (vv. 9, 12) we know that James had a prominent role in the Jerusalem church. According to Acts, James became the most influential leader in that church. It is not surprising, therefore, that Paul would have had some contact with him. What transpired during that visit Paul does not tell us. But we can be sure from his argument so far that Paul did not report to James as if James were the president of his mission to the Gentiles. While Paul was working for harmony in the church, he was working under a direct commission from God.

Paul confirms the complete reliability of his account so far with a legal oath (1:20). Under Roman law, an oath was used outside of court to indicate that one would be willing to resolve an issue in the courts. But why did Paul think it was necessary to take an oath to defend the veracity of his report? It seems reasonable to suppose that Paul took this oath because he was contradicting a false report of his part in the mission of the church, a report claiming that he had received his gospel and his authority to preach the gospel from the apostles in Jerusalem. Such a report may have been circulated in the churches in Galatia by those who were persuading the Gentile believers to live like Jews since that was the way of believers in the mother church in Jerusalem. If Paul was merely a messenger for that church, then an appeal to the example of that church was more authoritative than Paul's message. Of course these are simply speculations. But if Paul is right that "some false brothers had infiltrated" the church and opposed him (2:4), it is probably also true

1982:98; Fung 1988:74).

1:20 Sampley provides evidence that Paul's use of an oath is based on Roman judicial procedure and is "a forceful and even dramatic means to emphasize both the seriousness of the issue and his own truthfulness" (1977:481). Jesus' admonition against using oaths (Mt 5:33-37) was directed against the abuse of using oaths to mask untruthfulness. But Paul's oath indicates that he is willing to have his truthfulness tested by cross-examination in court.

that false reports had been circulated about him.

It is common, even expected, that public leaders in the church must respond to false reports about their ministry. The best answer to false reports is the truth—absolutely no lies. Not only is personal integrity at stake. The truth of the gospel is also at stake. And it can be defended only by unvarnished truthfulness.

Paul wraps up the record of his first visit to Jerusalem with a further denial of any personal involvement with the church of Jerusalem. Since he went to Syria and Cilicia after his first visit (1:21), he *was personally unknown to the churches of Judea that are in Christ* (v. 22). And since Paul was not within the orbit of the Jerusalem church, he was not under the supervision of the Jerusalem apostles.

What Paul did during his time in Syria and Cilicia between his first encounter with the apostles in Jerusalem (vv. 18-19) and his participation in the Jerusalem conference (2:1-10) is clearly stated in his quotation of the report circulated about him in the Judean churches: *The man who formerly persecuted us is now preaching the faith he once tried to destroy* (1:23). *Preaching* is actually a translation of "evangelizing." Paul was fully engaged in the work of evangelism. And the content of his message was *the faith,* a shorthand summary for the gospel of Christ.

The power of the gospel had transformed Paul from a persecutor of believers to a preacher of the faith. The light of the gospel that he had tried to snuff out had penetrated and illuminated his heart and was now shining brightly through his life and preaching. That was the report heard about Paul in the churches of Judea. What a contrast to the false, negative reports about Paul that were being circulated in the churches of Galatia.

In contrast to the Galatian churches, which were turning away from the gospel preached by Paul, the churches in Judea had praised God because Paul was preaching the gospel (v. 24). Although Paul had obviously not learned his gospel from the Judean churches, as he sufficiently demonstrates in the course of his argument, those churches recognized that the gospel Paul preached was *the faith,* the gospel they

---

2:1 If the word *again* is connected with the reference in 1:18 to the first visit to Jerusalem, then it appears to indicate that Paul is describing his second visit to Jerusalem in 2:1-10. But the conference described in 2:1-10 fits better with the record of Paul's third visit to Jerusalem, as described in the account of Acts 15:2. If in fact Acts 15:2 and Galatians 2:1

believed. When they measured Paul the preacher by the message he preached (just as Paul says every preacher should be measured—vv. 8-9) and found that he was faithful to the true gospel, they gave thanks to God.

The enthusiastic response of the Judean churches to Paul's gospel is certainly a rebuke to the present attitude of the Galatian churches. If only they would learn from the example of the Judean churches and evaluate preachers on the basis of their faithfulness to the true gospel, they would no longer be mesmerized by the troublemakers who had caused such confusion by their perversion of the gospel.

Paul really turns the tables on those troublemakers. They had apparently appealed to the practice of the Jerusalem church and the Judean churches to persuade the Galatian churches to adopt the Jewish way of life. But now Paul appeals to the example of the same churches. They had praised God when they heard the report that Paul now preached the gospel, the same gospel that had changed his life and theirs. Their example still stands as a challenge to churches today. Praising God when we hear that his faithful servants are preaching the gospel will keep our focus on the right thing: God's gracious work through the power of the gospel.

The Conference in Jerusalem (2:1-10) In the previous section of his autobiography (1:17-24) Paul has been describing the nature of his relationship with the original apostles in Jerusalem to show that he had been commissioned directly by God, not by the apostles, to preach the gospel to the Gentiles. He has worked independently from them; he is not their messenger boy. In fact his contact with them has been minimal. He did not visit them until three years after his conversion; and then he spent only two weeks with Peter in Jerusalem in order to get acquainted with him. On that trip to Jerusalem, the only other apostle he saw was James. After that time he remained unknown to the churches in Judea except for the good reports they heard about his evangelistic work in the

refer to the same visit, then Paul has omitted any reference to his second visit to Jerusalem as recorded in Acts 11:30 (if we grant the trustworthiness of the Acts account). Since Paul takes an oath that he is telling the truth (1:20), some commentators have felt that his account of his second visit in 2:1 must be harmonized with the account of the second visit in Acts

provinces of Syria and Cilicia. It was a long time before Paul met again with the apostles in Jerusalem, not until fourteen years after his conversion, or about eleven years after his first visit (2:1).

With these facts Paul has sharpened his rebuke for turning to a different gospel. It is ludicrous for the Galatians to discard Paul's gospel as if it were a secondhand, abbreviated version that needed to be supplemented with additional instructions from the Jerusalem apostles. Paul did not spend enough time with the original apostles in Jerusalem to get his gospel secondhand from them. Since Paul's gospel was given by revelation from God, the Galatian believers should have maintained unswerving loyalty to it.

So the direct revelation of the gospel to Paul has been established. But it appears from the next episode of his autobiography that Paul also wants to defend his gospel against another possible misunderstanding. Although it is true that he got his gospel by direct revelation, this does not mean that he preached his gospel without the approval and support of the original apostles and the rest of the church. Paul is not a visionary who simply wants to protect his claim to private revelations rather than building the unity of the church. Nor is he a pioneer missionary who works in isolation from the rest of the church.

Disruptive mystics and lone rangers have often split and splintered the church. People with exceptional gifts and strengths are sometimes prone to exercise their gifts in divisive ways. But Paul saw that the unity of the church was necessary for the success of his mission. So he worked hard to build unity on the basis of the gospel. In fact, his whole argument leads to the conclusion that his gospel to the Gentiles is the only sure foundation for the unity of the church (see 3:28). But that is jumping ahead. Our attention must be focused now on Paul's account of the Jerusalem conference that led to the church leaders' full support for Paul's gospel to the Gentiles (2:1-10). The agreement reached at the conference in Jerusalem demonstrated the power of the gospel Paul preached to unite the church. As we follow Paul's participation in this

---

11:30 (see Guthrie 1973:32; Bruce 1982:106; Longenecker 1990:45). But perhaps Cole is right in his suggestion that Paul considered the Acts 11:30 visit "as completely irrelevant to his argument, since it had nothing to do with theological matters, and thus deliberately omitted it without any intention of deceiving" (Cole 1989:101; see also Dunn 1993a:88).

conference, we will observe eight steps in the process which concluded with the giving of the *right hand of fellowship* (v. 9). We also can be agents of reconciliation in the church as we take these steps to unite the church to support God's mission to all nations.

First, we observe that Paul attended this conference with a team: he went with Barnabas and took Titus along also (v. 1). The unity of Jews and Gentiles in the church was demonstrated by the composition of Paul's team.

Barnabas was a highly respected Jewish Christian. According to Acts, his given name was Joseph, but the apostles gave him the nickname Barnabas ("Son of Encouragement") because of his gift of encouraging the early church (Acts 4:36). When Paul was excluded from the church in Jerusalem after his conversion, Barnabas was the only one willing to reach out to this dangerous former persecutor of the church, bring him into the circle of the apostles and believe in God's work of grace in his life (Acts 9:27). Later the Jerusalem church sent Barnabas to Antioch to supervise the mission to the Gentiles. Again, Barnabas was big enough to accept the radically new practice of including Gentile converts in the church, because his focus was the grace of God (Acts 11:22). Barnabas selected Paul to join him in that ministry in Antioch (Acts 11:25). The Christians in Antioch sent Barnabas and Paul with a famine relief gift back to the poverty-stricken church in Jerusalem (Acts 11:27-30). Sometime after their return from Jerusalem, the church of Antioch sent Barnabas and Paul on a missionary trip to Cyprus and southern Galatia (Acts 13:1—14:28). After their return from that trip, they were sent back to Jerusalem to work out the problem of Jew-Gentile relations in the church (Acts 15:1-35). This brief review of the account of Barnabas in Acts brings us up to the conference in Jerusalem, which is the subject of this section of Paul's autobiography. It is important for us to see from this account that one member of Paul's team was an outstanding Jewish Christian leader in the early church who was noted for his ability to be a bridge-builder between diverse factions of the church.

After all, Paul's oath in 1:20 only meant that he was telling the truth about his relationship with the apostles in Jerusalem; it did not necessarily indicate that he felt obligated to give an extensive report of all his trips to Jerusalem. For further discussion of this historical problem, see the introduction.

Titus, the other member of Paul's team, was a Greek Christian (2:3). Paul's inclusion of Titus on his team boldly expressed his conviction that it was not necessary for Greek Christians to change their ethnic identity by becoming Jews in order to be included in the church. The presence of Titus forced the conference to resolve the issue of discrimination against Gentile Christians. The conference could not remain neutral about the key issue. If Titus was forced to be circumcised in order to be accepted by the Jerusalem church, then it would be clear that Gentiles must become Jews in order to be accepted in the church. But if Titus was accepted by the Jerusalem church as a Gentile, then it would be clear that Gentiles were regarded as equal members.

Paul's team was a living illustration of the new freedom in Christ for Jews and Gentiles to build close friendships. His team was a microcosmic expression of the power of the gospel to break down the barriers that had separated Jews and Gentiles and to create a new unity in Christ—a unity that transcends the ethnic, cultural and social divisions in the world.

The best place to start building unity in the church is to start working with a team of diverse people who are united by their common faith in Christ and their mission. Finding the right people to serve on such a team is often difficult, but it's worth the effort, because it offers the opportunity to show the unifying power of the gospel.

Second, we observe that Paul went to the conference *in response to a revelation* (v. 2). None of the attempts to harmonize this reference to revelation with other references in Paul's letters and in Acts can claim to be more than a guess. But we must not miss Paul's point in making this reference to revelation. Here again we see his insistence that he was taking orders directly from God, not from human beings. Neither the Jerusalem apostles nor any other pressure group summoned Paul to

---

2:2 Acts reports that Paul received guidance by *revelation* in several different ways: through prophets (11:28; 21:10-11), by the Holy Spirit (13:2; 16:6-7; 20:22-23; 21:4), in dream visions (16:9; 18:9-10; 23:11; 27:23-24) and in estatic trances (22:17-21; see also 2 Cor 12:2-4).

Paul says he conferred with the leaders *privately*. If 2:1-10 describes the same event as Acts 15:2-21, then perhaps we may see Acts 15:6 as a reference to such a private meeting.

Paul's references to the original apostles as *those who seemed to be leaders* (v. 2), *those who seemed to be important* (v. 6) and *those reputed to be pillars* (v. 9) do not indicate that

Jerusalem for cross-examination. He went because God told him to go. Paul was not outward-directed, pushed and shoved by the changing whims of public opinion. Nor was he only inward-directed, driven by his own needs and ambitions. He was God-directed, led by the Spirit of God (see 5:18). When it comes to making peace in a church torn by conflict, we need peacemakers who are called children of God because they are sensitive and obedient to the voice of their Father (see Mt 5:9).

Third, Paul went to the conference in order to have his gospel evaluated. He set before the leaders in Jerusalem the gospel that he preached among the Gentiles (v. 2). The verb *set before* indicates that Paul was willing to present his ministry and message at the conference for discussion and debate. The fact that he had been given a revelation did not lead him to think that he was above evaluation.

Some people seem to think that when they deliver their word from the Lord, all discussion should stop. They do not allow any questions or debate about their message. They feel they have delivered the last and final word. But Paul did not approach this conference in that spirit. After all, he had nothing to fear from an evaluation of his gospel, and he had everything to gain. So he placed himself in the vulnerable position of facing a full review of his work by the senior leadership of the church. That must have been a humbling experience for Paul. But he did it to gain the Jerusalem leaders' approval of his Gentile mission. Those who are convinced of the truth of their message should not fear evaluation. They should welcome it.

When Paul says that he presented his gospel *for fear that I was running or had run my race in vain,* he does not mean that he had secret doubts about the validity of his Gentile mission and needed the apostles' assurance that he was running in the right direction. His confidence in God's call (1:1, 15-16) rules out such an interpretation. But Paul did

---

he was rejecting their apostolic authority but that he was calling into question an exaggerated importance that had evidently been given to them in the early church, an importance that threatened to place their personal authority above the absolute authority of the *truth of the gospel.* As Holmberg notes, "According to Paul every apostle is subordinated to the Gospel and is authoritative because and insofar as he is a faithful preacher of this one and only Gospel—not because he knew the historical Jesus or has access to old and reliable traditions about him" (1978:29).

recognize that his divine commission could not be effectively fulfilled if there was a division between his Gentile mission and the leaders of the church in Jerusalem. His God-given mission did not need to be authorized by them, but it would have been rendered fruitless *(in vain)* if it lacked their support. It was evident to Paul that if the mother church denounced and disowned his Gentile mission, his work of evangelizing the Gentile world would be frustrated. If the unity of all believers in the church was denied, the gospel for the Gentiles would be undermined. It was because Paul desired this unity that he presented his gospel to the leaders in Jerusalem, hoping that they would give their wholehearted support to his mission. In fact, that is just what they did.

Fourth, Paul strongly resisted those who challenged the essentials of the gospel. His willingness to present his gospel for evaluation did not mean that he was willing to compromise the truth of the gospel. For Paul, the truth of the gospel included his Gentile mission. And his Gentile mission presupposed the unity and equality of Gentile and Jewish believers in Christ. This basic presupposition was challenged at the Jerusalem conference when some *false brothers* tried to require that Titus be circumcised—in other words, become a Jew—in order to be included in the church. But since such a requirement denied the equality and unity of Gentiles and Jews in the church, Paul did not give in to them. As a result he is able to report to the Galatians that *not even Titus, who was with me, was compelled to be circumcised, even though he was a Greek* (v. 3). Titus was accepted as a Gentile believer; he did not have to become a Jew to be included. Paul's firm resistance to pressure protected the unity of the church.

Those who tried to get Titus circumcised were called *false brothers* by Paul because they were unwilling to accept Titus as a true brother. They would allow him to be included in the Christian family only if he became a Jew. The basis of unity in the church for them was race rather than grace. According to Paul, they *had infiltrated our ranks to spy on the*

2:3 Some suggest that although Titus was *not . . . compelled to be circumcised,* he was in fact voluntarily circumcised as a practical concession for the sake of the gospel (Duncan 1934:41-44). This view appears to be supported by the Western text (B) which omits the negative in verse 5. But all the most reliable early manuscripts support Paul's negative assertion in verse 5 *(we did not give in to them for a moment),* which clearly means that

freedom we have in Christ Jesus and to make us slaves (v. 4). To accuse them of being intruders and spies in the Jerusalem church implies that their primary loyalty was not to the gospel of Christ or the church. Rather than upholding the *freedom we have in Christ Jesus* to be accepted before God and by one another simply on the basis of God's grace, they required adherence to Jewish customs as the basis of acceptance.

The parallel between these intruders and the intruders in the Galatian churches is clear. In both cases their requirement to maintain a distinctive Jewish lifestyle denied the freedom of all believers to be included in God's family regardless of racial, cultural or social status. In both cases their message led to slavery—slavery to the values of the world.

But, Paul informs the Galatian churches, *we did not give in to them for a moment, so that the truth of the gospel might remain with you* (v. 5). Paul's refusal to give in to the demands of the intruders in the Jerusalem church protected the truth of the gospel for the Galatian Christians. If he had given in, they would also have been required to become Jews to be included in the church. As a result the truth of the gospel— that they were accepted by God as Gentile believers in Christ—would have been lost.

Unity in the church can be secure only when there is no compromise of the essentials of the gospel. Working toward unity does not mean a passive submission to misguided zealots. The truth of the gospel is nonnegotiable. Paul's account of his defense of the truth of the gospel against intruders in Jerusalem presents a challenge to his readers to do the same in Galatia. His purpose for recording this episode in his autobiography is to provide an example for the Galatian Christians in their own struggle against the demands of the intruders in their churches. The Galatians should not give in to them for a moment; the truth of the gospel must be preserved.

Fifth, Paul built the unity of the church on the truth of God's impartiality. Although he respected the leaders of the church in Jerusalem, he

he did not allow Titus to be circumcised (Betz 1979:89; Bruce 1982:112; Longenecker 1990:50).

2:4 The words *this matter arose* are in brackets in the NIV because they have been added by the translators to make sense of the Greek sentence, which contains neither a subject nor a main verb.

was not intimidated by them, because he knew that *God does not judge by external appearance* (v. 6). Paul recognized that the men he met with at the conference in Jerusalem were regarded as the spiritual giants in the church, *those who seemed to be important* (v. 6). Most people who met them were probably awestruck by the stories they had heard about their relationship with the Master, Jesus himself. It was well known that Peter and John were the disciples closest to Jesus; James was the brother of Jesus. But Paul subtly calls into question the original apostles' basis of authority. His repetition of a qualifying phrase to describe them (*those who seemed to be leaders* [v. 2]; *those who seemed to be important* [v. 6]; *those reputed to be pillars* [v. 9]) connotes a "mild irony." Paul was not impressed by their credentials: *whatever they were makes no difference to me* (v. 6). For God's assessment is not based on such external factors as temporal priority or temporary popularity: *God does not judge by external appearance* (v. 6). But God does judge; he judges on the basis of response to the gospel, Paul's message. Paul draws attention to the fact that those who were highly respected in the church agreed with his message (*those men added nothing to my message* [v. 6]). The authority of these leaders is relativized by Paul, subordinated to the standard of the gospel. Though they were *reputed to be pillars* (v. 9), their authority did not rest on their reputation but on their faithfulness to the *truth of the gospel* (v. 5).

Our attempts to build the unity of the church will fail if we are overawed by the impressive reputation of church leaders. We must remember that God does not measure persons by their public reputation, but by their response to the gospel. We must not be afraid to do the same. I once heard an artist say, "Great works of art, 'the originals,' are not judged by us; we are judged by them." Similarly, the gospel is not

2:6 The "theological axiom" that *God does not judge by external appearance* supports Paul's arguments elsewhere (Rom 2:11; Eph 6:9; Col 3:25) and undergirds Paul's position here that God does not favor the original apostles over himself just because they were the companions or even relatives of Jesus during his earthly ministry (see Bassler 1982:139-49).
2:7-8 The fact that Paul uses the name Peter in these two verses and the name Cephas in every other reference to Peter led Oscar Cullmann to suggest that Paul "here cites an official document, in the Greek translation in which the form Petros was used" (Cullmann 1953:20). The non-Pauline phrases "gospel of uncircumcision" (NIV: *gospel to the Gentiles*) and "gospel of circumcision" (NIV: *gospel . . . to the Jews*) also point to an underlying source. But the use of the first person indicates that "rather than quoting from the written protocol,

judged by great leaders; great leaders are judged by it.

We need to remember this as well when we are tempted to seek such a reputation for ourselves. Ultimately, we will be judged by our faithfulness to the gospel.

Sixth, unity is maintained in the church by keeping the focus on God's work. Paul says that when the leaders *saw* something (vv. 7-8) and *recognized* something (v. 9), they gave the right hand of fellowship to Paul and Barnabas and agreed that they should continue their ministry to the Gentiles. What they saw was God at work in Paul's ministry (v. 8). What they recognized was the grace given to him (v. 9). Just as the miraculous work of God in Peter's ministry validated his call to preach the gospel to the Jews, so also the miraculous work of God in Paul's ministry was irrefutable evidence that God had given him the task of preaching the gospel to the Gentiles (vv. 7-8).

It was precisely because these leaders were preoccupied with God's work, rather than human traditions and prejudice, that they were able to reach an agreement. Unfortunately, the reverse is too often true. A church is divided because the elders accuse the pastor of breaking with denominational traditions. It does not seem to matter to them that the church has doubled because God has saved many through the pastor's ministry. Another church is divided because some like contemporary choruses and others prefer traditional hymns. While they argue over their tastes in music, they lose sight of God's work in their midst. If only we could keep our eyes on what God is doing in our midst, we would be able to transcend the things that divide us and accomplish the tasks that God has given to us.

Seventh, unity at the conference in Jerusalem was based on a delineation of different spheres of responsibility. The leaders in Jerusalem

Paul reminds the readers of the agreements by using the terms upon which the parties had agreed" (Betz 1979:97; on the variation of the names Cephas and Peter in this autobiography, see also Kilpatrick 1983:318-26).

2:9 The order of the *pillars—James, Peter and John*—corroborates the dominant leadership role attributed to James in the Acts 15 account of the conference. The metaphorcial use of *pillars* may reflect the view of the early church that James, Peter and John were comparable to the patriarchs Abraham, Isaac and Jacob, who were often referred to in Jewish literature as the three pillars of Israel. Perhaps the term *pillars* is an echo of the tradition behind Matthew 16:18, where Peter's name is connected in some sense to the foundation ("pillar") of the church (Wenham 1985:26).

agreed that Paul and Barnabas should go to the Gentiles, while they would be responsible for the evangelization of the Jews (v. 9). The people groups to be evangelized were simply divided into two different spheres: the Jews and the Gentiles. We know from Paul's other letters and from Acts that he always had a burden for his own people, the Jews, and when he began his evangelistic work in a city, he always began in a synagogue. But he was clear about his primary calling to be the apostle to the Gentiles. We also know from Acts that Peter was the first apostle to evangelize Gentiles, when he went to the house of Cornelius. So the agreement reached at the conference cannot be viewed as a strict geographical or even ethnographical division of labor.

Nor did the agreement include resolutions about the extent to which Gentiles were free from the requirements of the law of Moses. The incident in Antioch described in 2:11-14 is sufficient evidence that such boundaries and definitions were lacking in the general agreement reached at the Jerusalem conference. It simply recognized and approved the different tasks that God had given to leading evangelists in the church. Paul's mission to the Gentiles was confirmed, and he was not required to change his message; uncircumcised Gentile believers in Jesus Christ were to be received as full members in the church.

No one of us can fulfill the Great Commission to disciple all the nations on our own. Laboring under the misconception that the Great Commission is the sole responsibility of any one person or any one organization leads only to competition and conflict. Harmony in the mission of the church must be built on the willingness of each of us to accept and fulfill the particular assignment given to us by God and confirmed by the leadership of the church.

Eighth, the unity of the church was maintained by practical service. The practical outworking of the basic agreement regarding Paul's mission to the Gentiles included the Jerusalem apostles' request that Paul and his team *should continue to remember the poor* (v. 10). Probably *the poor* meant, as Paul says in Romans 15:26, "the poor among the saints in Jerusalem." Most commentators have interpreted this request as an

2:10 See Paul's eagerness to raise support for the poor in Jerusalem in Romans 15:25-31, 1 Corinthians 16:1-4 and 2 Corinthians 8:1—9:15. See Holmberg 1978:35-43.

appeal for money to support the poverty-stricken church in Jerusalem. While financial help was needed by the Jerusalem church, the request may have had a broader reference to the special relationship between Paul's missionary outreach to the Gentiles and the Jewish church in Jerusalem. The leaders of the Jerusalem church supported Paul's mission to the Gentiles, but at the same time they asked Paul to keep the needs and welfare of the Jewish church in mind. His Gentile mission should support, not harm, the Jewish church.

Paul affirmed his eager desire to express the unity of the church by his practical support of the Jerusalem church (v. 10). We know from his letters to the churches in Corinth and Rome that a major theme of his teaching to his Gentile churches was their obligation to support the Jerusalem church. Paul saw the collection that he took from his Gentile churches for the Jewish believers in Jerusalem as an indispensable expression of the unity of the church. "For if the Gentiles have shared in the Jews' spiritual blessings, they owe it to the Jews to share with them their material blessings" (Rom 15:27).

From Paul's account of the Jerusalem conference we learn how to maintain the unity of the church so that the preaching of the gospel to different audiences in different cultures will be effective.

The Conflict in Antioch (2:11-14) The next episode in Paul's autobiography presents a painful contrast to the heartwarming expression of unity in the Jerusalem conference. Having just heard about the "right hand of fellowship" extended in verse 9, we now read in verse 11 that Paul opposed Peter to his face in Antioch.

How could such a conflict occur between Paul and Peter after they had reached an agreement to support one another? Some early church leaders (Origen, Chrysostom and Jerome) could not believe that this conflict really occurred. They explained that Paul and Peter must have staged the conflict to illustrate the issues at stake. Augustine, however, interpreted the story as a genuine conflict in which Paul established the higher claim of the truth of the gospel over the rank and office of Peter.

2:11-14 For a survey of the diverse interpretations given to this passage in the first five centuries of the Christian era, see Longenecker 1990:64-65.

Augustine was right. Paul was willing to endure the pain of conflict with Peter in order to defend the truth of the gospel. To understand the nature of the conflict and the issues involved, we will observe how the drama developed in four stages: (1) Peter's practice of eating with the Gentile Christians, (2) Peter's separation from Gentile Christians after the arrival of the delegation from James because of his fear of the circumcision group, (3) the separation of the other Jewish Christians from Gentile Christians because of Peter's influence, and (4) Paul's rebuke.

Peter's Practice of Eating with the Gentile Christians (2:12)
According to Paul's report about Peter, *before certain men came from James, he used to eat with the Gentiles* (v. 12). In Antioch's fully integrated congregation of Christian Jews and Gentiles, Peter had regularly followed the custom of eating with Gentile Christians. His practice of sharing meals with non-Jewish Christians must have also included sharing the Lord's Supper with them. Undoubtedly his presence at table fellowship with Gentile Christians was taken as an official stamp of approval on the union and equality of Jews and Gentiles in the church. We can imagine that the Gentile believers in the church were especially encouraged by Peter's wholehearted acceptance of them. This picture of Peter eating with Gentiles is consistent with the account in Acts of Peter's visit with Cornelius after he was taught by a special vision not to call anything unclean that God had cleansed (Acts 10:1—11:18). After that vision Peter knew that God approved of his table fellowship with Gentile believers. In fact, to refuse to eat with Gentile Christians would have been to go against the clear revelation he had received from God.

Peter's Separation from Gentile Christians (2:12) It is difficult to understand how anybody could have persuaded Peter to stop sharing common meals and the Lord's Supper with Gentile believers. But apparently that is exactly what certain men with connections to James did when they arrived in Antioch. Who were these men? Were they actually sent from James? Or were they members of James's circle in the church but without a direct commission from James? Fortunately for them, Paul

---

2:12 Robert Jewett's thesis that "Jewish Christians in Judea were stimulated by Zealot pressure into a nomistic campaign among their fellow Christians in the late forties and fifties" (1971:205) is accepted by Bruce (1982:31) and Longenecker (1990:74). Building on

cloaks them with anonymity. But he seems to lay on James the responsibility for their disturbance in the church in Antioch.

More important than the question of their identity, however, is the question of their message. What did they say that persuaded Peter to separate from the Gentile believers? The only clue we have is Paul's explanation that Peter separated himself from the Gentiles *because he was afraid of those who belonged to the circumcision group* (v. 12).

The circumcision group may be another way of referring to those who came from James—namely, Jewish Christians. But why would Peter fear a delegation of Jewish Christians from the Jerusalem church, since he himself was a "pillar" of that church and had already stood up against extremist factions in that church (see Acts 11:1-18; 15:7-11; Gal 2:9)? It seems much better to interpret Paul's reference to *the circumcision group* in the same way that we interpret his use of the same phrase in the immediate context. Three times in verses 7-9 the NIV translates the same phrase as "the Jews" in contrast to the Gentiles. So the reference to *the circumcision group* in verse 12 is simply another reference to non-Christian Jews. But still we have to ask why Peter would fear non-Christian Jews when he had been so fearless in his own proclamation of the gospel to them (see Acts 2:14-41; 3:17-26; 4:8-12; 5:29-32). Our answer to that question must be based on historical information outside of the text and some speculation.

It seems that during the late forties and fifties, Jewish Christians in Judea were facing bitter antagonism from Zealot-minded Jews for socializing with Gentiles. The fierce Jewish nationalism rampant in Palestine at that time led to harsh treatment of any Jew who associated with Gentiles. It is likely that the delegation from James simply reported to Peter that his open and unrestricted association with Gentiles in Antioch would cause (or had already caused) the church in Jerusalem to suffer greatly at the hands of *the circumcision group,* Jewish nationalists.

If Peter expressed his own reason for separating from the Gentiles in Antioch, he may well have voiced his concern about the detrimental effect his table fellowship with Gentiles had on the Jerusalem church's

---

Jewett's thesis, Dunn speculates that "Peter would recognize the importance of retaining a good standing in Jewish eyes, or at least of not needlessly offending those who were formulating Jewish attitudes and reactions in such threatening times" (1990:157).

mission to the Jews. When non-Christian Jews in Jerusalem heard that Peter, a prominent church leader, was eating with Gentiles in Antioch, they would not only turn away from the witness of the church but also become actively hostile toward the church for tolerating such a practice. Confronted by these practical concerns for his home church and its mission to the Jews, Peter acted against his own better judgment. He separated himself from the Gentiles.

The Separation of the Other Jewish Christians from Gentile Christians (2:13) All the Jewish believers in Antioch were subservient to Peter's authority and followed his example. As a result the church was split into racial factions: Jews were divided from Gentiles. It is important to note that Paul accuses Peter and the rest of the Jewish believers in Antioch of hypocrisy, not heresy: *the rest of the Jews joined him in his hypocrisy* (v. 13). Their action was inconsistent with their own convictions about the truth of the gospel. They were more influenced by their common racial identity as Jews than by their new experience of unity in Christ with all believers of every race.

The irrationality of their action is expressed in the verb Paul uses to describe the defection of Barnabas: *even Barnabas was led astray* (v. 13). Painful disappointment is expressed by that phrase *even Barnabas.* It is like Julius Caesar's "Et tu, Brutus?" Paul would have expected that Barnabas would remain loyal to him and his gospel even if everyone else turned away. After all, Barnabas, as the first pastor of the church in Antioch, had warmly welcomed Gentile believers. He had worked alongside Paul in that church and in their mission of planting Gentile churches in Galatia. He had stood with Paul in the Jerusalem conference. How could even loyal Barnabas deny the truth of the gospel now? Didn't he of all people know that Gentile believers were to be fully accepted? Yes, he must have known that. But the emotions stirred up in the crisis swept him along to act contrary to his convictions. And so along with the rest of the Jewish Christians he was guilty of hypocrisy: behavior inconsistent with basic beliefs.

It is sometimes frightening to see how otherwise sane and sensible people can be swept away by emotions in the midst of a church crisis.

2:14 Peter Richardson defends Peter's application of Paul's own principle of accommo-

In the heat of the conflict they lose all sense of perspective and proportion.

We should never underestimate the emotional power of national pride and racial ties. We should not be surprised that the Jewish Christians in Antioch put their own Jewish interests above the welfare of the church. Throughout the history of the church, conflicts and divisions have occurred because Christians have been more deeply influenced by their national interests or racial identity than their Christian convictions. Whenever we identify ourselves as American Christians, or British Christians, or Chinese Christians, or German Christians, we must be aware that being American, British, Chinese or German may easily become more important to us than being Christian.

Paul's Rebuke (2:14) Peter's response to the delegation from Jerusalem and his withdrawal from the integrated fellowship of the church has been exonerated by some who think he was appropriately sensitive to the demands of his own mission to the Jews and was simply accommodating himself to those he was trying to win to Christ. If Paul himself could "become all things to all men" to win some to Christ (1 Cor 9:19-22), then why was it wrong for Peter to follow the same principle of accommodation when he adapted himself to the preferences and sensitivities of his home church?

From Paul's perspective, however, Peter's action was not accommodation for the sake of the gospel; it was compromise of the essential truth of the gospel. And on that basis Paul was willing to confront Peter with the inconsistency and hypocrisy of his actions. This confrontation was not just a power struggle to see who would maintain control of the church. Paul did not assert his authority as an apostle directly appointed by Jesus Christ or as one of the senior leaders of the church in Antioch. Nor did he appeal to the authority of the decision of the Jerusalem conference (vv. 7-9). Paul's refusal to follow Peter's example as all the other Jewish Christians did and his open rebuke of Peter were based solely on the standard set by the gospel: *When I saw that they were not acting in line with the truth of the gospel, I said to Peter in front of them all* . . . (v. 14).

dation (1980:347-62). For a refutation of Richardson's interpretation, see Carson 1986:6-45.

Paul had the spiritual discernment to rise above the emotional trauma of the crisis: he *saw* the terrible consequences of Peter's action. Peter had contradicted the gospel. The gospel proclaimed that salvation for both Jews and Gentiles was by way of the cross of Christ and union with Christ. But Peter's separation from table fellowship with Gentile Christians implied that salvation for Gentiles required strict adherence to the law and incorporation into the Jewish nation. No doubt Peter would have denied that he meant to communicate this requirement to the Gentile believers. But how else could his action be interpreted? The Gentile believers could not help but conclude from Peter's withdrawal that they were lacking something, that they were unacceptable outcasts. If they wanted to enjoy fellowship with Peter and the mother church in Jerusalem, they would have to become Jews. Their experience of salvation would be incomplete until they became Jews and observed the Jewish law. Gentile believers would have seen these implications of Peter's action even if Peter did not.

Since the consequences and implications of Peter's action were so destructive to the unity and spiritual integrity of the church, Paul had no choice but to confront Peter *in front of them all* to prove that his action was wrong. A public confrontation is not pleasant. It can easily degenerate into a no-win situation. Usually there is a loss of face for all concerned. For that reason it is natural to avoid public confrontation at all costs. But when a leader avoids public confrontation with one who is causing others to lose their faith in the completeness of God's grace expressed in the gospel of Christ, the cost is the loss of their experience of God's grace. Paul was not willing for the church of Antioch to suffer that terrible loss.

Paul led Peter back to his own deepest convictions by asking him a question: *"You are a Jew, yet you live like a Gentile and not like a Jew. How is it, then, that you force Gentiles to follow Jewish customs?"* (v. 14). By his practice of eating with the Gentile believers when he came to Antioch, Peter had already demonstrated that even as a Jew he had complete liberty to *live like a Gentile and not like a Jew.* In other words, Peter had already made it clear that his convictions permitted him to be free from Jewish food regulations. But now his separation from table fellowship with the Gentile believers forced Gentiles *to follow Jewish customs.* So while Peter, a Jew, had the freedom to live like Gentiles, his recent act of separation from Gentiles robbed them of their own freedom to live like Gentiles! They were being forced to live like Jews if they wanted to remain in the same church with the Jewish Christians. Actually, the verb that the NIV translates as *to follow Jewish customs* would be more accurately translated as "to become Jews." For the Gentiles would have to do more than follow a few Jewish customs; they would have to become Jews in order to have table fellowship with Jewish Christians who were following Jewish law.

To put it simply, Peter's separation had violated his own conviction that the racial division between Jews and Gentiles should not exist in the church. As a consequence of his separation, Gentiles were not admitted to table fellowship with Jews in the church. And the only way for them to gain admission was to become Jews.

If we feel that Paul was unnecessarily harsh or rude for rebuking Peter in public, we need to recall that the freedom of all Gentile Christians and the whole future of the Gentile mission was at stake. What if Peter's separation had set a precedent for the future so that all Gentile Christians really were required to become Jews? From a human perspective, such a precedent would have spelled the end of the Gentile church. It is not conceivable that Gentile churches could have been planted or would have grown if this requirement would have been enforced. And furthermore, if the division along racial lines had been allowed, the church would never have been able to exhibit a new humanity unified by faith in Christ, which transcends the racial and social divisions in the world. The truth of the gospel would be negated by such division.

We need to be encouraged by Paul's courageous stand to take our own stand against Christians who repeat Peter's mistake in the church today. The church today is divided in many places along racial and social lines. A list of such divisions would be too long to enumerate. We must not allow them to continue. The consequences for the clear proclamation of the gospel are disastrous. Divisions in the church negate the truth of the gospel. Let us boldly take our stand to heal those divisions now.

Paul's Personal Affirmations (2:15-21) This social crisis in the church of Antioch was exactly the same as the crisis faced by the churches in Galatia: Gentiles were being forced to live like Jews in order to be acceptable to Jews. Behind this social crisis, however, a more fundamental theological issue was at stake: Is the truth of the gospel or is the law the basis for determining fellowship between Jewish and Gentile Christians? In this next section of his autobiography, Paul addresses this fundamental issue raised by the social crisis in the church of Antioch and the churches in Galatia. As we work through his theological arguments, we must not forget that he was responding to a social crisis: division in the church along racial lines. His complex theological definitions are aimed toward the practical goal of healing this racial division in the church.

We can follow Paul's affirmations if we observe that he first presents a point of agreement (vv. 15-16), then a point of disagreement (vv. 17-18) and then his own confession of faith (vv. 19-21). Although he expresses all of these affirmations in intensely personal terms, they provide a pattern for all Christians to follow.

A Point of Agreement (2:15-16) Paul begins with a point that all Jewish Christians acknowledged and affirmed. The subject of the verb *know* in verse 16 is given in verse 15: *we who are Jews by birth and not "Gentile sinners" know* . . . Paul is developing the same kind of argument that he used against Peter in verse 14. If Peter, being a Jew, lived as a Gentile and not as a Jew, how could he require Gentiles to live as Jews? Paul continues this line of reasoning by saying that if *we who are Jews by birth and not "Gentile sinners"* (v. 15) *know* that *we, too,*

2:15-21 Betz provides an outline (point of agreement, point of disagreement, theses, refutation) from his study of Hellenistic rhetorical handbooks of Paul's era (1979:113-14).

2:16 The verb *justified (dikaioō)* is a legal metaphor that speaks of God's judgment in favor of someone. "In Paul the legal usage is plain and indisputable. For Paul the word *dikaioun* does not suggest the infusion of moral qualities. It implies the justification of the ungodly who believe on the basis of the justifying action of God in the death and resurrection of Christ" (Schrenk 1964:15; see also Ziesler 1972:212). Since the Jew-Gentile contrast in verse 15 is intimately linked with the threefold use of the verb *dikaioō* in verse 16, Paul's point is that the judicial pronouncement of God that declares someone to be within the covenant people is not based on Jew-Gentile distinctions. The covenant is no longer conceived in nationalistic terms. As Cousar observes, "The context is a social setting. The specific point Paul wants to make in that context is that God's favorable judgment in Christ means by its very nature that Gentiles are included in the Christian community on no different level or no different terms than Jews" (1982:57).

believe in Christ Jesus in order to be justified by faith in Christ and not by observing the law (v. 16), then we must recognize that *"Gentile sinners"* can be justified only by faith in Christ Jesus, not by observing the law.

Jews considered themselves to be God's covenant people; Gentiles were considered to be *sinners* because they were not part of that covenant people. But Jewish Christians recognized that God's judicial pronouncement that someone is part of the covenant people is not based on this Jew-Gentile distinction. The covenant is no longer conceived in nationalistic terms. Even though as Jews they claimed a privileged status, now as Jewish Christians they knew that only those who believe in Jesus Christ are justified, declared by God to belong to the covenant family.

In the context of Paul's account of the disputes at Jerusalem (vv. 3-6) and Antioch (vv. 11-14), the phrase *observing the law* refers to circumcision and the Jewish purity laws. The Jewish people were identified by their observance of these laws. So what Paul is denying in this context is that identification with the Jewish people through observance of these distinctively Jewish practices is not the basis of membership in the covenant people of God. Paul is appealing to the common affirmation of Jewish Christians themselves that believing in Christ Jesus, not following "Jewish customs" (v. 14), is the basis of being justified. In the final clause of verse 16, Paul paraphrases Psalm 143:2 to show the universal scope of this affirmation of Jewish Christians: *by observing the law no one will be justified.* The main emphasis of Paul's argument here is that faith in

---

The phrase *observing the law* (literally "works of the law") has usually been defined either as a straightforward reference to actions performed in obedience to the Mosaic law (Bertram 1964:646; Moo 1983:91-92) or as a negative reference to legalism—the prideful attempt to establish one's own righteousness through observance of the law (Fuller 1980:88-105). But Dunn's interpretation pays more attention to the context: "they are simply what membership of the covenant people involves, what mark out the Jews as God's people; given by God for precisely that reason, they serve to demonstrate covenant status" (1990:194; see also 1993a:133-38).

Faith in Jesus Christ is interpreted by Longenecker as "the faithfulness of Jesus Christ" (1990:87; see his list of others who support his interpretation; see also Matera 1992:100-102 for a cogent defense of this interpretation). But the fact that Christ is the object of the verb *believe* in the main clause seems to indicate that Christ should be taken as the object of the noun *faith* in the clauses that precede and follow the main clause. See Burton 1921:121, Betz 1979:117-18, Bruce 1982:139 and Dunn 1993a:134-39.

Jesus Christ replaces and excludes Jewishness as the determining criterion for belonging to the people of God.

We will see that this point of agreement was confirmed by the experience of the Gentile believers at Galatia (3:1-5). Just as Jewish Christians came to know that they were justified by faith in Christ, and not by any Jewish privileges or customs, so Gentile believers experienced the Spirit, the sign of covenant blessing (3:14), by their faith response to the message of Christ, not by their acceptance of circumcision, Jewish food regulations or sabbath observance (see 4:10). The exclusion of observing the law as a basis for justification is developed more fully in 3:10-14. There *the law* is expanded to include all the works commanded by the Mosaic law.

A Point of Disagreement (2:17-18) Second, Paul summarizes the central point of disagreement in the dispute between himself and those who forced the Jewish Christians to separate from Gentile Christians. His summary of his opponents' accusations against him consists of two premises and a conclusion: first premise—*if, while we seek to be justified in Christ;* second premise—*it becomes evident that we ourselves are sinners;* conclusion—*does that mean that Christ promotes sin?* (v. 17). From the perspective of the opponents, while Paul was seeking justification in Christ, he was at the same time living like a sinner; therefore Christ promoted sin. In other words, if his identification with Christ led him into sin, then Christ was the cause of his sin.

Certainly Paul would accept the first premise. As he clearly states in verse 16, all Jewish Christians knew that they were justified not by observing the law but by faith in Christ. But would Paul have accepted the second premise of this accusation? That depends on how we interpret the second premise. The key to the interpretation of this premise is the meaning of the word *sinners.* Does this term refer to the preconversion status or the postconversion status of Jewish Christians? It might appear from the logic of verses 15-16 that *sinners* referred to the recognition of Jewish Christians before their conversion that they too, like Gentiles, were sinners and hence could attain justification only through faith in

---

2:17 Lambrecht (1991:491), Byrne (1979:145) and Bruce (1982:141) take *sinners* as a reference to the confession of Jewish Christians at their conversion that they were sinners just like Gentiles. Longenecker (1990:89; also Stott 1968:64) takes the term *sinners* as a

Christ. But this line of interpretation fails to provide a reason for the accusation that *Christ promotes sin.* After all, the recognition of one's sinful position and total dependence on God's grace was a basic tenet in Jewish faith. Within Judaism, the acknowledgment of sin and the forgiveness of sin through the sacrificial system did not imply that the sacrificial system promoted sin.

The interpretation of *sinners* as a reference to a preconversion recognition of sin also fails to fit the context of this passage. Paul is writing these words in response to the conflict in Antioch. The criticism of Paul, Peter and the other Jewish Christians in that conflict was not because of their admission of sin before or in their conversion experience, but because of their practice of breaking Jewish purity laws by eating with Gentiles. When we keep this context in focus, it becomes clear that the term *sinners* refers to postconversion activity. The Jewish Christians in Antioch were accused of sinning after their commitment to Christ. They were not accused of all kinds of immoral behavior: sexual immorality, deceitfulness, stealing and so forth. They were accused of a specific sin: breaking the law by eating with Gentiles. Such behavior put them on the same level as Gentiles; they were sinners outside the covenant people of God.

This interpretation makes sense of the accusation that Christ promotes sin. The accusers understood correctly that the Jewish Christians were eating with Gentile Christians because of their common faith in Christ. Therefore their faith in Christ led them into the sin of breaking Jewish purity laws. If identification with Christ promoted unlawful identification with Gentiles, then, it was argued, Christ promotes sin.

Paul frames this argument of the opponents in the form of a question and counters it with an indignant *Absolutely not!* (v. 17). Paul refuses to accept the conclusion that *Christ promotes sin* because he refuses to accept the second premise. From the perspective of his accusers, eating with Gentiles is sinful, because the law forbids it. But from Paul's perspective, eating with Gentile Christians is not sinful, because the gospel demands it. Withdrawal from table fellowship with Gentile Christians

charge by Paul's opponents that justification apart from the law will inevitably lead to libertinism and licentious living.

was hypocrisy; it was a violation of the truth of the gospel. The conclusion that *Christ promotes sin* is wrong, because what was judged to be sinful (eating with Gentiles) according to the law is not really sinful according to the gospel.

Paul's statement of the accusation leveled against his position in Antioch also reflects the argument of his opponents in the Galatian crisis. Just as the failure of Jewish Christians at Antioch to observe Jewish food regulations caused them to be demoted to the category of *"Gentile sinners,"* so the failure of Gentile Christians at Galatia to observe circumcision kept them, it was argued, from being promoted to the category of the children of Abraham. The point of attack was the common failure of Jewish Christians at Antioch and Gentile Christians at Galatia to keep the law.

Paul's countercharge to the accusations leveled against him is stated in verse 18: *if I rebuild what I destroyed, I prove that I am a lawbreaker.* The object of the verbs *rebuild* and *destroy* must be understood from the context. In verse 16 Paul affirms that observing the law is not the basis of justification. In verse 17 he denies that the law can be used as a valid basis for criticizing his practice of eating with Gentile Christians. And in verse 19 he affirms that through the law he died to the law. So it is his past relationship to the law that has been destroyed and must not be rebuilt.

The law can no longer be used as the basis for judging the practice of Christians (v. 17). To rebuild the law means to reinstate the law for the supervision of the Christian life. If the law is reinstated, then the Christian is proved to be a lawbreaker. Some have interpreted Paul's argument to be against rebuilding the law on the grounds that rebuilding the law will prove him to be a lawbreaker. In other words, the transgression of breaking the law is admitted only if the law is reestablished. If the law is established for supervision of the Christian life, then eating with Gentiles is sin, since it is forbidden by the law.

2:18 Betz (1979:121) and Bruce (1982:142) understand Paul to be against the rebuilding of the law, because the rebuilding of the law would prove him to be a transgressor for breaking the law. The interpretation that the rebuilding of the law is the real transgression is supported by Duncan (1934:69), Ziesler (1972:173: "the real sin is not infringing the law, but in disloyalty to Christ and to the new way of acceptability in and through him"), Lambrecht (1991:236: "There is a kind of identification between nullifying God's grace [v.

If we keep the context in mind, however, we will see that the transgression referred to by Paul in verse 18 is actually the rebuilding of the law rather than the breaking of it. According to verse 14, Peter's real transgression was that he did not live consistently according to the truth of the gospel. The gospel had destroyed all essential distinctions between Jews and Gentiles and rendered inoperative all laws that upheld those distinctions. Whoever observed all the Jewish law—and so maintained such Jew-Gentile distinctions—violated the truth of the gospel. Duncan makes this point:

> If it is regarded as "sin" for a Jewish-Christian to eat with a Gentile, it is sin only in the sense of a technical breach of a regulation; but if a Christian allows such a regulation to stand between him and eating with a brother-in-Christ, then he is breaking God's law in a much more heinous sense, for he is doing violence to the will of God as clearly revealed in Christ. (Duncan 1934:69)

In chapter 3 Paul develops the theological basis for his assertions here regarding the role of the law in the Christian life. Our study of that chapter will lead us to consider in more depth what Paul means when he asserts that "we are no longer under the supervision of the law" (3:25). We must note here, however, that the whole discussion of law and gospel is the result of a division between the Jewish and Gentile believers in the church. That racial division threatened the effectiveness of Paul's mission to the Gentiles. It is in defense of his God-given mission that Paul spells out the relationship between law and gospel. His goal is to prove that in Christ Jesus there is neither Jew nor Greek (3:28). The unity and equality of all believers in Christ is the foundational principle and overarching aim of Paul's entire argument.

Although it may be difficult to follow each step of his argument, we can at least appreciate the lengths to which he goes to defend the unity and equality of all believers in Christ. And the more we grow in our understanding of the steps in his argument, the more we too will be able

---

21a] and transgressing [v. 18b], in so far as one who nullifies God's grace by the same token transgresses the life command it contains. As a matter of fact, by the restoration of the Law Paul would destroy God's grace and become ipso facto a transgressor of the new command to live for God") and Longenecker (1990:91: "to revert to the Mosaic law as a Christian is what really constitutes breaking the law").

to protect the equality and unity of all believers in Christ.

A Personal Confession of Faith (2:19-21) The points of agreement and disagreement that Paul sets forth in response to the crisis in Antioch (and Galatia) are founded upon his own personal confession of faith in Christ (vv. 19-20). His faith in Christ involved both a death and a new life. When Paul says *Through the law I died to the law,* he is not speaking of physical death. In his vocabulary, to die to something means to have no further relation to it (see Rom 6:2, 10-11). So to die to the law means, in this context, to cease to be under the supervision of the law.

Paul's death to the law was accomplished *through the law* (v. 19). The phrase *through the law* is taken by some interpreters as a reference to Paul's own subjective experience under the law. The law led him to discover his inability to keep the law and its inability to make him righteous. Thus it was through the law that Paul was finally led to abandon the law as the means to righteousness and to seek salvation in Christ. But this interpretation is not warranted by the immediate context. Paul does not say in this context that he died to the law because of his terrible sense of guilt and frustration under the law. Instead he declares that his death was accomplished by identification with the cross of Christ—*I have been crucified with Christ* (v. 20). When we interpret *through the law* in light of this declaration, *I have been crucified with Christ,* then we can see that death to the law through the law is accomplished by identification with the death of Christ. Paul explains in the next chapter that the law pronounced a curse on Christ as he hung on the cross (3:13). In this sense Christ died through the law. By crucifixion with Christ, believers also die because of the curse of the law on the one who hangs on the cross—and so, in this sense, they also die through the law. The perfect tense of the verb *have been crucified* points to the permanent condition of Christians in relation to the law: we remain dead and fully punished. Therefore the law can no longer condemn us.

_____

2:19 Burton (1921:133) takes *through the law* as a reference to Paul's experience with the law: "The law by his experience under it taught him his own inability to meet its spiritual requirements and its own inability to make him righteous, and thus led him to abandon it and seek salvation in Christ." Additional support for the interpretation given above can be found in Hansen 1989a:107-8.

The result of dying to the law is a new kind of life, not a life of moral license, but a life for God—*that I might live for God* (v. 19). This new kind of life is not ego-centered but Christ-centered: *I no longer live, but Christ lives in me* (v. 20). This new life of faith is motivated and guided by the sacrificial love of the Son of God, *who loved me and gave himself for me* (v. 20). Participating by faith in the death of Christ *(I have been crucified with Christ)* and the resurrection life of Christ *(Christ lives in me)* is the only way to live for God. But attempting to attain righteousness through the law sets aside the grace of God and negates the value of Christ's death (v. 21).

In succinct, compact form, Paul's confession of faith expresses his own experience that Christ, not the law, is the source of life and righteousness. The reason for his personal confession was his insistence that Jewish and Gentile believers should not be separated as the law demands, but united as the truth of the gospel demands. His new spiritual identity—*I no longer live, but Christ lives in me*—is the basis of his new social identity: "There is neither Jew nor Greek . . . for you are all one in Christ" (3:28).

When we make Paul's confession of faith in Christ our own, we must keep in mind both the spiritual and social dimensions of our union with Christ. Without the social dimension, our faith in Christ degenerates into individualism. We then become interested only in our personal faith and neglect to maintain and express our union with all believers in Christ. Such individualism has been a root cause of constant division in the church. But without the spiritual dimension, all efforts to maintain unity in the church are fruitless. Not until we can truly know and experience the reality of Paul's affirmation—*I no longer live, but Christ lives in me*—will we be able to live in true harmony with our brothers and sisters in Christ. For until then we will be ego-centered, not Christ-centered.

The experience of union with Christ as expressed here by Paul is a

---

2:20 The first-person singular, *I,* sets forth Paul's own experience, "but in such a way that the words are meant to be universally valid for all true Christians" (Blass 1961:147). Paul's experience establishes "a paradigm of the gospel of Christian freedom" (Lyons 1985:171). Paul "offers his experience as a paradigm of the reversal inaugurated by the gospel" (Gaventa 1986:319). See also Koptak 1990:97-115.

mystical experience in the sense that it transcends rational explanation: direct, intimate communion with God in Christ cannot be fully described. This mystical experience, however, should not be confused with the mysticism prevalent in the Hellenistic mystery religions of Paul's day, or the mysticism of Eastern religions touted by New Age prophets in our day. Both Hellenistic and Eastern types of mysticism emphasize ascetic disciplines leading to absorption into the divine, negation of individual personality and withdrawal from objective reality. The mystical experience of union with Christ is not accomplished by human effort but granted by God's grace *(I do not set aside the grace of God);* it is not a loss of individual personality but a renewal of true personality *(the life I live in the body, I live by faith);* it is not a withdrawal into isolation but an involvement in service ("serve one another in love"—5:13).

Mystical union with Christ also needs to be understood from the historical perspective: it is not a totally subjective experience divorced from objective historical reality. Just as a person who becomes a citizen of the United States has decided to live within the historical reality created by events in Philadelphia on July 4, 1776, so the person who becomes identified with Christ has decided to live within the new historical reality created by the events of the cross of Christ and his resurrection. Paul places the subjective experience of faith in Jesus Christ in the context of God's redemptive work in history (3:6-25).

The practical outworking of union with Christ comes into focus in Paul's ethical appeal (5:13—6:10). There we find that the experience of union with Christ includes both passive (being led by the Spirit) and active (walking in the Spirit) dimensions. So it would be a mistake to take Paul's words *I no longer live, but Christ lives in me* as a proof text for total passivity in the Christian experience. The very next phrase underscores the necessity of active faith: *The life I live in the body, I live by faith in the Son of God* (v. 20). We do not become just empty pipes that God's power flows through, as I've heard preachers say. *I no longer live* as an egocentric person in obedience to all my selfish passions and desires, for Christ is now at the center of my life. Now *I live* in obedience

Notes: 3:1 *Bewitched* is found only here in the New Testament, but it is a common term in Greek literature for "witchcraft exercised through hostile looks or words" (Delling 1971:595: "the dangerous feature is that the Galatians have willingly yielded to these mato him, for he *loved me and gave himself for me.*

□ Paul's Exposition of Promise and Law (3:1—4:11)

The questions cut like a knife. "Why did you ever listen to such a crazy man? How could you believe such nonsense?" The talk-show host badgered the former members of the Branch Davidian cult with piercing questions after David Koresh and his followers destroyed themselves by fire in Waco, Texas.

Paul's questions in Galatians also cut like a knife. Having concluded his autobiography, Paul addresses his readers directly with a series of piercing questions. These questions are asked in a tone of rebuke and thus continue the rebuke section of the letter. Paul rebukes the Galatians for their foolishness. Their defection from the gospel was caused by their foolish confusion of gospel and law. Paul's rebuke for their foolish exchange of faith in the gospel for works of the law is then enforced by an exposition of Scripture (3:6—4:7) to clarify the relationship of the gospel and the law. After his exposition of Scripture, Paul turns to the Galatians and again rebukes them with questions (4:8-11).

My exposition of this passage will follow the flow of Paul's thought:

□ understanding the presence of the Spirit (3:1-5)

□ recognizing the children of Abraham (3:6-9)

□ facing the alternatives of curse and blessing (3:10-14)

□ understanding the promise (3:15-18)

□ understanding the law (3:19-25)

□ identifying the recipients of the promise (3:26-29)

□ moving from slavery to freedom (4:1-7)

□ returning to slavery again? (4:8-11)

Understanding the Presence of the Spirit (3:1-5) Paul's rebuke expresses deep concern for the Galatian believers. They have been poisoned by a perversion of the gospel. They appear to Paul like people who have come under the control of an evil magician and his demonic spells: *You foolish Galatians! Who has bewitched you?* (3:1). The Ga-

gicians and their influence without realizing to what powers of falsehood they were surrendering"). Betz (1979:131) and Burton (1921:144) see the use of this term by Paul as simply a rhetorical technique to depict negatively the false teachers who have confused the

latians are acquiescing to the demands of persuasive teachers of the law in order to attain spiritual perfection without realizing that they are being enslaved by demonic powers (see 4:8-9). Their quest for perfection through the law is a drugged illusion from which they must be wakened. But how? How is the spell to be broken?

Paul's methods are instructive. He pierces the fog of confusion in the Galatian churches with the searchlight of questions. Paul presses hard with questions to put the Galatians back in touch with their own experience of God. Questions come before dogmatic statements and authoritative commands. Questions are the way to start breaking the grip of illusions.

Paul's questions in 3:1-5 focus on three aspects of the Galatians' experience of the Spirit: their initial reception of the Spirit (vv. 1-2), their progress toward maturity by the Spirit (v. 3) and their experience of miracles by the Spirit (vv. 4-5).

Initial Reception of the Spirit (3:1-2) Paul takes the Galatians back to their first exposure to the message of Christ crucified. In verse 1, which is one sentence in the Greek text, the reminder of their vision of Christ crucified is set over against their foolish acquiescence to a bewitching influence. In other words, Paul is asking them how they could have succumbed to any other influence, no matter how charming and intoxicating, after they had once seen Christ portrayed as crucified.

This initial question reveals the nature of Paul's evangelistic preaching as he founded the churches in Galatia. His use of the term *portrayed* means that his preaching was like painting a picture with words or putting up a public poster for all to see. The perfect tense of the verb *crucified* indicates that Paul's vivid portrayal of Christ crucified was not only of the historical event but also of the present, saving power of the cross of Christ for all who believe in him.

Paul's first question drives us along with the original readers back to

---

minds of the Galatians. In their view Paul is not expressing a belief in the reality of magical powers or demonic influence. Neyrey, however, asserts that "Gal 3:1 is no different from 2 Cor 11:3, 13-15, where Paul accuses his rivals, the 'super-apostles' at Corinth, of being Satan disguised as an angel of light. This charge of demon possession is a formal 'witchcraft accusation,' a technical term for the accusation that Paul's rivals are either the devil himself or persons controlled by him" (1988:75). Neyrey overstates the case to claim that Paul is speaking of demonic possession and witchcraft. There is no evidence that his opponents

the foot of the cross of Christ. This is the place to find release from any enchantment that draws us away from Christ. We need a renewed vision of Christ crucified if we are to gain freedom from illusions of perfection through law observance, for such a vision is a vivid reminder that the cross, not human achievement, is the basis of God's blessing. Paul's questions move from the experience of the preaching of the cross of Christ (v. 1) to the experience of the Spirit (vv. 2-5). The two are linked: the cross opens the door for the Spirit, and the experience of the Spirit is the result of faith in the message of the cross of Christ.

The Galatian believers are taken back to the beginning, when they first received the Spirit by believing the message of the cross of Christ: *I would like to learn just one thing from you: Did you receive the Spirit by observing the law, or by believing what you heard?* (v. 2). The evidence of the Spirit's entrance into their lives in that conversion experience must have been undeniably clear for Paul to use it as a reference point in his argument. Their baptism (3:27) and the full assurance of the Father's love given by the Spirit (4:6; compare Rom 5:5; 8:15-16) left an indelible mark on their life. The reference to miracles in verse 5 is evidence that they also experienced outward manifestations of the Spirit's presence.

The readers are taken back to the roots of their spiritual experience to remind them that the beginning was a gift of God's Spirit. The renewal of this perspective destroys the delusion that God's blessing depends on joining a group (in this case the Jewish people) or attaining a certain level of moral excellence (observing the law of Moses). The Galatian converts were excluded from the Jewish nation, and they had not observed the law; but there was no denying that they had experienced God's blessing, the gift of his Spirit.

Paul formulates his question in verse 2 as a sharp antithesis designed to break the bewitching spell of the intruders by showing the contradic-

---

were part of an occult movement. Nevertheless, it is clear from Paul's other letters that he viewed demonic influence as a very real danger (1 Cor 10:19-21; 2 Cor 4:4; 11:3, 13-15; Eph 6:11-12; 2 Thess 2:9-10; 1 Tim 4:1). And Galatians 4:8-9 indicates that Paul was concerned that the Galatians were being enslaved by demonic powers. The troublemakers in Galatia appeared to Paul as unwitting agents of demonic deception. "This bewitchment, then, is nothing other than a dementing by the devil, who inserts into the heart a false opinion, one that is opposed to Christ" (Luther 1979:195).

tion between the Galatians' recent interest in *observing the law* and their initial experience of *believing what you heard* (see also v. 5). The readers are confronted with a clear choice between mutually exclusive alternatives. They are not permitted to accept the both-and synthesis of the intruders. It is an either-or choice.

The meaning of the alternatives needs to be clarified. We have already observed in our study of 2:15-16 that *observing the law* has specific reference to regulations of the Jewish community which maintained their distinctive national identity. In other words, Paul is reminding his converts that they did not need to become Jewish proselytes in order to receive the Spirit in the first place (v. 2) or to experience the continuous outpouring of the Spirit and miracles in their lives (v. 5).

The meaning of the phrase *observing the law* is further clarified by the reference to *human effort* in verse 3. Actually, *human effort* is the NIV translation of the word "flesh" in this verse. At the end of the letter Paul tells the Galatian believers that the intruders in their churches "want you to be circumcised that they may boast about your flesh" (6:13). In that reference "flesh" refers to circumcised flesh. In other words, the intruders want to be able to boast that the Gentile believers have become Jews. So in the light of this understanding of "flesh" in verse 3, *observing the law* refers principally, though not exclusively, to circumcision of the flesh and other practices that serve as marks of Jewish identity. Paul is saying that it is not necessary to take on a new racial or cultural identity

---

3:2 *Believing what you heard (ex akoēs pisteōs)* should be interpreted in the light of the parallel text in Romans 10:16-17, where Paul's use of *akoē* is determined by his quotation of Isaiah 53:1, "who has believed our message" *(akoē)*. Paul's comment on this Old Testament text employs *akoē* to mean "message" or "what is heard": "faith comes from the message *(akoē)* and the message *(akoē)* by the preaching of Christ" (Bruce 1982:149; Hays 1983:146). Romans 10:17 teaches that the message, the proclamation of the gospel, creates or evokes faith (cf. Rom 1:16; 1 Cor 1:18; 2:4; 1 Thess 1:5). As Lull notes, "Preference should be given to the interpretation which does justice to the double emphasis in the context on Paul's missionary preaching on the one hand, and the act of faith on the other" (1980:56).

3:3 The parallelism "beginning . . . completing" (NIV: *beginning . . . trying to attain your goal*) occurs also in Philippians 1:6 ("he who began a good work in you will carry it on to completion until the day of Christ Jesus"), where it refers to the beginning and completion of the Christian life, both accomplished by God. The verb *to complete* or *to perfect* is also used in 2 Corinthians 7:1 to depict the process of sanctification: "Let us purify ourselves . . . perfecting holiness out of reverence for God." Paul has the process of perfection in mind in Galatians 3. In other words, he is talking not simply about justification but also about

in order to experience the Spirit.

Progress Toward Maturity by the Spirit (3:3) Not only was the beginning a gift, but progress is also a gift, as the question in verse 3 indicates. The contrast between *beginning with the Spirit* and *trying to attain your goal* by the flesh (remember that the NIV translates "flesh" as *human effort*) sets up the antithesis between spirit and flesh which recurs in 4:29, 5:16-23 and 6:8. In 4:23 and 29 the son born according to the flesh ("born in the ordinary way") is a reference to Jews who hold to the Sinai covenant (4:24) and to the present Jerusalem (4:25) as the basis of their identity. These are the same ones who desire to boast in circumcised flesh—in other words, in the proselytization of Gentile believers at Galatia (6:13). We need to keep this historical conflict in mind so that we do not slip into an interpretation derived from Greek dualism where the spirit is good and the body (flesh) is inherently evil. Paul's specific point is that the Galatians' alternative is between living by the Spirit, whom they received when they believed the message of Christ crucified, and seeking perfection by circumcision (and other rites such as food laws and sabbath observance), which would identify them as proselyte Jews. Trying to attain perfection by the flesh in that context meant the attempt to attain spiritual status by conforming to Jewish customs in order to become Jews.

Sincere Christian people have often felt that belonging to a specific cultural or religious group would enhance their spiritual status. They

---

sanctification. It will be important to keep this scope of reference in mind when we consider Paul's discussion of the role of the law in the Christian life. We need to remember that he is talking about the role of the law not only as it relates to justification but also as it relates to sanctification.

"Flesh" (NIV: *human effort*) in 3:3 refers specifically to the circumcision of the flesh, but a broader meaning is also implied here by the antithesis to the Spirit. O'Donovan aptly defines flesh in this context as "an alternative source of strength to the Spirit . . . an autonomous human power" (1986:12). It is interesting to compare and contrast two churches described by Paul—the Galatian and Corinthian churches. The former was preoccupied with the law and was characterized by legalism; the latter abandoned the law and was characterized by libertinism. The flesh was the root problem in both cases. "So we find the flesh taking occasion not only of law but of freedom to assert itself against the Spirit" (O'Donovan 1986:12). The superreligious ascetic separated from all obvious sins of excess may be just as dominated by "flesh" ("autonomous human power") as the derelict enslaved to the most sordid vices.

have sometimes conformed to extreme requirements just to gain acceptance. All such efforts to achieve spiritual progress are classified here by Paul as merely *human effort* (NIV), efforts of the flesh. Paul's question in verse 3 reminds us that our beginning in the Christian life was based on our response of faith to the message of Christ crucified and the consequent experience of the Spirit, and our progress in the Christian life must be on the same basis.

Miracles by the Spirit (3:4-5) Paul's emphasis in this context on the positive experience of the Spirit probably indicates that his question in verse 4 should be interpreted as another reference to God's gracious work by his Spirit in their lives. The word translated *suffered* by the NIV also has a positive meaning. The NEB translates it in this way: "Have all your great experiences been in vain?" Since the verses before and after verse 4 speak of the gift of the Spirit and the occurrence of miracles, it seems that Paul is asking them if all these marvelous spiritual experiences have not had a positive effect in their lives. Their acceptance of the message of the Judaizers makes Paul wonder whether they have learned anything at all from all the great things God has been doing in their midst: of what value is the gift of the Spirit if you strive for perfection without the direction or power of the Spirit?

But Paul cannot accept that God's gracious provision of the Spirit and his miraculous work will be in vain, so he adds the disclaimer at the end of verse 4: *if it really was for nothing.* Such a great experience of God's work cannot be for nothing. The Galatians must be shaken out of their stupor. They must think deeply again about the implications of their own wonderful experience of God's activity in their lives.

In verse 5 the present tense of the participles in the Greek text ("the one who gives . . . the one who works") points to the unchanging

---

3:4 *Suffered (paschō)* is used in a positive sense ("to experience"), according to W. Michaelis, "only when there is an addition to this effect or, very rarely, the context makes it sufficiently plain" (1967:950). But he inexplicably asserts that the word has a negative sense in Galatians 3:3. While it is true that Paul's usage of this word is usually with the negative sense (1 Cor 12:26; 2 Cor 1:6; Phil 1:29; 1 Thess 2:14; 2 Thess 1:5), in each case the context clearly points to the negative sense. The immediate context in Galatians 3:1-5, however, seems to point in the direction of a positive meaning (for support of the positive sense here see Cole 1965:90, Hendriksen 1969:114 and Longenecker 1990:104).

3:5 With the reference to *miracles (dynameis)* in the experience of the Galatian churches,

character of God. He always gives and works in this way. The word translated *give* was used in marriage contracts to express the husband's commitment to provide faithful and generous support for his wife. God is the faithful husband caring for his bride. The experience of God's continuous and generous supply of his Spirit to the Galatian believers is linked with his work of miracles in their midst. Though Paul anticipates that the Spirit will produce inward moral qualities in those led by the Spirit (5:22-23), his focus here is primarily on outward manifestations of the Spirit's presence in miracles. Paul recounts such overwhelming evidence of God's gracious work in order to draw his readers away from their present fixation on the stringent requirements of the teachers of the law.

A review of God's gracious work among his people by his Spirit releases us from imperious demands for religious performance. God's performance, not ours, must be the object of our faith and hope.

It is important to observe how central the experience of the Spirit is in Paul's entire argument. The arguments from Scripture in 3:6-29 are bracketed by two passages (3:1-5 and 4:1-7) in which Paul describes the experience of the Spirit in the Galatian communities: *Did you receive the Spirit* . . . (3:2); *After beginning with the Spirit* . . . (3:3); *Does God give you his Spirit* . . . (3:5); "God sent the Spirit of his Son into our hearts, the Spirit who calls out, '*Abba*, Father' " (4:6). The undeniable presence of the Spirit in the Galatian church is presented as irrefutable evidence that these Gentile believers who call God "Abba! Father!" are true children of God.

The undeniable presence of the Spirit among Gentile believers who were not observing the Mosaic law must have been an electric shock to

we learn that they were charismatic communities in the sense that they were enjoying outward manifestations of the power of the Spirit on a regular basis. Burton says that "the apostle has in mind chiefly the charismatic manifestation of the Spirit which attests itself in *dynameis* [miracles] and other kindred manifestations" (1921:151). Paul's point here is that miracles were freely given and accomplished by God without any human effort. Paul gives us no basis for manipulative efforts to make miracles happen. But we can expect, on the basis of this verse, that God will continue to work in miraculous ways by the power of his Spirit in the midst of his people who look to him in confident, quiet trust.

the Jewish Christian teachers. It was their expectation that the Holy Spirit would be experienced only by righteous Jews who faithfully kept all the law of Moses. In the Mishnah, the codification in the second century A.D. of Jewish customs and traditions, we find this kind of thought about the Holy Spirit: "Rabbi Phineas ben Jair says, 'Heedfulness leads to cleanliness, and cleanliness leads to purity, and purity leads to separatism, and separatism leads to holiness, and holiness leads to humility, and humility leads to shunning of sin, and shunning of sin leads to saintliness, and saintliness leads to the Holy Spirit.' " But in the experience of the Galatian Christians, the demonstration of the Spirit's presence came before they were even taught the law or tried to live by its requirements.

God delights in doing miracles for new Christians who believe his promises. They may have much to learn before they can live saintly lives, but at least they know that the Spirit of God is with them, because when they pray with simple faith, God answers their prayers with miracles. During his twenty-two years in Afghanistan, J. Christy Wilson observed that "there is nothing greater than a demonstration of the Spirit's power to convince Muslims of Christ's power. Muslims love to argue. Yet when they see the power of God manifest and the sick healed in the name of Jesus, they come to Christ more readily." When I read such reports of God's gracious, miraculous work by his Spirit, my own faith is renewed.

Paul reminds the Galatian Christians of God's miraculous work in their lives so that their faith will be renewed. His questions call for a reaffirmation of faith. The alternatives are posed so that Christians will be compelled by their own experience of the Spirit to choose the right answers: "Not by observing the law, but by believing what we heard about Christ crucified!" "Not by flesh, but by the Spirit!" This clear choice will break the spell of any bewitching influence. It is a choice that needs to be reconfirmed every day.

Identifying the Children of Abraham (3:6-9) Just as the converts in Galatia were struggling to understand how their new faith in Christ affected their identity, so I have heard Chinese Singaporean Christians struggle to define their identity as Christians in response to constant negative references in the media to "Christian/Western values." This equation of Christian values and Western values implies that when Chinese people become Christians, they abandon their Chinese identity and become Westerners. Unfortunately, conversions to the Christian faith *are* often accompanied by such a change in cultural identity, which seems to be required by strong Western influences both in society and in the church. As a result there is often a painful confusion of identity. "I feel like I'm not really a true Christian unless I give up my Chinese identity and become thoroughly Westernized," one young Chinese Christian man told me. "But I don't understand why I have to adopt so much of the Western culture and deny my own Chinese heritage in order to be a true Christian."

Similar questions have been raised in every age and culture as converts to the Christian faith wrestle to understand their identity as Christians. Even in so-called Christian countries, Christians need to discern the difference between their identity as God's children and the identity offered by the dominant forces of the surrounding culture.

It is helpful in the context of this discussion about the Christian's sense of identity to reflect on Paul's response to the identity crisis faced by the Galatian Christians. They were adrift in a no man's land between the pagan temples and the Jewish synagogues. They belonged to neither. They had abandoned the gods and religious practices of the temples. But they did not attend the Jewish synagogues, nor were they welcome there, even though they read the Jewish Scriptures and believed in a Jewish Messiah. As new Christians without a clear sense of identity, they were easily persuaded that if they acquired a Jewish identity they would belong to the people of God. They were probably reminded that the mother church in Jerusalem was a law-observant Jewish church. So if they really wanted to belong to the true church, they would have to be Jewish. They were in the process of receiving circumcision and the law so that they could belong to the people who claimed to be the true recipients of God's blessing.

In Galatians 3:6-9 we see how Paul defines the identity of the Galatian believers: he compares them to Abraham (v. 6), then he identifies them as children of Abraham on the basis of a common family characteristic (v. 7); he confirms that identification by quoting Scripture (v. 8), and on that basis he includes them in the family blessing (v. 9). Our own sense of identity can be clarified and strengthened as we trace the steps in this identification process.

Compared to Abraham (3:6) After his questions in 3:1-5, designed to evoke a reaffirmation of faith, Paul points to the story of Abraham's faith: *Consider Abraham.* Since Abraham is the father of God's people, his experience with God establishes a guide to the will of God for his people. If the experience of the Galatians can be shown to correspond to the experience of the patriarch, then their experience conforms to the will of God. Verse 6 begins with a comparative conjunction (missing in the NIV): [Just as Abraham] *believed God, and it was credited to him as righteousness.* Paul shows the striking similarity between the experience of the Galatians, who believed the preaching of the cross and received the blessing of the Spirit, and the experience of the great patriarch of God's people, who believed God's promise and received the crediting of righteousness. Paul draws two significant parallels between the Galatians' experience and Abraham's experience: the human response of faith and the divine blessing enjoyed by those who believe.

The human response of faith. The Galatian believers were being excluded from the family of Abraham because they did not have the required membership badge: circumcision and works of the law. "After all," they had probably been told, "circumcision is the sign of the Abrahamic covenant, and Genesis 17 declares that anyone without this sign is to be cut off from the covenant family. So you uncircumcised Gentiles

---

3:6 Note how Paul uses the narrative pattern to guide the Galatians' thinking in the evaluation of their experience. Too often Paul has been viewed as a systematic theologian who developed a list of abstract theological concepts. Not so. Paul's theology is usually expressed along a story line. When he speaks of sin and death, he tells the story of Adam (Rom 5:12-20). When he speaks of promise and faith, he tells the story of Abraham (Rom 4; Gal 3). All stories point to the story of Christ (see Hays 1983:213). There is a narrative structure to Paul's theology. We are not so much required to contemplate abstract concepts as we are invited to enter the narrative of God's relationship with his people. At this point in his letter, Paul draws his readers into the story of Abraham to show them how they are like the father of God's special people. "Paul describes the situation in terms of sacred history. The demonstration from Scripture follows the history of Israel" (Ebeling 1985:171).

The Jewish interpretation of Genesis 15:6 ("Abram believed the LORD") in Paul's day understood the faith of Abraham as equivalent to his righteous behavior, namely, his acceptance of circumcision, his observance of Mosaic law and his faithful obedience when tested

cannot possibly be included in the Abrahamic family and blessing. You don't belong!" It must have been very upsetting, as it always is, to be excluded from the blessing of God and the fellowship of God's people on the basis of racial, social and religious entrance requirements.

But Paul quotes Genesis 15:6 to prove that faith is the only entrance requirement for full membership in the family of God. The close parallel between verses 5 and 6 of Galatians 3 sets Abraham's faith in contrast to the works of the law. Keeping all the requirements of the law is not the way to belong to the covenant family of God. Faith is the way to enter into a relationship with God.

The content of Abraham's faith is not specified in verse 6, but in verse 8 Paul asserts that the gospel was announced in advance to Abraham, the gospel of blessing for Gentiles. So it is not stretching the text at all to draw the conclusion that Paul sees Abraham's faith as a response to this gospel of blessing for the Gentiles. The context of Genesis 15:6 indicates that the content of Abraham's faith was God's promise of an innumerable offspring. One clear night God challenged Abraham to count the stars. Then God gave Abraham his promise: "So shall your offspring be" (Gen 15:5). When Abraham heard God's promise, he believed. His faith was a response to God's promise.

The content of the Galatians' faith is essentially the same. Their faith is believing what they heard (vv. 2, 5). What they heard was the gospel of blessing for Gentiles through the cross of Christ. So the comparison of the response of faith of Abraham and the Galatians points to a remark-

(Hansen 1989:79). We can see this interpretation in the Old Testament Apocryphal books (Sirach 44:19-21; 1 Macc 2:50-52) and in the New Testament (Heb 11:17; Jas 2:21-23). According to this interpretation, Abraham's faithfulness was credited to him as righteousness because it actually *was* righteousness, faithful obedience to God's will (Ziesler 1972:104). But Paul reads Genesis 15:6 through the lens of his and the Galatian converts' experience of faith in Christ (2:16-20; 3:1-5)—faith in the saving act of God, not faithfulness in human acts of obedience. "His knowledge of Christ opened a new way in which he found the true meaning of Scriptures" (Ellis 1957:149). His interpretation fits with the emphasis in the original context on Abraham's faith as trust in the promises of God (see Gen 15:1-6).

Paul's definition of faith as faith in Christ implies that he did not interpret the phrase *it was credited to him as righteousness,* as his opponents probably did, to mean that Abraham's faith was reckoned to be equivalent to Abraham's righteous behavior. From Paul's perspective, the crediting of righteousness is the gracious act of God by which Abraham is accepted and established within a covenant relationship with God.

able similarity that cannot be denied. No wonder, then, that Paul commands the Galatians to draw the appropriate conclusion from this comparison with Abraham: they belong to the Abrahamic family. But before we look at that conclusion, we need to examine the other side of the comparison.

The divine blessing. Believing what was heard is the basic parallel between the experience of the Galatians and the experience of Abraham. But by quoting the entire text of Genesis 15:6, Paul also sets up a parallel between the bestowal of the Spirit upon the Galatians and the crediting of righteousness to Abraham. This parallel points to the close connection between the bestowal of the Spirit and the crediting of righteousness. Paul's line of argument seems to be that the observable experience of the bestowal of the Spirit is evidence of the unobservable act of God's judicial acquittal that brings the believer within the covenant relationship. Miracles (3:5), the heart-cry of "Abba" (4:6) and the fruit of the Spirit (5:22-26) provide solid evidence of the bestowal of the Spirit. And the bestowal of the Spirit indicates that the crediting of righteousness has taken place.

Paul takes his readers back to the beginning of the story of God's family. Abraham believed God: that was how the covenant relationship with God began. As Paul argues throughout this chapter, the terms of the relationship have not been changed. This comparison with Abraham demonstrates the unity of the Bible. Receiving the blessing of God by faith is the central theme of the entire story of God's people, from the first page to the last.

Identified as Children of Abraham (3:7) The comparison drawn in verse 6 between the experience of Abraham and that of the Galatians requires the conclusion of verse 7: *Understand, then, that those who believe are children of Abraham.* The common family trait of faith is the decisive factor. Anyone characterized by that trait is definitely identified as a member of the family.

We might have expected the conclusion in verse 7 that God credits

---

3:7 When Paul calls the Galatian believers *children of Abraham,* he is giving them one of the favorite titles of Israel (see Mt 3:9; Jn 8:39). The use of this title for the church points to continuity between Israel and the church and unity in the plan of salvation for all of God's people.

righteousness to all those who are of faith. That conclusion would have been more closely related to the previous verse's quotation of Genesis 15:6. But the fact that Paul's conclusion has to do with the identity of the children of Abraham shows that this was the major concern. The troublemakers insisted that circumcision was the indispensable sign of the covenant family. Paul uses Genesis 15:6 to prove that only those who believe can legitimately make the claim that they belong to the people of God as children of Abraham.

Faith is the true sign of covenant. In the context Paul clearly defines *faith* as faith in Jesus Christ (v. 16). So now identification with Christ by faith, rather than identification with the Jewish nation by circumcision and works of the law, provides the basis of belonging to God's covenant family.

The continuity between Israel, the "children of Abraham," and the church is clearly stated here: Christians have roots; they have a clear identity; they belong to the ancient people of God that began with Abraham.

Confirmed by Scripture (3:8) The radical conclusion drawn from Genesis 15:6 is confirmed by a second quotation: *The Scripture foresaw that God would justify the Gentiles by faith, and announced the gospel in advance to Abraham: "All nations will be blessed through you"* (v. 8). It was not enough to show that those who believe are the children of Abraham. Paul proves that the principle of righteousness by faith attested for Abraham in Genesis 15:6 is explicitly extended by Scripture itself to the Gentiles. In Paul's quotation the phrase *all nations* from Genesis 18:18 is inserted in place of the phrase "all the families" (NIV "all peoples") in Genesis 12:3. This combination of texts in his quotation indicates that Paul's primary purpose is to demonstrate that Scripture witnesses to the inclusion of the Gentiles in the blessing promised to Abraham.

Paul interprets the promise of the blessing of all Gentiles in Abraham as a prophecy of what actually happened in his mission to the Gentiles.

3:8 This promise of blessing for Gentiles in Abraham *(through you)* would have been interpreted by Jews to mean that Gentiles could receive the blessing when they were incorporated among the descendants of Abraham by circumcision and the observance of the Mosaic law (Betz 1979:142). But Paul takes the promise as a prophecy of the result of

We must not forget that Paul wrote this letter as a missionary. He was called to take the good news about Jesus to the Gentiles. When he did so, he saw the incontestable evidence that God accepted the Gentiles who believed the gospel. It was clear that God justified them by faith. The evidence that this had happened was the bestowal of the Spirit on these Gentile converts. Paul had learned from his missionary experience that *God would justify the Gentiles by faith* (v. 8). In the light of that missionary experience, Paul understood the Old Testament promise of blessing for the Gentiles as a description and validation of his ministry.

Scripture *foresaw* what happened to the Gentile believers in Galatia. And because Scripture foresaw that God would justify Gentiles when they believed the gospel, Scripture *announced the gospel in advance to Abraham.* The gospel announced in advance to Abraham was a gospel of blessing for Gentiles. That was the gospel Paul preached to the Gentiles! To say that Scripture *foresaw* and *announced the gospel in advance* is to personify Scripture. The written text is treated as a person who sees and speaks. Paul's personification of Scripture means that for him the written text expresses the voice of God: what Scripture says, God says.

Included in the Family Blessing (3:9) The blessing promised to Abraham for all nations is appropriated by *those who have faith.* This application in verse 9 of verse 8's quotation from Scripture is parallel to the application in verse 7 of the Scripture quotation in verse 6. Both applications have as subject *those who have faith.* Two related descriptions are given of those who have faith: they *are children of Abraham* (v. 7), and they *are blessed along with Abraham, the man of faith* (v.

---

his missionary efforts in Galatia: the Galatian believers received the Spirit by faith in Christ. In verse 14 Paul clearly states that their experience of the Spirit is the fulfillment of the promised blessing of Abraham.

The personification of Scripture, so that Scripture foresees and speaks, also occurs in Galatians 3:22 and 4:30, and Romans 4:3, 9:17, 10:11 and 11:2.

3:9 Jewish interpreters of the Old Testament would have described Abraham as "the faithful man" rather than *the man of faith.* But Paul's focus is on the similarity between the Christians' and Abraham's trust in the gracious promise of God. (The exact nature of this similarity is explained in Romans 4.) Association with Abraham is no longer based on physical relationship and keeping of the Mosaic law, but on the spiritual kinship of faith in God, who gives and fulfills his promise of blessing.

9). The point Paul is making from his exposition of the Old Testament narrative of Abraham is that the Galatian believers are Abraham's children and recipients of Abraham's blessing.

What exactly is this blessing? In the Old Testament story God promised to bless Abraham with innumerable offspring and a land in which they would dwell. But in the context of Paul's application of this story, the blessing enjoyed by those of faith is transformed into a twofold spiritual blessing. In verse 8 Paul's introduction to the scriptural promise clearly equates the justification of the Gentiles by faith with the blessing. And the presence of the Spirit described in verses 2, 5 and 14 is presented as the observable evidence that the Galatian believers are recipients of the blessing. So justification and the gift of the Spirit are two dimensions of the blessing presented by Paul. God's declaration that Gentile believers are accepted as righteous and God's demonstration of his presence by his Spirit in the midst of the Galatian churches constitute the blessing enjoyed by faith.

Faith has been the emphasis in this section. Noun and verb forms of *faith* occur seven times in verses 1-9. No longer will anyone be excluded from the blessing on the basis of race; those of faith from all nations enjoy the blessing. Abraham is now the prototype of the universal people of faith, not simply the progenitor of the Jewish race. So it is not necessary to belong to the Jewish race to participate in the blessing of Abraham. All that is necessary is faith like Abraham's.

Just as the Galatian believers did not need to take on a Jewish identity in order to be Christians—their true identity as full members of the family of faith was based on their faith in Christ, not on their racial or social status—so today believers in every nation need to be encouraged

---

In the Old Testament narrative the blessing is often presented in terms of offspring as numerous as the stars and the land of the Cannanites for Abraham's offspring to enjoy (Gen 12:1-2, 7; 13:14-18; 15:5-6, 18; 17:4-8, 16-21; 18:18; 22:17). Just exactly how God would bless the Gentiles who were not Abraham's offspring was a question contemplated by the Jews. In a rabbinic commentary we read: " 'And in thee shall all the families of the earth be blessed.' Now if that is meant in respect of wealth, they are surely wealthier than we! But it is meant in respect of counsel: when they get into trouble they ask our advice, and we give it to them" (Genesis Rabbah 39:12; see Hansen 1989:128-47). Paul went far beyond any of the rabbinic commentaries when he defined the blessing for the Gentiles in the light of Christ and his missionary experience as justification and the gift of the Spirit.

to find their true identity in Christ, not in the attainment of a new ethnic identity.

The Alternatives: The Curse and the Blessing (3:10-14) "Two roads diverged in a yellow wood," Robert Frost tells us in his poem "The Road Not Taken." He took "the one less traveled by," and that "made all the difference."

But choosing a road only because it is less traveled seems to be a risky basis for navigation through life. How can we be sure that we are on the road to blessing?

When we read Galatians 3:10-14 we are struck by the antithesis of two words: *curse* and *blessing*. In this section Paul describes two alternative roads: the first leads to a curse (v. 10), the second to blessing (v. 14).

Faced by this fork in the road on their journey, the Galatian Christians had difficulty knowing which way to take. Some Jewish Christians were pointing to the well-traveled road that had been taken by the Jewish people for centuries. "Join us in the Jewish way of life," they said. "Only if you identify yourselves with us and come with us will you find blessing." They emphasized the noble, distinctive traditions of the Jewish nation.

But Paul argues in this passage that identification with the Jewish nation by observing the Mosaic law is not the way that leads to blessing. In fact, the claim that blessing depends exclusively on national identity leads to a terrible curse. Identification with Christ is the only way that leads to true blessing.

Four quotations from Scripture are used as signposts at this fork in the road to indicate which way leads to a curse and which way leads to blessing. We may label these four signposts with four words: *curse* (v. 10), *faith* (v. 11), *law* (v. 12) and *cross* (vv. 13-14).

Of course today we do not face pressure to turn to the Jewish way of life. But there are people similar to the intruders in Galatia who want to map out for us the way that leads to blessing. The road they point to is defined in terms of cultural customs.

3:10 Most interpreters assume that Paul has left unstated the implicit minor premise: no one has in fact fulfilled all the law (see Lightfoot 1957:137; Burton 1921:164; Stott 1964:79; Schreiner 1984:159). Another interpretation is that prideful legalism, self-glorification

The signposts that Paul placed in the fork of the road for the Galatian believers can direct us today.

Signpost 1: Curse (3:10) The first signpost issues a harsh warning to *all who rely on observing the law* They are *under a curse.* The warning is based on a quotation from the law itself: *Cursed is everyone who does not continue to do everything written in the Book of the Law* (see Deut 27:26). In Deuteronomy a long list of terrible curses concludes with severe warnings of complete destruction (Deut 30:11-20). Since the curse is the result of failure to do the law, it must be assumed by Paul that *all who rely on observing the law* fail to do the law. In fact, Paul explicitly asserts at the end of his letter that "not even those who are circumcised obey the law" (6:13).

In the context of the Galatian dispute, when Paul refers to *all who rely on observing the law* he is speaking about those who are persuading the Galatian believers to enter their circle by keeping the law. Paul seems especially concerned to prove to the Galatians that the very ones who are inviting them to join the group of lawkeepers are under a curse, since they actually are lawbreakers. If the lawkeepers themselves are under a curse for having failed to keep all the law, then the risk of incurring a curse is even greater for Gentile believers who accept only certain items of the law in order to identify with the Jewish nation. An acceptance of requirements such as circumcision and sabbath keeping obligates them to keep the whole law (5:3). And if *all who rely on observing the law* cannot keep the whole law (see 2:14 and 6:13), then surely the Galatian believers will not be able to do so either. Hence they will surely come under a terrible curse for failure to keep the whole law. Paul points to this curse to dissuade Galatian believers from seeking membership among those *who rely on observing the law* and so placing themselves under the curse of the law.

If you join a group known for untainted fundamentalism and uncompromising separatism in order to be sure of God's blessing, beware! Since no one, not even the most saintly, ever kept the whole law, even the members of this group are under a curse for failure to keep

---

through religious actions, is cursed (Fuller 1980:88-97). But since the curse is the result of failure to do the law, Paul's assertion that "all who rely on observing the law are under a curse" makes sense only if, in fact, all fail to do the law (see Moo 1983:97-98).

the whole law.

Signpost 2: Faith (3:11) On the second signpost at the fork in the road we find an inscription from the prophet Habakkuk, *The righteous will live by faith* (v. 11, from Hab 2:4). Since faith is the way to righteousness, law cannot be the way. So, Paul says, *clearly no one is justified before God by the law.* This signpost tells us that faith and law are not the same way, but two different ways.

The Galatian believers were turning to the way of law because they thought by keeping the requirements of the law they could gain entrance into the Jewish nation and thus be assured of acceptance as God's people. But *clearly* acceptance by God, justification before God, cannot possibly be found through the law: according to the Scriptures, righteousness comes by faith.

Signpost 3: Law (3:12) Paul must have realized that his readers would find it difficult to understand why faith and law are two different ways and why only faith, not law, leads to righteousness (acceptance by God). So he sets up a third signpost that repeats the antithesis between faith and law and supports that antithesis by a quotation from Leviticus 18:5 regarding the nature of the law: *The law is not based on faith; on the contrary, "The man who does these things will live by them."*

The fundamental nature of law is that it requires doing. When Paul refers to law here, he cannot mean the whole of the Pentateuch (the five books of Moses). The whole of the Pentateuch (law in the broad sense) is primarily concerned with faith in God. Paul has already quoted from Genesis 15:6, which describes the way of faith exemplified by Abraham. In Galatians 3:12 *law* must be taken in the narrow sense as a reference to the specific divine requirements given to the Jewish people through

---

3:11 In the original setting, Habakkuk 2:4 is God's reply to the prophet's cry for judgment against the Babylonians. God will judge the wicked at the appointed time (Hab 2:3), but in the meantime "the righteous will live by his faith" (2:4).

The Hebrew text of Habakkuk 2:4 reads, "The righteous will live by his faith" (or "faithfulness"). The LXX text has two readings: "the righteous will live by my [God's] faithfulness" and "my righteous one will live by faith" (or "faithfulness"). Paul's quotation does not contain the personal pronoun *his* of the Hebrew text or the personal pronoun *my* of the Greek text. It is unclear whether Paul takes the phrase *by faith* adjectivally to modify the noun *the righteous (the righteous . . . by faith)* or adverbially to modify the verb *live (will live by faith).* Both possibilities fit with Paul's argument. As Bruce (1982:162) notes,

Moses. In the context of Leviticus 18 the *things* to be done are the "decrees and laws" God gave Israel at Mount Sinai so that the Israelites would be distinguished from the Egyptians and Canaanites (Lev 18:1-4). In the Galatian dispute, *the law* refers to a set of requirements (specifically circumcision, food laws and sabbath laws) imposed on Gentile believers which would identify them with the Jewish nation and set them apart from Greeks and Romans.

Paul is not making an abstract, absolute contrast between believing and doing. His rebuke is aimed at the folly of doing the works of the law as a means of participating in the life and blessing of the covenant people of God. The law is not of faith, because it demands doing the works of the law as the way to life, whereas it has just been demonstrated (v. 11) that righteousness by faith is the way to life. The law demands perfect obedience (v. 10) and offers life on the basis of this perfect obedience (v. 12), but in itself the law is incapable of imparting life or righteousness before God (v. 21). So Paul puts up a stop sign in front of those who want to follow the law as the way to life. You can't get to life that way. Life is found only through faith in Christ.

Signpost 4: Cross (3:13-14) On the fourth signpost we see the cross of Christ. The only way to be delivered from the curse of the law is to turn in faith to the cross of Christ. In large letters this signpost announces the fact that *Christ redeemed us from the curse of the law by becoming a curse for us.* How Christ became a curse for us is explained in the citation from Deuteronomy 21:23: *Cursed is everyone who is hung on a tree.*

Cursed is everyone . . . the first signpost reads in its proclamation of condemnation on all for failure to keep all the law. *Cursed is everyone . . .* the fourth signpost reads in its proclamation of redemption by the

"Righteousness by faith is for Paul so closely bound up with true life that the two terms— 'righteousness' and 'life'—can in practice be used interchangeably (see v. 21)."

3:13 In the original context, Deuteronomy 21:22-23 refered to hanging a dead corpse of convicted criminal on a tree after his execution. Such exposure was clear evidence of God's curse. In the time of Christ this text was also applied to the crucifixion of a living person on a tree or pole (see Fitzmyer 1978:493-513).

To take the first-person plural pronoun *us* as an exclusive reference to Jewish Christians, as some interpreters do (see Hays 1983:116-17; Donaldson 1986:94-112), runs counter to Paul's entire argument that all Christians, Jews and Gentiles, are united by redemption in Christ (see Hansen 1989a:123; Longenecker 1990:121).

One who hung on a tree. By hanging on a cross, Jesus came under the burden of the curse that all deserve for failure to keep all the law. By bearing the total burden of the curse himself, Jesus set us free from the terrible weight of the curse.

The Jewish Christians who were pestering the Galatian believers had drawn two circles: the circle of blessing for Jews and the circle of the curse for Gentiles. The Galatian believers were moving from the circle of Gentiles to the circle of Jews so that they could be free from the curse and obtain the blessing. But Paul has demonstrated from the law itself the surprising fact that the circle of Jews is also under a curse for failure to keep all the law. Transferring from the Gentile circle to the Jewish circle is no way to escape the curse of the law. The only way for Jews and Gentiles to escape the curse of the law is to turn to Christ.

The fourth signpost points toward the blessing of Abraham and the promise of the Spirit. Verse 14 tells us that the reason Christ set us free from the curse of the law was to open the way for us to participate in the promised blessings to Abraham. The parallelism of the two phrases in verse 14 indicates that the blessing given to Abraham is equivalent to the promise of the Spirit. When the Galatian believers received the Spirit by faith in Christ crucified (vv. 1-2), they were recipients of the blessing promised to Abraham. The reference to the Spirit brings the argument back full circle to the beginning of the chapter. Since the Galatian believers are already recipients of the promised blessings to Abraham but are now trying to keep the law in order to obtain the blessings they already have, they deserve to be called foolish (v. 1).

Why would you be so foolish as to take the road toward a curse when you were already on the road to blessing?

3:14 Williams demonstrates that "throughout Galatians 3 and 4 when Paul speaks of the promise or the promises he has in mind one fundamental divine pledge, the promise of the Spirit" (1988:713). The close connection between receiving the Spirit and being justified by faith in 3:1-14 indicates that "the experience of the Spirit and the status of justification are, for the apostle, inconceivable apart from each other. . . . Those persons upon whom God bestows the Spirit are justified" (Williams 1987:97). Cosgrove sees 3:1-14 as the key passage that sets forth the agenda for the entire letter: the conditions for sustaining or promoting life in the Spirit (1989:86).

3:15 Attempts have been made to locate the source of Paul's example of *a human covenant* in Greek (Behm 1964:129), Roman (Taylor 1966:58-76) and Jewish (Bammel

Understanding the Promise (3:15-18) My parents set up irrevocable trust agreements for each of us seven children. Once the trust papers had been signed, they could not be annulled or changed. These irrevocable trusts demonstrate our parents' generous, unconditional love for us.

In Galatians 3:15-18 Paul uses a similar legal document to illustrate the nature of the Abrahamic covenant: *Brothers, let me take an example from everyday life. Just as no one can set aside or add to a human covenant that has been duly established, so it is in this case* (v. 15). This "irrevocable trust agreement" that God made with Abraham is described in terms of the beneficiary of the trust (v. 16), the date of the trust (v. 17) and the condition for inheritance (v. 18). Our study of these terms of the Abrahamic covenant will enable us to appreciate the gracious, unconditional nature of God's love for us.

The Beneficiary of the Trust (3:16) Paul carefully examines the terms of the Abrahamic covenant and notes that the promises of this covenant were made to Abraham and to his seed. The term *seed,* Paul explains, is not plural but singular. Therefore the covenant designated one person, not many people, to be the recipient of the promises. That one person, says Paul, *is Christ.*

Except for the lawyers among us who enjoy the minutiae of legal arguments, Paul's discussion may seem to be over our heads. But if we understand Paul's hidden agenda, we will be able to grasp the reason for this technical argument about one term in the Abrahamic covenant. We have to realize that Paul's definition of *seed* contradicts the Jewish nationalistic interpretation of this term. Jews were convinced that the term *seed* referred to the physical descendants of Abraham, the Jewish people. Therefore they believed it was absolutely necessary to belong

1960:313-19) legal practices. Although the evidence is inconclusive, Bammel appears to have made his case that the example in Paul's thought is a Jewish legal procedure in which the property passes immediately into the possession of the beneficiary. This type of will is irrevocable.

3:16 Our understanding of *one* (NIV: *one person*) in 3:16 must fit with Paul's declaration to all Christians in 3:29, "You are Abraham's seed." Thus, as Wright suggests, "the singularity of the 'seed' in v. 16 is not the singularity of an individual person contrasted with the plurality of many human beings, but the singularity of one family contrasted with the plurality of families which would result if the Torah were to be regarded the way Paul's opponents apparently regard it" (1991:163).

to the Jewish nation in order to receive the blessings promised to Abraham.

In Jewish literature the generic singular *seed* was usually interpreted as a collective singular, referring to the nation of Israel. But *seed* was also understood by the rabbis to be a specific singular, referring to an individual—for example, Isaac or David or Solomon. Paul's attention to the grammatical form of this term is very much like the rabbinic practice of exegesis. But Paul's interpretation is based on his conviction that Christ is the sole heir and channel of God's promised blessing. So while he uses common Jewish methods of exegesis, Paul's messianic interpretation of *seed* restricts the reference to Christ and negates the common nationalistic interpretation. It is no longer necessary to be in the Jewish nation to be a recipient of the promises; it is necessary to be in Christ.

Paul is just as exclusive as his Jewish counterparts, but his exclusivity is not based on ethnic identity. Since Christ is the heir of the promises, all those and only those who are in Christ by faith are beneficiaries of the irrevocable trust agreement God made with Abraham (v. 29).

We can see by the way Paul uses the term *seed* in verse 29 that his emphasis on its singularity in verse 16 does not restrict the *seed* to one individual person. Christ, the one seed of Abraham, includes within himself a new community of all believers where there are no racial, social or gender divisions. Just as the seed is one (v. 16), so "you are all one in Christ" (v. 28). So the emphasis on the oneness of the seed in verse 16 prepares the way for the emphasis on the unity of all in Christ in verse 28. Whereas the law made a division between Jews and Gentiles, Christ, the promised seed of Abraham, is the center of a new unity of Jews and Gentiles. The people of God are no longer identified by ethnic origins, but by union with Christ.

The Date of the Trust (3:17) Legal documents are signed and dated. Dates establish the precedence of one document over another. In the case of a will, a subsequent codicil or new will can annul or change the terms of the previous document. So lawyers search to make sure they

---

3:17 Exodus 12:40 gives *430 years* as the figure for Israel's captivity in Egypt, whereas Genesis 15:13 (also Acts 7:6) has 400 years for that same period of enslavement. The rabbis resolved this apparent discrepancy by taking the 430 years as the time between Abraham's

have the document with the latest date which overrides all previous documents.

In the case of an irrevocable trust agreement, however, subsequent documents cannot overturn the terms of the original document. Paul has this type of document in mind. He carefully notes that the date on the irrevocable trust agreement made with Abraham places that covenant 430 years before the Mosaic law. If the Mosaic law and the Abrahamic covenant had the same date, then one might suppose that the Mosaic law should be included in the understanding of the terms of the Abrahamic covenant. But the fact that the Mosaic law came 430 years after the Abrahamic covenant indicates that the two should be clearly distinguished from each other and that the terms of the Abrahamic covenant should not be confused with or changed by the terms of the Mosaic covenant.

This distinction between the time of the confirmation of the promise to Abraham and that of the giving of the law stands in stark contrast to the rabbinic claim that Abraham knew and kept even the minutest details of the Mosaic law. In Jewish tradition the Mosaic law had been inseparably linked with the Abrahamic covenant. Influenced by this perspective, the Galatian believers had come to think that it was necessary to keep the Mosaic law to inherit the blessings promised to Abraham. In Paul's view, those who seek the inheritance through the law have failed to recognize the precedence of the promise in salvation history. They have failed to realize that because the law came 430 years after the promise it could not annul or be attached to the promise as a condition of inheriting the promised blessings.

Since Paul equates the promise and the gospel, the distinction he sees between promise and law is also a distinction between gospel and law. Those who minimize or deny this contrast between gospel and law need to consider the radical nature of Paul's distinction.

The Condition for Inheritance (3:18) When my parents set up the trust agreements for their seven children, we were all very young and could not have possibly fulfilled any conditions to merit the gift of

reception of the covenant and Moses' reception of the law and the 400 years as the period of Israel's captivity in Egypt (see Betz 1979:158). Paul apparently accepted the rabbinic explanation.

inheritance that they provided for us. It is true that we grew up in a home marked by high standards and strict discipline. But if someone supposed that our inheritance depended on living up to the high standards set in the home, we could easily demonstrate that such a supposition was ridiculous. In the first place, none of us has been able to keep all the high standards set for us. In the second place, the irrevocable trust agreements were established for us before the standards were communicated to us. So we are beneficiaries by sheer grace.

Paul is concerned to demonstrate the unconditional nature of the promises made to Abraham. He points out the incompatibility between receiving the inheritance as a gift on the basis of a promise and receiving it as a payment for keeping the law: *For if the inheritance depends on the law, then it no longer depends on a promise; but God in his grace gave it to Abraham through a promise.* The categories of payment and gift are mutually exclusive. Since the gift character of the promised inheritance is clearly established, the inheritance cannot be received as a payment for keeping the law. This logical argument is developed by Paul to drive home his rebuke for the foolish error of viewing something as a payment which had already been received as a gift.

Understanding the Law (3:19-25) Paul suddenly stops the flow of his argument and asks a question: *What, then, was the purpose of the law?* (v. 19). This question reflects Paul's awareness that his argument so far would lead his readers to wonder whether he has denied any purpose to the law. If the inheritance of the promised blessing does not depend on the law, as Paul has just declared (v. 18), then why was the law given by God? Paul's answer is important for us as we wrestle with similar questions regarding the application of the Mosaic law. How should Christians relate to the Mosaic law today?

In this section Paul first asks his major, initial question regarding the purpose of the law and replies briefly (vv. 19-20), then asks a supplementary question regarding the relation of the law to the promise of God and supplies an explanation (vv. 21-22), and finally presents two images to illustrate more fully God's purpose for the law (vv. 23-25).

What Was the Purpose of the Law? (3:19-20) Paul's brief reply to this question points to (1) the negative purpose of the law, (2) the temporal framework for the law and (3) the mediated origin of the law.

1. According to Paul, the law has a negative purpose: *It was added because of transgressions* (v. 19). Paul has already demonstrated what the law does not do: it does not make anyone righteous before God (v. 11); it is not based on faith (v. 12); it is not the basis of inheritance (v. 18). So if the law is divorced from righteousness, faith and inheritance of the blessing, to what is law related? Paul says that the law is related to transgressions. A transgression is the violation of a standard. The law provides the objective standard by which the violations are measured. In order for sinners to know how sinful they really are, how far they deviate from God's standards, God gave the law. Before the law was given, there was sin (see Rom 5:13). But after the law was given, sin could be clearly specified and measured (see Rom 3:20; 4:15; 7:7). Each act or attitude could then be labeled as a transgression of this or that commandment of the law.

Imagine a state in which there are many traffic accidents but no traffic laws. Although people are driving in dangerous, harmful ways, it is difficult to designate which acts are harmful until the legislature issues a book of traffic laws. Then it is possible for the police to cite drivers for transgressions of the traffic laws. The laws define harmful ways of driving as violations of standards set by the legislature. The function of traffic laws is to allow bad drivers to be identified and prosecuted.

2. The temporal framework for the law is clearly established by the words *added . . . until the Seed to whom the promise referred had come* (v. 19). Paul has already emphasized that the Mosaic law was given 430 years after the Abrahamic promise (v. 17). The word *added* implies that the law was not a central theme in God's redemptive plan; it was supplementary and secondary to the enduring covenant made with Abraham. As the word *added* marks the beginning point for the Mosaic law, the word *until* marks its end point. The Mosaic law came into effect at a certain point in history and was in effect only until the promised *Seed*, Christ, appeared. There is a contrast here between the permanent validity of the promise and the temporary nature of the law. On the one hand, the promise was made long before the law and will be in effect long after the period of the law; on the other hand, the law was in effect for a relatively short period of time limited in both directions by the words

added and *until.*

As we shall see in our study of the next few sections of the letter (see 3:23-25; 4:1-4), Paul's presentation of the temporal framework for the law is a major theme of his argument for the superiority of the promise fulfilled in Christ over the law. This theme differs radically from the common Jewish perspective of his day, which emphasized the eternal, immutable nature of the law. But Paul's Christocentric perspective led him to see that Christ (the promised Seed), not the law, was the eternal one.

3. Paul designates the origin of the law in his statement that *the law was put into effect through angels by a mediator* (v. 19). By this Paul does not mean that the law was given by angels rather than by God. He is merely pointing to the well-known Jewish tradition that God gave the law through the agency of angels as well as *by a mediator,* namely Moses. References to the agency of angels in the giving of the law can be found in the Greek version of Deuteronomy 33:2 and Psalm 68:17. We can also see this tradition about angels in Acts 7:53 and Hebrews 2:2.

The presence of angels and the mediation of Moses in the giving of the law were understood by the Jewish people to signify the great glory of the law. But Paul argues that the giving of the law through a series of intermediaries, angels and Moses, actually demonstrates the inferiority of the law. His argument is cryptic and enigmatic: *A mediator, however, does not represent just one party; but God is one* (v. 20). Literally, this sentence reads, "But a mediator is not one, but God is one." A contrast is being made between the plurality of participants in a process of mediation and the oneness of God. In the larger context of Paul's argument here, there is also the implied contrast between the promise given directly by God to Abraham and fulfilled in Christ, the seed of Abraham, and the law given through numerous intermediaries.

3:19 The Hebrew text behind the Greek version of Deuteronomy 33:2 is ambiguous (the NIV footnote to Deuteronomy 33:2 reads, "The meaning of the Hebrew for this phrase is uncertain"). In any case, the Greek version translates the clause "at his right hand were angels with him." That translation and the association of the "chariots of God" with Sinai in Psalm 68:17 determined the Jewish understanding of the giving of the Mosaic law *through angels.*

3:20 The sentence *A mediator, however, does not represent just one party; but God is one* is "one of the most obscure in the letters of Paul" (Callan 1980: 549). Lightfoot claims that

By faith the Galatian converts have already entered into the experience of the Spirit (vv. 1-5), which is the fulfillment of the promise (v. 14). Evidently they are now being persuaded that if they observe the rituals of the Jewish people, they will experience new dimensions of spiritual life and blessing—that if they become members of God's people, the Jews, they will be guaranteed intimacy with God. Paul warns them that the circumstances of the giving of the law demonstrate otherwise. The law had a mediated origin. Thus the law does not provide direct access to God. Only the fulfillment of the promise in the bestowal of the Spirit to those in Christ guarantees direct access to God (see 4:4-8).

Paul's affirmation of the common confession of all Jews that *God is one* (v. 20) implies a contrast between the universality of God and the particularity of the law. The particular focus of the law is specified by its mediation through the angels and Moses to the Jewish people. The preachers of the false gospel in Galatia limited the sphere of God's blessing to the Jewish nation. Their message implied that God is the God of the Jews only. But the unity of God means that he is the God of the Gentiles as well as the God of the Jews (see Rom 3:29-30). The universality of God is clearly expressed in the promise for "all nations" (Gal 3:8). The bestowal of the Spirit on Gentiles who had not become Jews was irrefutable evidence for the universality of God.

Moses, the mediator of the law, brought in a law that divided Jews from Gentiles; therefore he was not the mediator of "the one," the one new community promised to Abraham (v. 8) and found in Christ (v. 28). Christ, not Moses, is the mediator of the unity of all believers in Christ—Jew and Greek, slave and free, male and female.

These arguments against the supremacy of the Mosaic law should not be interpreted to mean that Paul is antinomian, totally against the law. He is, after all, showing that the law had an important place in the

there are 250-300 interpretations of this passage (1957:146). The text of the commentary above builds on two interpretations: (1) Any transaction that requires mediation is inferior to direct communication, and therefore the law is inferior because it was given by way of mediation (see Betz 1979:171-72; Ebeling 1985:190). (2) Moses, the mediator of the law, is not the mediator of the one united family of God; he is only the mediator of the law to the Jews; but God is one, and therefore there must be one family of God in which Jews and Gentiles are one (see Wright 1991:169-70).

redemptive plan of God. But the giving of the law was not the final goal of God's plan. The law was an essential step, but only a step, toward the ultimate fulfillment of God's promises in Christ. Christ is the beginning, end and center of God's plan.

In the churches in Galatia the law was supplanting the central place of Christ. The churches were becoming law-centered. It was necessary, therefore, to put the law back into its rightful place. Its purpose is negative: to point out transgressions. Its time is limited: 430 years after the promise, until Christ. Its origin is mediated through angels and Moses: it does not provide direct access to God, and it divides Jews from Gentiles.

Is the Law Opposed to the Promises of God? (3:21-22) This question is an understandable response to Paul's stark contrast between the law and the promise (vv. 15-18) and his confinement of the law to a limited role in God's historical plan (vv. 19-20). People who were preoccupied with the supreme value of the law must have been stunned by such a devaluation of it. How could Paul speak against the law? Was the logical conclusion of his line of reasoning the position that the law stood in opposition to the promise? *Absolutely not!* says Paul. Since both the law and the promise were given by God, they must be complementary rather than contradictory in the overall plan of God. Paul explains the relation of the law to the promise in a two-part answer to the question. First, he presents a contrary-to-fact hypothesis that ascribes a positive role to the law (v. 21). Second, he turns from hypothesis to the reality of the law's negative role (v. 22).

In order to clarify the relation of the law to the promise, Paul poses a contrary-to-fact hypothesis: *If a law had been given that could impart life, then righteousness would certainly have come by the law* (v. 21). The very way that Paul phrases this hypothesis (as a contrary-to-fact conditional statement) indicates that he does not for a moment think the law can impart life. By *life* Paul means living in right relationship with God (see 2:19: "that I might live for God"). If the law could empower one to live in a right relationship with God, *then righteousness would certainly have come by the law.* This was in fact the position of the rival teachers in the Galatian churches. They were promoting the law as the way to live for God. It was actually their position that set the law in direct opposition to the promise; it contradicted the gospel. For as Paul has already said

(2:21), "if righteousness could be gained through the law, Christ died for nothing!"

It is only when the law is given a positive role that it is directly opposed to the promise fulfilled in Christ. You are faced with an absolute contradiction if you are told that only by believing in the cross of Christ will you be able to live in a right relationship with God and then you are told that only by keeping the law will you be able to live in a right relationship with God. And that is precisely what the Galatian believers were being told by the rival teachers. But Paul does not accept the false hypothesis of a positive role for the law. Since believing the gospel has already been proved to be the only way to receive life in the Spirit and righteousness (3:1-18), such a positive role for the law is excluded.

The strong adversative conjunction *but* at the beginning of verse 22 indicates that Paul is turning from the unreal hypothesis of a positive role for the law to the reality of the negative role of the law: *but the Scripture declares that the whole world is a prisoner of sin* (v. 22). In reality, the law has the negative function of condemning everyone. Literally, Paul says that "the Scripture imprisoned all under sin." Probably Paul has in mind Deuteronomy 27:26, the specific Scripture he quoted in verse 10: "Cursed is everyone who does not continue to do everything written in the Book of the Law." This citation from the law summarizes the purpose of the law: to demonstrate that all are sinners and to put all sinners under God's judgment. Paul's emphasis on the universality of human sin (v. 22) and the universality of God's judgment on all sinners (v. 10) reduces Jews to the same status as Gentiles—*the whole world is a prisoner of sin.* So identification with the Jewish people by circumcision and observance of the Mosaic law does not remove one from the circle of "Gentile sinners" (2:15) and bring one into the sphere of righteousness, blessing and life. Rather, it leaves one imprisoned under sin.

But we are not left as condemned sinners under the curse of God. The law was given to show that all humanity is held under the bondage of sin, *so that what was promised, being given through faith in Jesus Christ, might be given to those who believe* (v. 22). Now we can see how the law and the promise work in harmony to fulfill the purpose of God. The law puts us down under the curse; the promise lifts us up in Christ. We are left with no exit under the condemnation of the law so that we might find our freedom only by faith in Christ. The law imprisons *all*—both Jews and Gentiles—under sin to prepare the way for including all believers in Christ—both Jews and Gentiles—in the blessing promised to Abraham.

So the law should not be viewed as contradictory to the gospel. By reducing all to the level of sinners, the law prepares the way for the gospel. But neither should the law be viewed as if it were the same as the gospel. The law has a negative purpose: it makes us aware of our sin. But it does not, indeed it cannot, set us free from bondage to sin. The promise of blessing comes only through faith in Christ.

The Law Is a Jailer and a Disciplinarian (3:23-25) Paul expands and dramatizes his explanation of the negative function of the law by personifying the law as a jailer and a disciplinarian. In his portrayal of the roles given by God to the law, Paul shows that these negative roles are a necessary part, but only a temporary part, of the entire drama of God's plan of salvation.

The law took the part of God's jailer on the stage of history: *before this faith came, we were held prisoners by the law, locked up until faith should be revealed* (v. 23). Notice the important shift of focus from universal to particular: in verse 22 the whole world is declared by Scripture to be *a prisoner of sin,* but in verse 23 Paul says *we were held prisoners by the law.* In the first case the law is related to all people without distinction, Jews as well as Gentiles. All are condemned as sinners by the law. In the second case the law is related to Jews. For a certain period of time, Jews in particular were held as prisoners under law. When we read the Mosaic law we can see how every aspect of Jewish life was restricted, restrained and confined by the law. In this sense the law was a jailer over the Jews.

It is essential to distinguish between these two functions of the law: the universal condemnatory function and the particular supervisory function. Every person in the whole world of every time and every race is under the condemnation of the law given in Scripture. The law makes it clear that everyone is a prisoner of sin in order that it may be absolutely

3:24 Recent study of the phrase "the law was our pedagogue" (NIV: *the law was put in charge to lead us*) confirms the negative picture of the pedagogue: he did not have a positive, educative role, but a negative role of punishing wrongdoing. On the stage he was

clear that the salvation promised by God can be received only by faith in Jesus Christ (v. 22). That is the universal condemnatory function of the law. The condemning sentence of the law against all humanity can never be overturned. It stands as a permanent indictment of the sinful rebellion of *the whole world* against God.

The Mosaic law was given not only as a permanent standard for all humanity but also as a temporary system to supervise a particular people. As we read through the Mosaic law we are impressed with a complex system of laws that were set in place to guide the conduct of the Jewish people. According to Paul's imagery in verse 23, the law functioned as a jailer to lock up the Jewish people in a vast system of legal codes and regulations. But that lockup was meant to be only temporary. Verse 23 begins and ends with clear references to the time when the imprisonment within the system of Mosaic law would end: *before this faith came . . . until faith should be revealed.* Of course Abraham had faith in God long before the Mosaic law, as Paul emphasized in 3:6. But the specific nature of *this faith* that Paul has in mind has just been stated in verse 22: *faith in Jesus Christ . . . Before this faith came, we [the Jewish people] were held prisoners by the law, locked up until faith [in Jesus Christ] should be revealed.* The function of the law as a jailer is not permanent; it is limited to a certain period in history.

The temporary function of the law is also described by the image of a disciplinarian. *So the law was put in charge to lead us to Christ* (v. 24). The NIV here is more a loose paraphrase than a word-for-word translation. The NRSV is an excellent, literal translation of this phrase: "Therefore the law was our disciplinarian until Christ came." Behind the English word *disciplinarian* is the Greek word *paidagōgos,* from which we derive *pedagogue.* The first meaning listed in Webster's Third New International Dictionary for *pedagogue* is "a teacher of children or youth"; the second meaning given is "one (as a slave) having charge of a boy chiefly on the way to and from school in classical antiquity." In Paul's day the pedagogue was distinguished from the teacher *(didaskalos).* The pedagogue supervised, controlled and disciplined the child; the teacher

easily recognized by his rod. To be under the pedagogue was to be under the rod (Betz 1979:177-79; Longenecker 1990:146-49; 1982:53-61; Lull 1986:481-98; Young 1987:150-76).

instructed and educated him.

A fascinating dialogue between Socrates and a boy named Lysis high-lights this distinction. Socrates begins the conversation by asking Lysis, "Do they [Lysis's parents] let you control your own self, or will they not trust you in that either?"

"Of course they do not," he replied.

"But someone controls you?"

"Yes," he said, "my pedagogue here."

"Is he a slave?"

"Why certainly; he belongs to us," he said.

"What a strange thing," I exclaimed: "a free man controlled by a slave! But how does this pedagogue exert his control over you?"

"By taking me to the teacher," he replied.

Josephus tells us of a pedagogue who was found beating the family cook when the child under his supervision overate. The pedagogue himself was corrected with the words: "Man, we did not make you the cook's pedagogue, did we? but the child's. Correct him; help him!"

These examples of the use of the term *pedagogue* in Greek literature point to the common perception of this figure in the Hellenistic world: he was given the responsibility to supervise and discipline the conduct of children. He did not have the positive task of educating the child; he was only supposed to control the behavior of the child through consistent discipline. The point of Paul's use of this image in depicting the law is that the law was given this supervisory, disciplinary role over the Jewish people. But the supervisory control of the law was only "until Christ" (*to Christ* in NIV). This phrase has a temporal meaning, as we can see from the parallel phrase in the previous verse: *until faith should be revealed.* In the outworking of God's plan of salvation in history, the period when the Jewish people were under the supervisory control of the law was followed by the coming of Christ. The supervisory discipline

---

3:25 This verse is at the center of a major debate that began at the inception of the church and continues unabated today. On one side of the debate are those who contend for a continuing supervisory role of the law in the life of a Christian. On the other side are those who emphasize Christian freedom from the supervision of the law. A good survey of the early participants in this debate is given in the introduction of Longenecker's commentary (1990:xliii-lvii). Westerholm's book *Israel's Law and the Church's Faith* offers an excellent evaluation of recent positions in the debate and his own synthesis of the complex issues

of the law over the people of God came to an end when Christ came.

The purpose of the disciplinary function of the law was to demonstrate that God's people could only be justified by faith: *that we [the Jewish people] might be justified by faith* (v. 24). Under the constant discipline of the law, the Jewish people should have learned how impossible it was to keep the law. The law constantly beat them down like a stern disciplinarian, pointing out all their shortcomings and failures. The pain of this discipline was designed to teach them that they could only be declared righteous by God through faith.

In verse 25 Paul draws a conclusion that demolishes any argument that Christians ought to live under the supervisory control of the law: *Now that faith has come, we are no longer under the supervision of the law.* The Galatian believers were evidently succumbing to arguments that their life in Christ should be lived under the supervisory discipline of the Mosaic law. But to live under the supervision of the Mosaic law is to live as if Christ had not come. Now that Christ has come, we live, as Paul has already affirmed in 2:20, "by faith in the Son of God." To live by faith in Christ sets us free from the supervision of the law.

Since Paul is still speaking here in the first-person plural *(we)* his primary reference is to the freedom that Jewish believers now experience from the supervision of the law because they have put their faith in Christ. If Jewish believers are no longer under the supervision of the law, then it is surely foolish for Gentile believers in Christ to put themselves under the law's supervision. No wonder Paul began this chapter with the rebuke "You foolish Galatians!" They have received the Spirit by believing the gospel, but now they are trying to make progress in their spiritual life by observing the law. But their attempt to observe the law as if they were now under the supervision of the law is not progress; it is retrogression to the period in history before Christ came.

We have some friends who immigrated from a country under dicta-

---

involved. The position taken in this commentary is basically that of Martin Luther. In his commentary on this verse he insists that "we are free from the law, from the prison, and from our schoolmaster; for when faith is revealed, the law terrifies and torments us no more" (1979:343). Does this mean we are free to sin? Absolutely not! "For as Christ came once corporally at the time appointed, abolished the whole law, vanquished sin, destroyed death and hell, even so he comes spiritually without ceasing, and daily quenches and kills those sins in us" (Luther 1979:344).

torship to North America. Their move to the States marked a turning point in their history. They no longer live under the tyrannical government of their former country. Now they are under a new government. It would make no sense for them to start living again as if they were under the supervision of their former government.

Similarly, Paul sees the turning point in his life to be the time when he put his faith in Christ. Before that time he lived under the supervision of the Mosaic law. But after he put his faith in Christ, his life was lived by faith in Christ, under the supervision of Christ. He had immigrated (see Col 1:13) to the kingdom of Christ.

Of course those friends who have now immigrated to America cannot assume that they are now free to do whatever was forbidden in their former country. Although they cannot be prosecuted under the laws of their former country for murder or theft, they are now bound by the laws of their new country not to murder or steal. Our new life in Christ is not under the supervision of the law; it is under the rule of Christ by his Spirit. Freedom in Christ from the supervisory rule of the Mosaic law empowers us to "live for God" (2:19).

The Unity of All Recipients of the Promise (3:26-29) We now encounter a dramatic shift of focus. Paul has been talking in the first-person plural ("we") of the past experience of the Jewish people, who were "locked up" under the Mosaic law (vv. 23-25). Now he turns to the privileged position of the Galatian Christians *(you are all . . . all of you . . . you are all),* who are all united in Christ (vv. 26-29). Union with Christ is the main emphasis of each verse: *faith in Christ Jesus* (v. 26), *baptized into Christ . . . clothed . . . with Christ* (v. 27), *one in Christ Jesus* (v. 28), *belong to Christ* (v. 29).

This sharp contrast between the negative consequences of imprisonment within the system of Mosaic law and the positive privileges of union with Christ reinforces Paul's rebuke for foolishness at the beginning of the chapter. In the light of this contrast, how foolish it is to think

3:27-28 These verses are probably based on a baptismal liturgy used in the early church (Betz 1979:184; Longenecker 1984:32). This supposition helps to explain why verse 28 includes references to slave-free and male-female categories, when neither of these categories has direct relevance to the argument of Galatians. This means that the declaration that observing the law could possibly enhance the privileged relationships Christians already enjoy because of their union with Christ Jesus. Imprisonment under the law (vv. 19-25) has been replaced by new relationships *in Christ.* These new relationships in Christ are both spiritual (vv. 26-27) and social (vv. 28-29).

New Spiritual Relationships in Christ (3:26-27) In the old set of relationships under the law, Jews were the children of God and Gentiles were sinners (see 2:15). But now Gentile Christians are *all sons of God through faith in Christ Jesus.* This must have been a shocking declaration for a Jew to hear. In Jewish literature, *sons of God* was a title of highest honor, used only for "the members of righteous Israel, destined to inherit the eschatological blessings" (Byrne 1979:174). But now Gentiles—the rejected, the outsiders, the sinners, those who do not observe the law—are called *sons of God.* Indeed this is a "new creation" (6:15). How could a Gentile ever be called a child of God? Paul's answer is clear—*through faith in Christ Jesus* (v. 26). Since Christ Jesus is the "Son of God" (2:20), all who by faith are in Christ are also *sons of God.*

The next verse points to the basis for the new spiritual relationship depicted by this title, *sons of God:* they are children of God because they have been united with Christ in baptism and, as a result, clothed with Christ. In the light of his repeated emphasis on faith in this context, Paul cannot possibly mean that the ritual of baptism by itself, apart from faith, would accomplish union with Christ. Only when there is genuine faith in Christ is baptism a sign of union with Christ. Paul is reminding the Galatian Christians of their baptism in order to renew their sense of belonging to Christ. That ceremony of initiation into Christ and the Christian community points to the solid foundation for their new relationship as children of God. Moreover, their baptism has led to being *clothed . . . with Christ.* This metaphor, probably drawn from the ceremony of rerobing after baptism, pictures the reality of complete identification with Christ. In the Old Testament there are frequent references to being clothed with righteousness, salvation, strength and glory

of the unity and equality of all believers in Christ was a central affirmation of the early church.

In our interpretation of Paul's phrase *baptized into Christ* we need to avoid two extremes. On the one hand, to take these words to mean that baptism in itself is the effective means

(2 Chron 6:41; Job 29:14; Ps 132:9, 16, 18; Prov 31:25; Is 51:9; 52:1; 61:10; Zech 3:3-5). And in other letters Paul uses this metaphor of putting on clothing to mean taking on the virtues of Christ (Col 3:12; 1 Thess 5:8). As baptism pictures the initial union with Christ by faith, being clothed with Christ portrays our participation in the moral perfection of Christ by faith. As the hymnwriter put it, Christians are "dressed in his righteousness alone, faultless to stand before the throne." That is why Christians can be called the children of God: in Christ they truly are the members of righteous Israel.

The title *sons of God* and the two ceremonies of baptism and being clothed with Christ point to the reality of our new relationship with God in Christ.

New Social Relationships in Christ (3:28-29) The new vertical relationship with God results in a new horizontal relationship with one another. All racial, economic and gender barriers and all other inequalities are removed in Christ. The equality and unity of all in Christ are not an addition, a tangent or an optional application of the gospel. They are part of the essence of the gospel.

Equality in Christ is the starting point for all truly biblical social ethics. The church that does not express this equality and unity in Christ in its life and ministry is not faithful to the gospel. Paul's own immediate concern is to make sure that the racial equality of Jews and Gentiles is implemented in the church. Gentiles were being demoted to a second-class status because they were not Jews. This expression of racial superiority was a violation of the essence of the gospel. Similarly, any expression of social class superiority (the free over the slaves) or gender superiority (men over women) violates the truth of the gospel. *There is neither Jew nor Greek, slave nor free, male nor female, for you are all one in Christ Jesus* (v. 28). All the divisions and prejudices that matter so much in the world are abolished in Christ.

---

to union with Christ would make faith unnecessary. But Paul's great emphasis on faith in this chapter (the Spirit is received by faith—3:2) negates the position that baptism is effective apart from faith. On the other hand, to take Paul's emphasis on faith to mean that baptism in water is an optional, unnecessary symbol negates the full value of this phrase: *baptized into Christ*. Paul saw faith and baptism united as the way to become a Christian. Although the presence of the Spirit received by faith in the gospel, not water baptism, is the guarantee of salvation, baptism is the believer's appropriation of salvation. For further

This radical affirmation of unity and equality in Christ is a deliberate rejection of the attitude expressed by the synagogue prayer in which the worshiper thanks God for not making him a Gentile, a slave or a woman. Such an attitude of superiority contradicts the truth of the gospel, the good news that there is equality and unity of all believers in Christ.

When men exclude women from significant participation in the life and ministry of the church, they negate the essence of the gospel. Some will argue that the equality Paul defends here is only in the "spiritual" sphere: equality before God. But Paul's argument responds to a social crisis in the church: Gentiles were being forced to become Jews to be fully accepted by Jewish Christians. Paul's argument is that Gentiles do not have to become Jews to participate fully in the life of the church. Neither do blacks have to become white or females become male for full participation in the life and ministry of the church.

The equality of all believers before God must be demonstrated in social relationships within the church if the truth of the gospel is to be expressed. F. F. Bruce puts it succinctly: "No more restriction is implied in Paul's equalizing of the status of male and female in Christ than in his equalizing of the status of Jew and Gentile, or of slave and free person. If in ordinary life existence in Christ is manifested openly in church fellowship, then, if a Gentile may exercise spiritual leadership in church as freely as a Jew, or a slave as freely as a citizen, why not a woman as freely as a man?" (Bruce 1982:190).

Paul draws the conclusion to his argument in verse 29: *If you belong to Christ, then you are Abraham's seed, and heirs according to the promise.* Since the Galatian Christians belong to Christ, they are directly related to Abraham and recipients of the blessing promised to Abraham. Since full membership in the covenant people of God, "the seed of Abraham," is granted and maintained simply by union with Christ by faith, there is no longer any need for the law as the means to secure or

---

discussion of Paul's view of baptism see especially Ridderbos (1975:396-414) and his references to other works.

The important implications of Paul's phrase *male nor female* for women's ministry are developed by Longenecker (1984:70-93). When Fung says that "Paul's statement is not concerned with the role relationships of men and women within the Body of Christ but rather with their common initiation into it through (faith and) baptism" (1988:176), he seems to have forgotten the social context of Paul's teaching.

maintain that status. Any attempt by the Galatian Christians to gain status or receive blessing by observing the Mosaic law is foolish, since they have already been included within the realm of full inheritance in which there is no racial, social or gender hierarchy.

Moving from Slavery to Freedom (4:1-7) The contrast presented in the previous chapter between imprisonment under the law (3:23-25) and new relationships in Christ (3:26-29) is now clarified by an illustration drawn from a household where sons were treated as slaves until they received the full rights of sons at the age of maturity. First, the slavelike condition of the sons while they were still minors is described and applied to the human condition (4:1-3). Second, the sending of God's Son to liberate slaves and make them sons is announced (4:4-5). Third, the full rights of sons are disclosed (4:6-7).

When Sons Were the Same as Slaves (4:1-3) Paul gives us a portrait of a young boy in a wealthy home. This boy is the legal heir and future master of the entire estate. But as long as he is a child, his life is just like that of a slave. *He is subject to guardians and trustees.* They supervise him, discipline him and control him. Their orders regulate and restrain his behavior. He is under their authority *until the time set by his father,* when he will be free from their control and enjoy his full rights as heir and master of the family estate.

It is clear that Paul constructed this illustration to dramatize what life was like under the supervision of the law. But since he has already used the images of a jailer (3:23) and a disciplinarian (3:24-25) to dramatize the supervisory function of the law, why does he add yet another illustration of life under the law? To appreciate the reason for Paul's use of this additional illustration, we need to understand that Jewish Christians must have been astonished that their history under the Mosaic law had been compared to being imprisoned by a jailer and controlled by a disciplinarian. Paul himself would not have accepted such a description

---

4:3 The two most common interpretations of the phrase *basic principles of the world* are (1) elementary teachings of the basic principles of religion (Lightfoot 1957:167; Barclay 1976:383; Bruce 1982:193-94; Longenecker 1990:166) and (2) demonic forces that control this evil age (Delling 1964:670-87; Betz 1979:204-5). The first interpretation is favored by two impressive lines of argument. First, the use of the phrase to denote demonic forces is

of Jewish history before his conversion. After all, the Jews had been redeemed from slavery in the exodus. In fact, when God set the Jewish people free, he had called them his "son" (Ex 4:23). The giving of the law began with the announcement of freedom for God's people: "I am the LORD your God, who brought you out of Egypt, out of the land of slavery" (Ex 20:2). If God had redeemed his people from slavery, how could their whole existence under the Mosaic law until Christ be depicted in terms of slavery? It would certainly be appropriate to view the Gentile condition in terms of slavery, but surely not the Jewish condition. Such thoughts would have been in the minds of Jewish Christians and had probably been expressed to the Gentile Christians as well. No doubt the Gentile Christians had been told that only those who united with the Jewish people under the law could truly participate in the freedom God gave to his offspring, the people of Israel.

In this illustration Paul clarifies the condition of the Jewish people under the law. This is a much more positive image of slavery than the images of a jailer and a disciplinarian. Even in the best of homes, sons who are loved by their father and destined to be heirs of his estate go through a period of supervision. It is entirely appropriate for immature heirs to be subject to the care of guardians. Obedience to their guardians is evidence of their love for their father. But it would be inappropriate for sons to be kept under the supervision of guardians once they had reached the age of maturity. It is not a mark of disloyalty for sons to eagerly anticipate the day set by their father when they will no longer be subject to guardians but will enjoy their full rights as sons. Once that day comes, their love for their father will not be expressed through subjection to guardians but by a free expression of love from the heart of mature sons.

This illustration makes the point that even the Jewish people, the rightful heirs of God's promises to Abraham, experienced a certain kind of slavery for a period of time. In verse 3 Paul applies his illustration to

---

not found in the literature of the Pauline or pre-Pauline period (Belleville 1986:65). So the theory that Paul is referring to demonic forces rests on a questionable foundation. Second, the use of the phrase as a reference to elementary teachings fits very well with the metaphor of a pedagogue in 3:24 and the picture of a young child under supervision in 4:1-2. See especially Belleville 1986:64-69.

the real historical experience of God's people: *So also, when we were children, we were in slavery under the basic principles of the world.* This picture of slavery under *basic principles of the world* continues the series of images representing slavery under the law: "held prisoners by the law" (3:23), "under the supervision of the law" (3:25), *subject to guardians and trustees* (4:2). So in some sense Paul understood the *basic principles of the world* as equivalent to the Mosaic law. Although the Mosaic law was given by God, it was not God's last and ultimate revelation. It was necessary, but only elementary teaching: it was the ABCs of God's revelation. To be subjected to the discipline of learning the ABCs is good and proper for an elementary student, but to be kept forever at that level of education would be a tragic kind of slavery.

Now Paul has established his thesis that all of God's people, the Jews as well as the Gentiles, came to the inheritance of salvation in Christ out of a similar situation of slavery. As we will see in our study of verses 8-10, Paul views the Gentile Christians' attempt to observe the Mosaic law as a return to slavery under "weak and miserable principles." By their subjection to Mosaic law they are returning to their preconversion slave-like condition. The slavery of Gentiles under "weak and miserable principles" (v. 9) before their conversion and the slavery of Jews under the Mosaic law (the *basic principles of the world* [v. 3]) before Christ were certainly not similar in all respects. The pagan Gentiles were not enslaved to the Mosaic law; Jews were not enslaved to pagan idolatry. But these two situations of slavery were the same in one respect: Jews and Gentiles were enslaved to something less than the immediate knowledge of God enjoyed by Christians (see vv. 6, 9).

So when Paul says in 4:3 that *when we were children, we were in slavery under the basic principles of the world,* he is emphasizing how even Jews were caught in the universal condition of slavery. In this common condition of helplessness, all alike are completely dependent on the liberating grace of God.

How Slaves Became Sons (4:4-5) Slaves were set free to enjoy the full rights of sons only because God acted in history: *when the time had*

4:4 The combination of the eschatological statement *when the time had fully come* and

fully come, God sent his Son. This reference to the time of God's action in history is directly related to *the time set by his father* (v. 2) in the previous illustration and concludes a whole string of references to God's time schedule: "until the Seed . . ." (3:19); "before this faith . . . up until faith" (3:23); "now that faith . . . we are no longer . . ." (3:25). When God sent his Son, the former period of universal slavery ended; a new era of freedom was inaugurated.

God's plan of salvation cannot be understood merely in static terms as a logical system of ideas: revelation, God, human nature, Christ, salvation, church. God's redemptive work must be understood in the framework of his actions in history. God gave an irrevocable promise to Abraham; 430 years later God gave the law through Moses; at a time God had set, he sent his Son. The relationship of these acts of God in history provides the framework for understanding the redemptive work of God. Of course this does not mean that we should abandon systematic theology; we can develop logical expositions of the meaning of salvation. But we should always remember that the narrative structure of God's work in history is the substructure of all truly biblical theology.

The confusion of the Galatian Christians was the result of their failure to understand the narrative structure of the redemptive work of God. In their attempt to inherit the blessing promised to Abraham by keeping the Mosaic law, they failed to understand that the Mosaic law had been given 430 years after the Abrahamic promise and could not change the terms of the promise or be a condition for inheriting the promised blessing (3:15-18). In their attempt to make progress in their spiritual life by observing the law after believing the gospel, they failed to understand that supervision under the law ended when faith in Christ came (3:23-25).

At the center of this narrative framework is the narrative of the gospel story itself: *God sent his Son, born of a woman, born under law, to redeem those under law* (4:4-5). Here we have a simple confessional statement of the essence of the gospel story: the incarnation and birth of Christ, his perfect life of obedience under the law, and his redemptive

the Christological statement *God sent his Son* points to what Ridderbos calls "the fundamental structure" of Paul's teaching (1973:49-53).

death on the cross.

The phrase *God sent his Son* is taken by some interpreters as merely a reference to the prophetic mission of Jesus. As the prophets of old were sent by God, so Jesus was sent by God for a special redemptive mission. The background may be found in the parable Jesus told about the wicked tenants of the vineyard (Mk 12:1-12): the owner of the vineyard (God) first sent messengers (prophets), who were killed by the tenants (Jewish leaders); then he sent his own son (Jesus), who was also killed. But in light of Paul's other references to the preexistence of the Son (see 1 Cor 8:6; Phil 2:5-8; Col 1:15-17), we may also see here an affirmation of the deity of Jesus. Before the incarnation, the preexistent Son was commissioned by God to set slaves free and make them children of God.

The next phrase, *born of a woman,* points to the incarnation and full humanity of Jesus. The Son of God was sent to be one with us in our humanity. He was God's Son and he was Mary's son—the one and only God-man. He was also *born under law.* The phrase *under law* cannot mean legalism, keeping the law to earn salvation. Jesus certainly did not live his life under the misconception that he had to keep the law to earn his salvation. To be born under law means to be born a Jew under obligation to keep the requirements of the Mosaic law. From his circumcision eight days after his birth to his celebration of Passover with his disciples just before his death, every detail of Jesus' life was under the direction of the law. His perfect obedience to God the Father, as God's Son born of a woman, fulfilled all the requirements of the law. God's Son took our place as a human being to offer a perfect obedience to God on our behalf.

To be *born under law* also means to experience the curse of the law against all who fail to observe all that the law requires (see 3:10). Although Jesus did fulfill all the requirements of the law, he still experienced all the conditions of sinful humanity under the curse of the law. He was subject to temptations, suffering, loneliness, and finally, on the cross, God-forsakenness and death.

The twofold purpose of the Son's full participation in our humanity,

4:5 The privileges and responsibilities of adoption were defined by Roman law (see Lyall

his perfect fulfillment of the law and his experience of the curse of the law on our behalf is given in the next two phrases: *to redeem those under the law, that we might receive the full rights of sons* (v. 5). Christ is uniquely qualified to fulfill these two purposes. Because he is the Son of God, he is able to give the position and rights of his sonship to sinful people. Because he became fully human, he is able to represent and redeem all humankind. And because he rendered perfect obedience to God and bore the curse of God against the disobedient, he is able *to redeem those under the law.* If being *under law* means being under obligation to keep the law and under the curse of the law for not keeping it, then *to redeem those under the law* means to set them free from both the obligation to keep the law and the curse of lawbreaking. When Paul says that Jesus was *born under law, to redeem those under law,* he means, as Calvin puts it, that "by putting the chains on himself, he takes them off the other." By taking the obligation and curse of the law upon himself, he set us free from both the obligation and the curse of the law.

The two verbs in verse 5, *redeem* and *receive,* present both sides of our relationship with God: God has already acted in history to set us free; for our lives to be changed by his action we need to respond in faith. Our response to God's action is depicted here as receiving *the full rights of sons.* This phrase in the NIV is a good translation of a legal term that means "adoption as sons." Adoption was defined by Roman law and widely practiced in Roman life. Several Roman emperors adopted men not related to them by blood in order to give them their office and authority. When a son was adopted, he was in all legal respects equal with those born into his new family. He had the same name, the same inheritance, the same position and the same rights as the natural-born sons. God sent his Son, who by his divine nature was the Son of God, in order that we, who are not his children by nature, might be his children by adoption and thus *receive the full rights of sons.* We have the same name, the same inheritance, the same position and the same rights as the one who is Son of God by virtue of his divine nature.

There is a shift in Paul's images here from the picture of a son who

1969:459; see also Schweizer 1972:398).

is treated like a slave until he reaches a certain age (vv. 1-2) to the picture of a slave who becomes a son by adoption (v. 5). The first picture clarifies the contrast between the two stages of redemption in history. The sending of the Son concluded the stage of slavery under law and inaugurated the new era when sons receive their inheritance. The second picture focuses on the nature of sonship itself. We are adopted as God's children by the sending of the Son of God.

Enjoying the Full Rights of Sons (4:6-7) Now Paul describes the way that children experience their full rights: *Because you are sons, God sent the Spirit of his Son into our hearts* (v. 6). The change from first person *(we)* to second person *(you)* shows that the adoption received by *those under law* (v. 5) was also received by the Gentile converts. The confession of faith of Jewish Christians is now the confession of Gentile Christians. Though Gentiles were not *under law* in the same way the Jewish people were, Paul's point is that they too were set free from the tyranny and curse of the law by the sending of God's Son. And by faith in Christ, they too have entered into a new relationship with God which involves the enjoyment of the full rights of sons and daughters of God. Now their life is to be lived not "under law" but "in Christ."

The striking parallelism between *God sent his Son* and *God sent the Spirit of his Son* rivets our attention on God's gracious initiative. Just as our position as sons and daughters was secured by God's action in sending his Son, so our experience as sons and daughters is the result of God's action in sending the Spirit of his Son. We could do nothing to attain to the position of sons and daughters; we can only receive the gift of adoption by faith. We could do nothing to produce an experience as sons and daughters; the action of God in sending the Spirit of his Son into our hearts enables us to enjoy our new relationship with God our Father.

Paul makes it very clear that there is only one condition for the experience of the Spirit in our hearts: *Because you are sons, God sent the Spirit of his Son into our hearts.* There is no other prerequisite for this

---

4:6 On the significance of knowing God as "Abba, *Father,*" see the excellent book by Thomas Smail, *The Forgotten Father:* "Out of his relationship to his Father Jesus found the strength and obedience for all his living and dying; to him we have to look for definition of both God's fatherhood and our sonship. . . . The Spirit opens up to us the holy of holies

experience of the Spirit besides receiving the gift of adoption. We do not need to go through a series of steps, recite special prayers or meet extra conditions. God sends the Spirit of his Son into our heart for one reason: because he adopted us into his family. To view adoption and reception of the Spirit as two separate stages in the Christian life tears apart the reciprocal relation of adoption and the sending of the Spirit. Paul's unique title for the Spirit here, *Spirit of his Son,* emphasizes the unity of the experience of adoption and the experience of the Spirit.

Just as verse 5 teaches us that the gift of adoption is ours when we receive it, so verse 6 teaches us that the sending of the Spirit into our hearts is experienced when we pray: the Spirit sent *into our hearts* is *the Spirit who calls out,* "Abba, *Father." Abba* is an Aramaic word for "father" used by a child in intimate conversation within the home. When children addressed their father as *Abba,* they were expressing affection, confidence and loyalty. One of the most remarkable aspects of the life of Jesus was that he addressed God as *Abba* in his prayers and taught his disciples to do the same. So striking and significant was Jesus' addressing God as *Abba* that even in Greek-speaking churches Jesus' Aramaic word for Father was heard as the believers called out to God in prayer. They called God *Abba* because the Spirit of Jesus was assuring them within their hearts, the control center of their emotions and thoughts, that they were children of the Father.

To know at the deepest level of our being that God is our Father and we are his sons and daughters is not the result of theological research or moral achievement, but the result of God's sending the Spirit of his Son to speak to us and to convince us that despite all our guilt, fears and doubts, the Father of Jesus is our Father too. To know God as our Father in this way is not merely intellectual apprehension of a doctrine, not merely warm feelings about God, but a life-transforming conscious awareness of the reality of our intimate relationship with God our Father.

Paul is certainly not talking here about addressing God as Father in

and bids us enter, and become sharers in Jesus' relationship to the Father. At the springs of our being, deeper than emotion or even intellect, although moving and informing both, he cries to us and in our fear and unbelief convinces us that the Father of Jesus is our father too. And as he does it all life begins to change and become new" (1980:44).

a formal liturgy in which there is no real involvement of the heart and will and mind. Nor is he talking about addressing God with an easy familiarity, as in prayers where God is addressed as "Daddy" in a chummy, casual way with no sense of awe or reverence. We must remember that when Jesus addressed his Father as *Abba* in the garden of Gethsemane, he was expressing both confident trust and willing obedience. " '*Abba*, Father,' he said, 'everything is possible for you. Take this cup from me. Yet not what I will, but what you will' " (Mk 14:36). So if the Spirit of the Son is moving us to call God *Abba*, then we will be expressing the same confident trust and willing obedience of the Son to the Father. All that Jesus did and said flowed out of his relationship with his Father. His sense of identity (who he was) was not based on his ministry (what he did), but just the reverse: he did what he did because he knew who he was. Likewise, the witness of the Spirit within us that God is our Father and we are his children is the center and fountainhead of all our Christian life and ministry.

People all around us are having identity crises. They are trying to find out who they are. They go for therapy to discover their inner selves; they search for their roots; they try to build their sense of self-worth on the foundation of their achievements. But far more important than any of these ways of finding out who we are, we need to experience the great gift of God the Father, the gift of his Spirit who tells us that we are children of God our Father. This experience of our identity before God is not necessarily a sensational or emotional experience. It is simply an experience of the Spirit's inner witness as we pray from our hearts to God.

We should always be amazed that when we pray we are included in the conversation of the Triune God. When we call God "*Abba*, Father," we are reminded by the very word *Abba* that Jesus used this name for God the Father in his prayers. We can address God as Father only because his Son gives us the right to do so. And we can exercise our right to call God Abba only by the activity of his Spirit within us who calls out, "*Abba*, Father." We call God *Abba* through the Son and in the power of the Spirit.

We will always find it difficult to explain the doctrine of the Trinity. But in prayer we experience the life and love of the Triune God. What an amazing privilege that we should be included in the conversation within the Trinity through prayer!

Verse 7 sums up Paul's argument to this point: *So you are no longer a slave, but a son.* The witness of the Spirit within convinces us that we are sons and daughters, children of God. Sons and daughters are no longer "held prisoners by the law" (3:23), "no longer under the supervision of the law" (3:25) and no longer *subject to guardians and trustees* (4:2). Sons and daughters are free from the control of the law. This does not mean that sons and daughters are free to do anything. They are now under the direction of the Spirit, who brings them into such close communion with God that they call him *Abba.* Sons and daughters who live in communion with the Father under the direction of the Spirit do not need the law to guide and discipline them. They are directed by a far superior power: the power of the Spirit.

To live under the direction of the law, as the Galatian believers were attempting to do, was sheer folly. "You foolish Galatians!" You are sons and daughters, not slaves. Why turn to the direction of the law when you have the direction of the Spirit? The tragedy of the Galatian situation was that believers who had entered into a love relationship with the Father by the activity of the Spirit in their lives were now acting like slaves, not like sons and daughters. They were relating to God on the basis of keeping his law rather than worshiping and serving him in the freedom and power of the Spirit of his Son. It is the same tragedy of the elder brother in Jesus' parable of the prodigal son. Although he served his father dutifully, he never called him "Father" or related to him as a son. He thought and acted like a slave: "All these years I've been slaving for you and never disobeyed your orders" (Lk 15:29).

I have greater appreciation for Paul's argument here now that my two sons are full-grown and no longer minors. I no longer attempt to restrict their behavior with the set of rules they had to follow when they were still young. In fact, if at this stage of their lives they responded to me simply on the basis of keeping my rules, I would be disappointed. What I long for now is for them to relate to me as mature sons. When they express love and respect to me simply because that is the desire of their heart, I am deeply grateful and filled with joy.

The consequence of being a son is inheritance: *Since you are a son,*

God has made you also an heir (v. 7). The Galatian believers had been told that they must be related to the descendants of Abraham through observance of the law in order to inherit the promises God made to Abraham. But Paul has now demonstrated how faith in Christ makes one a child of God and so an heir of God. None of us can make ourselves children or heirs of God. Only God can make slaves into sons and daughters, and sons and daughters into heirs.

The promise of inheritance is the promise of the Spirit. Paul said in 3:14 that the blessing of Abraham came upon the Gentiles: they received the promised Spirit. What greater inheritance could there be than the presence of the Spirit of God, *the Spirit of his Son,* within our hearts? The Spirit of his Son not only assures us that we are beloved children of the Father; he also makes us like his Son. We are most like the Son of God when we totally identify with him in Gethsemane and are able by his Spirit to pray "*Abba,* Father." When Christ prayed "*Abba,* Father" in Gethsemane, he was expressing complete trust in his Father and his willingness to endure the cross in obedience to his Father. He was looking ahead with confident, obedient trust to both the cross and the resurrection. When we are sure of our adoption by the witness of the Spirit within, we will also be living in the power of the inheritance of the Spirit, who is in the process of making us like Christ in his death and resurrection. Every day something of his cross will be seen in us as we die to self. Every day something of his resurrection life will be seen as he lives through us. One day, after a final death and a final resurrection, we will be completely like him. That is our inheritance as the children of God.

I once heard a son speak at his father's funeral service about his inheritance. He said, "The greatest inheritance my father left me was not what he had but what he was. He was a man of integrity; he was humble and often admitted his own failures. He was generous and compassionate. Above all, he was a man of deep faith in God. That's the inheritance that I most treasure, the inheritance of the character of my father." As children of God, we can say the same. Our greatest inheritance is not the abundance of things the Father gives us, but the character of his Son which the Spirit of his Son is forming within us.

Returning to Slavery Again? (4:8-11) Paul began his rebuke for foolishness with a series of searching questions that called the Galatian believers to reexamine their experience of God's miraculous work by his Spirit in their lives (3:1-5). He ends this section of his rebuke for foolishness in the same way. He has just reminded them that in their experience of the Spirit they have begun to communicate with God as their *Abba,* Father (v. 6). Now he asks his readers questions that point to the contrast between their present knowledge of God as his children and their former ignorance of God as slaves. The essence of the father-child relationship that they now enjoy is reciprocal knowledge: the Father knows his child; the child knows the Father. But in their attempt to observe the law they are actually turning from their intimate knowledge of God as his children and returning to the slavery they experienced in their former pagan way of life when they did not know God.

To help them see the foolishness of their ways, Paul first reminds them of their former condition of ignorance when they were enslaved by pagan idolatry (v. 8). Second, he draws their attention again to the knowledge of God which they now enjoy in their new relationship with God (v. 9). Third, he asks them why they are returning to slavery by observing the law (vv. 9-10). Finally, he expresses his deep concern for them (v. 11).

When You Did Not Know God (4:8) Immediately after expressing the amazing truth that Galatian believers are no longer slaves but children of God (vv. 6-7), Paul contrasts what they are now by God's grace with what they were before they believed the gospel: *Formerly, when you did not know God, you were slaves to those who by nature are not gods* (v. 8). *Those who by nature are not gods* were the objects that pagan Gentiles worshiped as gods. They might have been stone or wooden idols made by craftsmen. Or they have been the mythical beings, such as Zeus or Aphrodite, that the idols represented. Or they might have been demonic spirits that enslaved those who worshiped these idols and mythical beings. But whether the gods of the Gentiles were carved idols, mythical figures or demons, Paul rejects their divine status. They do not have the essential attributes of God; they are finite, created things, not the infinite Creator. In Romans 1 Paul expands his teaching on pagan worship: "They exchanged the truth of God for a lie, and worshiped and served created things rather than the Creator" (Rom 1:25).

People today, no less than the pagan Galatians in Paul's day, continue to worship and serve created things rather than the Creator. As a result of placing other things in the place of God, people, whether ancient or modern, do not know God. When Paul says *you did not know God,* he is not talking about theoretical knowledge. As we can see in the next verse, he is talking about the experiential knowledge of personal relationship. Human religious and philosophical efforts to know God are not able to lead us to an experiential knowledge of God. As Paul said to the Corinthian Christians, "In the wisdom of God the world through its wisdom did not know him" (1 Cor 1:21).

Now That You Know God (4:9) According to Paul, the result of conversion from paganism to Christ is the knowledge of God. But again we are quickly informed that what Paul means by knowledge is a personal encounter initiated by God: *now that you know God—or rather are known by God* (v. 9). Our knowledge of God is the result of his knowledge of us. Throughout the Bible, the joy of God's people is that God knows them. "O LORD, you have searched me and you know me," the psalmist sings (Ps 139:1). Jeremiah begins his prophecy with the certain knowledge that God knows him: "The word of the LORD came to me, saying, 'Before I formed you in the womb I knew you' " (Jer 1:4-5). By contrast, the worst fate of all is to be unknown by the Lord. There are no more terrible words than the words "I never knew you. Away from me!" (Mt 7:23).

To be known by God is to be chosen and loved by him. Because he chose to know us as his own people, we know him as our God. This is the knowledge of personal relationship, a relationship initiated and sustained by God's grace.

This kind of knowledge was vividly illustrated for me one night as I was traveling by train from London to Cambridge. The man next to me pointed at the name of the author on the book I was reading and said, "He's a good bloke."

"Really?" I said. "Do you know him?" I was surprised, because the author of the book was John Polkinghorne, former Cambridge professor of mathematical physics and now the president of Queens College of Cambridge University, a world-renowned scientist and theologian; and the chap next to me on the train did not look or sound like either a colleague or a student of this great scholar.

"Oh yes, he knows me!" he asserted proudly. "I serve his table at the college." He was obviously delighted not only that he knew this famous author but also that he was known by him.

Although I have read several of Polkinghorne's books and read articles about him, I could not claim to enjoy the relationship that this chap had with him, even though he confessed that he had never read a word by him or about him.

The Galatian believers could also delight in knowing God and being known by him, even though they had not read his book. This was the knowledge of a love relationship. As Paul said to the Corinthians, "The man who loves God is known by God" (1 Cor 8:3).

Why Are You Returning to Slavery? (4:9-10) It must have come as a shock to the Galatian Christians to read these words. After all, they had no intention of returning to their former way of life in paganism. On the contrary, they were attempting to make progress in their new spiritual life by learning and observing the Mosaic law, which prohibited pagan idolatry. Yet now Paul is asking them why they are *turning back to those weak and miserable principles. Do you wish to be enslaved by them all over again?* he asks.

Paul's words *all over again* raise the alarming possibility that turning to the observance of the Mosaic law after conversion to Christ is actually comparable to taking up a pre-Christian position of pagan worship. Furthermore, Paul's use of the phrase *those weak and miserable principles* to describe both the Galatian believers' observance of law after their conversion and their pagan religious experience is parallel to his use of "the basic principles of the world" to describe the pre-Christian condition of the Jewish people under the law of Moses (v. 3). The only way to understand Paul's equation of observing the law and pagan worship is to recognize that whenever the observance of law takes the place of Christ as the basis of relating to God, it is as reprehensible as pagan worship.

Pagan religions are *weak and miserable principles.* They are *weak* because they do not have the power to overcome the guilt and power of sin; they are *miserable,* poor and impotent because they cannot impart a new life. In the same way the Mosaic codes are *weak and miserable principles.* The Mosaic law "declares that the whole world is a prisoner of sin" (3:22), but it is powerless to set anyone free from the chains of sin. And the Mosaic law is not able to impart life (3:21). Therefore to substitute observance of the Mosaic law for complete reliance on Christ is just the same as returning to pagan worship.

An illustration of the *weak and miserable principles* to which the churches in Galatia were turning is given by Paul in verse 10: *You are observing special days and months and seasons and years!* Evidently the Jewish calendar had been instituted in the Galatian churches. They were planning to observe the regulations for weekly sabbath days, monthly new moon festivals, annual festivals like Passover, Pentecost and Tabernacles, and the sabbatical years. They must have been led to believe that their observance of these holy days and festivals would draw them closer to God. What foolishness! How could people who have already received adoption as children of God and are praying *"Abba,* Father" in the Spirit, people who know God and are known by him, start to depend on the observance of holy days for their relationship with God? Isn't this obviously a return to those *weak and miserable principles* that characterized their lives in paganism?

My Chinese colleagues at Trinity Theological College in Singapore have recently been expressing their concern that some Chinese churches are sounding more Confucian than Christian. Their point is that Chinese Christians are in danger of turning their faith into a version of Confucianism, which was what they followed before their conversion to Christ. In their Confucian background they maintained high moral standards. But they were not able to enter into a personal relationship with God by their moral achievements. In fact, they experienced unresolved guilt for not being able to live up to their own standards. When they first met Christ, they focused on their newfound personal relationship with God the Father, which they enjoyed through faith in Christ by the presence of his Spirit in their lives. But slowly their center of attention changed.

4:10 The specific celebration signified by each term in the list of *special days and months and seasons and years* is the subject of much debate. Since similar lists of terms are found in various strands of Jewish literature, and since the central requirement of the Judaizers was for the Gentile Christians to receive circumcision, which was a specifically Jewish requirement and certainly not a requirement in Gnostic and pagan religions, it is safe to

They put more and more emphasis on the high moral standards of their Christian faith. They began to lose sight of what God had done for them in Christ and began to concentrate on what they must do to inherit "the good life." They were especially drawn to the Old Testament's legal codes. Then they formulated those moral laws in the familiar terms of their own Chinese cultural background. So my colleagues shake their heads with concern when they say of some fellow believers, "I'm afraid they sound more Confucian than Christian."

Paul's Expression of Concern (4:11) Paul treats the change of direction in the Galatian churches as an extremely serious matter. He is deeply troubled and upset. He even wonders if all his efforts in planting these churches will prove to be in vain.

Are we as grieved as Paul was when our churches begin to put the observance of law at the center of their life and worship? Are we so troubled when Christians put more emphasis on keeping certain traditions rather than on growing in their relationship with the Father through Christ in the power of the Spirit? Does our lack of concern for Christians who have become law-centered rather than Christ-centered indicate that we do not even recognize that a change has taken place or understand how destructive such a shift of focus can be?

With his expression of heartfelt concern for his converts, Paul closes the entire rebuke section of his letter. His rebuke for disloyalty to the gospel (1:6-10) was followed by his autobiographical account of his own loyalty to the gospel (1:11—2:21). His rebuke for foolishness regarding the gospel (3:1) was followed by his explanation of the Galatians' conversion experience and an exposition of Scripture (3:2—4:11) in order to show the relation of the gospel to the law. He will now move to his request for a change of direction.

□ REQUEST SECTION (4:12—6:10)

In Paul's day, letters that were written to rebuke someone for misbehav-

---

assume that Paul was referring to Jewish festivals, not Gnostic or pagan festivals (for a summary of the discussion see Hansen 1989a:170-71). Perhaps the list of four terms is intentionally vague and open in order to cover all kinds of celebrations observed by the Jews (so Burton 1921:234; Longenecker 1990:182).

ior often ended with a request for a renewal of friendship and a change of behavior. For example, one short papyrus letter from Paul's time reads: "I am surprised that you did not see your way to let me have what I asked you to send by Corbolon, especially when I wanted it for a festival. I beg you to buy me a silver seal and send it to me with all speed." Here we see the same form as Paul's letter to the Galatians. First there is an expression of rebuke ("I am surprised . . ."—see Gal 1:6) and a statement of the cause of rebuke ("that you did not see your way to let me have . . ."). Second there is an expression of request ("I beg you . . ."—see Gal 4:12) followed by imperatives ("buy . . . send").

At 4:12 Paul turns from rebuke to request: *I plead with you, brothers, become like me, for I became like you. Become like me* is the first imperative in Galatians. It sets the focus for the rest of the request section of the letter. This personal appeal (4:12-20) is followed by a scriptural appeal (4:21-31). Then Paul sets forth his authoritative appeal (5:1-12) followed by his ethical appeal (5:13—6:10).

□ Personal Appeal (4:12-20)

In order to understand Paul's personal appeal—*become like me*—we need to see how the entire rebuke section of the letter (1:6—4:11) establishes the background for this appeal. Paul rebuked the Galatian believers for disloyalty to the gospel (1:6). Under the influence of false teachers, they were turning from the true gospel and following another gospel which required circumcision and observance of the law for inclusion in the people of God. Paul reinforced his rebuke for disloyalty to the true gospel by telling the story of his own loyalty to the truth of the gospel (1:11—2:21). Since he was called by God to preach the gospel to Gentiles, he firmly resisted anyone who excluded Gentiles on the basis of the law. Paul also rebuked the Galatian Christians for foolishness about the gospel (3:1-5). In their confusion they thought that works of the law were required to enjoy the blessing of God. Paul undergirded his rebuke for foolishness by an exposition of the promise

---

Notes: 4:12 Parallels from first-century Greek letters to illustrate how the rebuke-request form of Paul's letter to the Galatians conformed to the conventions of letterwriting in his day are provided by Hansen (1989a:30-47; see also Longenecker 1990:184-89). Paul used a common letter form to express his rebuke for foolishness about the gospel and his request

to Abraham fulfilled in Christ (3:6—4:11). Since Gentile Christians were children of Abraham and included in God's promise to Abraham because they believed in Christ, they could not be excluded from the blessing of God on the basis of the law.

This extended rebuke sets the stage for his initial request: *Become like me.* Of course this is a plea for reunion with Paul, for identification with him. But in light of all that Paul has said already in his letter, it is clear that he is asking for more than empathy; he is saying more than "Put yourselves in my place" (NEB). He is calling for the Galatians to imitate him in his loyalty to the truth of the gospel (see 2:5, 14). He is challenging them to die to the law so that they might live for God (see 2:19-20). He is pleading with them to be as free as he is from the tyranny of the law, and to enjoy with him all the benefits of the gospel (the Spirit, righteousness, blessing, adoption and inheritance of the promise) which are already available by faith in Christ (see 3:6—4:7). He is demanding that they resist the false teachers who are trying to bring them under the tyranny of the law.

The challenge—*become like me*—is needed precisely because they are not like Paul. They are giving into the persuasive teaching of the law teachers. Because they have been preoccupied with getting circumcised in order to belong to God's people and using Jewish law to guide their lives, they are drifting from their single-minded devotion to Christ. What they need is a renewal of their experience of union with Christ. The first step toward that renewal is the imitation of Paul.

To us it may seem presumptuous and risky for Paul to challenge people to imitate him in order to draw them back to Christ. Most of us would rather say, "Don't follow me, follow Christ!" We are too aware of our own inconsistencies and failures to set ourselves up as models for the Christian life. But this was Paul's way. He said to the Corinthians, "Follow my example, as I follow the example of Christ" (1 Cor 11:1). Paul was well aware that the imitation of Christ needs to be illustrated in the experience of our peers. Without mentors who show us what it

to follow his example of obedience to the truth of the gospel.

Paul often urged his converts to imitate him (see 1 Cor 4:16; 11:1; Phil 3:17; 1 Thess 1:6). When he called for others to follow Christ, he led the way.

means to follow Christ in the rough-and-tumble of our contemporary world, imitation of Christ often seems an otherworldly, unattainable ideal. But when someone like ourselves gives us a living model to follow, we have a tangible, realizable pattern to guide us.

After his command, Paul gives four reasons to follow his example.

Paul's Identification with the Gentile Galatians (4:12) The first reason Paul gives to his readers for following his example is his identification with them: *for I became like you* (v. 12). In his evangelism of the Galatians, Paul did not preach at them from a distance. He entered into their culture, adapted to their ways and became one with them. Even though he was a Jew, trained as a Pharisee to be totally separate from Gentiles, he lived like a Gentile in order to reach the Gentiles for Christ. His practice of identification illustrated the principle he enunciated in 1 Corinthians 9:19-22: "I make myself a slave to everyone, to win as many as possible. To the Jews I became like a Jew, to win the Jews. . . . To those not having the law I became like one not having the law . . . so as to win those not having the law. To the weak I became weak, to win the weak. I have become all things to all men so that by all possible means I might save some."

The same practice of identification is necessary today, if we are going to communicate the gospel effectively to people. We must put ourselves in their place, eat what they eat, dress as they dress, talk their language, experience their joys and sorrows, and enter into their way of thinking. If we want people to become like us in our commitment to Christ, then we must become one with them.

One of the best examples of identification I've ever seen is a woman who lives in a country closed to all missionary activity. She lives with a large family. Except for participating in their religious practices, she has totally identified with the way this family lives. The government is sponsoring her to write the ancient legends of the people in a simple format for children to learn. As she has researched and written these stories, she

---

4:13 Paul's *illness* was viewed by Ramsay (1962:94-97) as malaria that Paul contracted in the lowland marshes of Pamphylia before he went to the higher plateau of Pisidian Antioch to recover; Wrede (1907:22-23) and others speculated that Paul's illness was epilepsy. Luther understood Paul's mention of illness here as a reference to all that he suffered in his body because of constant physical persecution (1979:409).

has been able to enter into the mind of the people. They love the way she retells their favorite stories. In a quiet and very effective way she has been able to lead people to commit their lives to Christ because she first became one with them.

Paul's identification with the Galatians served as a compelling reason for them to stand with him in his commitment to Christ and freedom from the law. After all, if Paul as a Jewish Christian was willing and able to live like them, then it was clear that living like a Jew or a Gentile is not what matters. What matters is simply faith in Christ.

The Galatians' Identification with Paul (4:12-16) After reminding the Galatians of his identification with them, Paul recalls how they identified with him during his first visit. Their early enthusiastic response to him was a good reason for them to return to their "first love."

In the last phrase of 4:12, Paul reassures his readers: *You have done me no wrong.* Since he moves right on to remind them how well they treated him when he was with them the first time, Paul is probably telling them that he is still thankful for their kindness toward him, despite whatever may have happened during the recent crisis. Sometimes when a friendship is strained in a time of crisis, it is helpful to stir up memories of the initial warmth of the relationship. That is what Paul does here. And his description of the way he was received by the Galatians sets forth an admirable pattern for the way all true ministers of God ought to be received.

Paul recalls that it was because of an illness that he first preached the gospel to the Galatians (4:13). We often wonder what kind of illness Paul had. The suggestion that he had some kind of eye problem is supported by his statement in verse 15 that the Galatians were so concerned for him that they would have given him their own eyes if they could have done so. And Paul's use of "large letters" when he wrote (see 6:11) is also taken as evidence that he had eye trouble. Since I had eye surgery as a child and still struggle with poor eyesight, I've been encouraged by the

---

When Paul says *I first preached,* does he mean "the first of two" occasions of preaching, or does he mean only an earlier occasion of preaching? The first interpretation is based on the use of the term *first (proteron)* in classical Greek and could signal the date of the letter relative to the narrative in Acts. But the latter meaning is more probable, since *first (proteron)* simply meant "earlier" in Hellenistic Greek.

thought that the great apostle was able to do so much even though he may have had eye trouble. But I must admit that there is insufficient evidence to be dogmatic about this theory. Paul's statement that the Galatians would have been willing even to give him their eyes is probably an idiomatic way of complimenting them for their compassion and generosity. And his use of large letters when he wrote was his way of emphasizing his point.

Of course there have been many other attempts to determine what illness Paul had. Some say he had malaria; others suggest epilepsy. If Paul had all the illnesses that our commentaries say he had, he was a very sick man indeed. The truth is, we have insufficient evidence to make an accurate diagnosis. But we should not let all the speculation about the nature of his illness distract us from Paul's perspective that even his illness was an opportunity to preach the gospel. It is common to view illness as a hindrance to preaching the gospel or an excuse not to do our duty. But Paul realized, as he says in a letter to the Corinthian church, that God's grace is sufficient for us in our weakness—in fact, that God's power is best expressed through our weakness.

Verse 14 indicates that Paul's illness was repulsive. It would have been understandable if the Galatians had turned away from him in disgust. But even though his illness was a trial for them to bear, they did not treat him with contempt or scorn. *Instead,* Paul exclaims with gratitude, *you welcomed me as if I were an angel of God, as if I were Christ Jesus himself* (v. 14). Of course Paul does not mean that the Galatians actually regarded him as an angel of God or as Christ Jesus himself. The repeated *as if* introduces two exaggerated comparisons that compare how the Galatians initially welcomed Paul to the welcome they would have given an angel of God or Jesus Christ himself. And yet Paul was like an angel of God, since he was an apostle sent from God (1:1), so the Galatians were right to give him a welcome due to an angel of God. And Paul was so identified with Christ (2:20) that those who welcomed him also welcomed Christ himself.

In the Galatians' reception of Paul we see a wonderful example of the way to receive a messenger from God. In our day people want to listen to someone who has a good "TV image." If preachers' outward appearance is appealing, they get a big audience. But if they were ugly and sickly, as tradition tells us Paul was, then most people would switch channels to find a more attractive image. But the Galatians' reception of Paul was not based on outward appearances. If they had responded to Paul simply on the basis of his physical attractiveness, they would have rejected him with contempt. Instead they evaluated the messenger on the basis of his message and then welcomed him with open arms. For his message was the redemptive love of God expressed in Christ Jesus.

Verses 15 and 16 present a contrast: the Galatians had given Paul a royal welcome, but suddenly their attitude toward him changed drastically. *What has happened to all your joy?* he asks. The question looks back longingly to those joyful days when Paul first preached the gospel in Galatia. Paul reminds them that they would have gone to any extreme to help him during those days; they would have torn out their eyes for him if they could have done so. Since the eyes were considered the most precious parts of the body, this is a graphic, idiomatic description of the Galatians' devotion to Paul at the beginning of their relationship. But now their relationship has turned sour. The cause for the Galatians' change of attitude is given by Paul in verse 16. Although the NIV puts this verse in the form of a question, it should be taken as a statement of Paul's description of the Galatians' fickle change of heart: "So now I have become your enemy by telling you the truth!" No doubt the truth Paul refers to here is the truth contained in this letter: his rebuke for desertion from the true gospel (1:6) and foolishness about the gospel (3:1).

The dramatic shift from the Galatians' warm welcome to their cold rejection of Paul serves as a sober warning to both pastors and their churches. Pastors should not be so naive as to think they will always receive a warm welcome if they consistently teach the truth. In fact, teaching the truth will always run the risk of alienating some people. And people in the church need to be aware that their initial positive response to pastors who teach the truth will be severely tested when the truth cuts like a two-edged sword. During such a time of conviction, people need to maintain their loyalty to their pastors precisely because they have the courage to preach the truth even when it hurts.

The Rival Teachers' Ulterior Motive (4:17-18) The negative example of the rival teachers provides another reason for following Paul's example. They were exclusive and divisive in their relationships. They had launched an aggressive campaign to win the allegiance of the Galatian Christians—*but,* Paul declares, *for no good.* They were jealous leaders who envied the Galatian Christians' affectionate relationship with Paul. So they sought *to alienate* the Galatian believers from Paul. Literally, the verb *alienate* means "shut out" or "exclude." Although Paul does not actually say from whom this exclusion was desired, his focus here on his relationship with his readers indicates clearly that the rival teachers intended to alienate the Galatian Christians from Paul.

All too often leaders in the church seem to be more interested in the exclusive personal attachment of their followers to themselves than in the spiritual growth and unity of the entire body of Christ. Of course, as Paul admits in verse 18, it is not wrong to be zealous to win the affection of others, as long as it is for their welfare. But by the very way Paul states this general principle, he calls us to be careful lest we court the affections of others for our own selfish advantage or are courted in such a way ourselves.

Paul's Ultimate Concern (4:19-20) In contrast to the selfish motive of the rival teachers, Paul expresses his own deep, heartfelt concern for his *dear children.* He portrays himself as a pregnant mother, *again in the pains of childbirth.* This rather shocking maternal image captures the extent of Paul's identification with these Christians. In his love for them, he has had to go through labor pains for them twice: when he preached the gospel to them the first time, and now *again* as he seeks to bring them back to the true gospel. This is more than any mother must go through for her child. But Paul tells his children in the faith that he is willing to endure labor pains for them not just twice but *until Christ is formed in you.*

Actually, there is a sudden shift of images here. Paul views himself as a pregnant mother delivering her children, but now he views the Galatians themselves as pregnant people bearing Christ as an unformed fetus in their wombs. Paul is enduring the pains of childbirth for them until Christ is fully formed within them. From a scientific point of view this may seem like a very strange conjunction of images, but Paul's point is

---

4:17 The words *from us* are in brackets in the NIV because they are not in the Greek text, but it makes good sense to add them in translation, since the context indicates that

clear: because he loves his converts with a sacrificial love, he will endure any pain until the full image of Christ is seen in them.

The contrast between Paul and the rival teachers is striking. Their selfish motive is to attach the Galatians to themselves so that they will be the center of attention; Paul labors to attach them to Christ so that the full moral character of Christ will be expressed in them. Paul's personal appeal, *become like me,* must be interpreted in the light of this contrast. It is not simply a demand for personal attachment to Paul. It expresses his longing for the Galatians to be able to declare wholeheartedly with him, "I no longer live, but Christ lives in me!"

It is not surprising that the image of Paul's maternal love for his children is followed by an expression of his wish to be with them and change his tone (v. 20). If he were with them, he would want to change from his tone of rebuke for their past foolishness and give them parental counsel for their future conduct. In fact, he does that in his letter, which is a substitute for his personal visit. Up to this point in his letter, his dominant tone has been one of rebuke. But now that he has called for a renewal of their friendship in this paragraph (vv. 12-20), he turns his attention to instructions. Yet still he has a heavy heart, for he is *perplexed* about them (v. 20). What will their foolishness lead them to do? What will be the outcome of their confusion? Such questions move Paul to give clear directions in the rest of his letter, to guide his readers out of their slavery to false teaching into the freedom of the true gospel of Christ.

We cannot help but be moved by Paul's passion for his people. He feels their pain; he identifies with their struggle. He has the heart of a good mother caring for her newborn. May God raise up evangelists and pastors like him in our generation.

□ Scriptural Appeal (4:21-31)

After his personal appeal ("become like me"), Paul begins to give specific direction to the Galatians. He does this first of all by taking their own perspective: since they *want to be under the law,* Paul asks if they

---

Paul's opponents wanted to alienate the Galatian believers from Paul.

are aware of what the law says to them (v. 21). His opening question is a clue that although the Galatians have expressed their desire to keep the regulations of the Mosaic law, they have not yet fully understood or accepted all the obligations of the law. We know from verse 10 that they are already trying to observe the Jewish calendar. And we will see in 5:2 that some of them have gotten circumcised. But Paul has to inform them in 5:3 that once someone is circumcised, he is under obligation to keep the whole law. At this point in his letter Paul takes their position and says, as it were, "Well, now if you really want to keep the law, let me tell you how the law applies to your situation."

Paul's application of the law to their situation is taken from the story of Abraham's two sons, Isaac and Ishmael. When we read through Paul's use of Scripture in this section, we encounter a strange allegorical interpretation. In all of the New Testament, there is perhaps not a more difficult passage to interpret. This passage has often been used to accuse Paul of twisting and distorting Scripture. Betz says that this passage "has strained the credulity of the readers beyond what many people can bear" (1979:244). Paul explicitly calls attention to his method of interpretation in verse 24: *these things may be taken figuratively*. A more accurate translation of this phrase than the NIV would be "these things are now being interpreted allegorically." Paul must have inserted this reference to his method of interpretation because he knew that his use of this method of interpreting the biblical text would cause difficulty for his readers. In order to appreciate what Paul is doing here, we need to get an overview of the passage, to look at the whole before looking at the parts. Let's consider Paul's purpose for his allegorical interpretation, the false teachers' interpretation and Paul's method of interpretation.

You can often tell the purpose of a book by simply reading its introduction and conclusion. Paul introduces his interpretation of the Old Testament text by pointing out the difference between the two sons of Abraham: one was born of the slave woman in the ordinary way, while

---

Notes: **4:21** C. K. Barrett's supposition that Paul's opponents were using the Hagar-Sarah story in their circumcision campaign is also supported by Bruce (1982:218), Longenecker (1990:199-200, 218), Drane (1975:43-44) and Barclay (1988:91).

The distinction between allegorical and typological is rejected by James Barr (1966:103-11). Barr emphasizes that allegorization does not necessarily mean a nonhistorical perspec-

the other was born by the free woman as the result of a promise (vv. 22-23). Paul concludes his interpretation with these words: *Therefore, brothers, we are not children of the slave woman, but of the free woman* (v. 31). His introduction and conclusion make it clear that his primary purpose is to identify the Galatian Christians as the true children of Abraham, the children of the free woman, the children of promise. As we have seen already, the primary point of Paul's argument in chapter 3 was also to answer this question of the identity of the Galatian Christians: "If you belong to Christ, then you are Abraham's seed, and heirs according to the promise" (3:29). So when we examine the details of Paul's allegorical interpretation, we need to keep in mind this central point to understand where Paul is headed.

When we consider the context for the allegory in the broader setting of the entire letter, we can also see that Paul constructed the allegory to call for decisive resistance to the false teachers. Paul began the body of his letter by rebuking the Galatians for giving in to the pressure of troublemakers who were leading them to accept a false gospel (1:6-7). In his autobiography Paul illustrated how he decisively resisted pressures from Jewish Christians at Jerusalem (2:3-5) and at Antioch (2:11-14) similar to those faced by the Galatian churches. The request section of the letter begins with the initial request of the letter in 4:12, "become like me," which calls for the Galatians to resist the false teachers just as Paul had resisted the false brothers. His own stand against those "Ishmaels" is now supported by the command of Scripture (Gen 21:10 in Gal 4:30), and Paul asks his converts to follow this command as well. To those who *want to be under the law* (v. 21) Paul gives a specific command to follow: *Get rid of the slave woman and her son* (v. 30). In 5:1 Paul paraphrases the call for decisive resistance expressed by the command of Genesis 21:10 in his own words: "It is for freedom that Christ has set us free. Stand firm, then, and do not let yourselves be burdened again by a yoke of slavery."

tive. It is true that Paul's use of the Hagar-Sarah story builds on the historical framework, but there is also an interpretation derived from the text of Genesis 21 which goes beyond the historical account and points to a symbolic meaning (see Longenecker 1975:49). See Hays (1989: 86-87) for a helpful explanation of Paul's "ecclesiocentric hermeneutic" in this passage.

So Paul's purpose for his allegorical interpretation of Genesis 21 is to identify the Galatian Christians as the children of freedom and to instruct them to resist those who would lead them into slavery under the law.

We might well wonder why Paul chose such a text to prove that Gentile Christians were the true descendants of Abraham. After all, on the surface it would seem that Paul had to use extreme measures to make the text serve his purpose. In fact, the text seems to fit the position of the false teachers better. We can easily imagine that Jewish Christians would have claimed that as Jews they were the sons of Isaac, the legitimate children of Abraham, while the Gentiles were like the Ishmaelites, illegitimate children. As the children of Isaac, the son of promise, the Jewish Christians could have gone on to claim that only those who attach themselves to the true people of God by circumcision and keeping the law can ever hope to inherit the promises of God. They would probably have threatened expulsion to all those who refused to live under the yoke of the law, as all full members of the Jewish Christian community were expected to live. They might have also claimed that the mother church in Jerusalem supported their teaching.

This line of speculation seems reasonable enough. But did the false teachers actually use the text in that way? Of course we cannot know for sure, but there seems to be good evidence that they did. First of all, the one undisputed fact in Paul's description of the rival teachers' campaign in the Galatian churches is their promotion of circumcision: they "are trying to compel you to be circumcised" (6:12). Since the law establishes circumcision as the sign of the Abrahamic covenant (Gen 17:10-14), and since circumcision and the Abrahamic covenant are closely linked in all strands of Jewish literature, it is difficult to imagine how the opponents could have promoted circumcision without referring to Abraham.

Second, the way Paul develops his allegory of Abraham's two sons immediately after his comment that the Galatians desire to be under the law (4:21) suggests that he was confronted by teachers who equated Abrahamic descent with being under the law. In fact, in the Jewish literature of Paul's day one of the most celebrated characteristics of Abraham was his perfect obedience to the Mosaic law.

Third, the way Paul introduces the Abraham story itself with the formula *it is written* (v. 22) is a clue that he is responding to the rival teachers' use of the same passage. Usually this formula introduces a quotation. But here it simply introduces a very brief summary of the Abraham story, which spreads over a number of chapters of Genesis: *Abraham had two sons.* It appears that the Gentile believers in Galatia have already been told the story.

Fourth, the women are introduced as *the slave woman* and the *free woman.* Which slave woman and which free woman? Paul seems to assume that his readers already know that the slave woman is Hagar, the free woman Sarah.

In light of this evidence for the false teachers' own use of the Abraham story, including the Hagar-Sarah story, we can safely conclude that Paul deemed his allegorical treatment of the Hagar-Sarah story necessary "because his opponents had used it and he could not escape it. His so called allegorical treatment of Abraham was evoked not by a personal love of fantastic exegesis but by a reasoned case which it was necessary that he should answer" (Barrett 1982:162). When we work through Paul's interpretation, it will be helpful to keep in mind that it is a rebuttal of a number of strong points in the rival teachers' argument.

If we hope to understand Paul's allegorical treatment of Scripture, we need to describe the method he used. Paul's statement that he was interpreting the Hagar-Sarah story allegorically does not automatically decide the question as to the exact nature of his exegetical method. Some of the early church fathers, such as John Chrysostom and Theodore of Mopsuestia, insisted that by "allegorical" Paul actually meant "typological." Many later commentators have taken the same view. R. Hanson's definition of these terms helps to sharpen the distinction between allegory and typology: "Typology is the interpreting of an event belonging to the present or recent past as the fulfillment of a similar situation recorded or prophesied in Scripture. Allegory is the interpretation of an object or person or number of objects or persons as in reality meaning some object or person of a later time, with no attempt made to trace a 'similar situation' between them" (1959:7). On the basis of this definition, we can see that Paul used both a typological method and an allegorical method in his interpretation of the Hagar-Sarah story.

Paul saw a real correspondence between the historical situation of the two sons of Abraham and the two sorts of descendants of Abraham in his own day—those born according to the flesh and those born according to the Spirit. This correspondence is emphasized by the grammatical construction of 4:29: *At that time . . . It is the same now*. Then, as now, the son according to the flesh persecuted the son according to the promise. Paul depicts the hostile activities of the troublemakers in Galatia in Galatians 1:7, 3:1, 4:17, 5:7-10 and 6:12-13. Since the Galatian believers were the persecuted and not the persecutors, they were obviously the children of the free woman through the promise. They were experiencing the fulfillment of a situation in the life of Isaac recorded in Genesis 21. On the basis of this real correspondence between the historical event in the life of Isaac (the type) and the fulfillment of that event in the present life of the Galatian churches (the antitype), Paul rephrases the words of Sarah in Genesis 21:10 as a divine command for the Galatian churches: *But what does the Scripture say? "Get rid of the slave woman and her son, for the slave woman's son will never share in the inheritance with the free woman's son"* (4:30). Galatians 4:31 is the natural conclusion Paul draws from this interpretation: *Therefore, brothers, we are not children of the slave woman, but of the free woman.*

Typological interpretation, such as this appears to be, is grounded on the conviction that God acts in similar ways in different periods of history and that the event of salvation in Christ is the fulfillment of history, law and prophecy. From this perspective, persons and events associated with the event of salvation in Christ will be seen to correspond to the original situation. Seen in this light, Paul's application of the Genesis account to the Galatian churches is based not on arbitrary, fanciful definitions but on actual parallels in history: *At that time . . . It is the same now.*

But when we turn to verses 24-27, we see Paul using an allegorical method of interpretation. For the correspondence between Hagar and Mount Sinai and the present Jerusalem is not a historical correspondence.

Among Jewish thinkers, Philo of Alexandria, a contemporary of Paul, was the most prominent practitioner of allegorical interpretation. Philo saw the Old Testament as primarily a book of symbols that have hidden meaning beyond the literal, historical sense. His allegorical interpretation of these symbols was guided not by the constraints of the text but by his desire to demonstrate that the Jewish Scriptures contained the essence of Greek philosophy. In his interpretation of the Hagar-Sarah story, Sarah represents virtue and true wisdom, whereas Hagar represents general education. So Philo uses the allegory to contrast the superior value of true wisdom, which is found in the sacred Scriptures, to general education, which prepares one for secular work. In that allegory Isaac is the true philosopher trained in holy Scriptures; Ishmael is the sophist, unable to perceive eternal ideals.

Paul, of course, is not using the text as Philo did, to expound Platonic philosophical principles. Nevertheless, he is giving a meaning to the various terms of the text in an allegorical fashion. The theological framework for Paul's allegorical interpretation comes from his Abraham argument in chapter 3. In that argument Gentile converts were identified as true children and heirs of Abraham on the basis of the promise given to Abraham and the fulfillment of that promise in their experience of the Spirit. The Abraham argument also set out a contrast between the Abrahamic covenant as the means of life and righteousness and the Sinaitic covenant as the means of slavery.

Thus when the Genesis account is interpreted allegorically, it is not surprising that Sarah and her counterpart—the Jerusalem above, our true mother—should be identified as the mother of the Galatian believers in Christ. It follows naturally enough that Sarah can also be equated with the covenant of promise—a promise that included Abrahamic blessings for Gentiles as the seed of Abraham.

All these equations are built on the exposition of the gospel in the light of Old Testament texts in Galatians 3. In other words, Paul's allegorical definitions in Galatians 4 do not determine or form the basis of his theology but are derived from his theology, which has already been developed in the previous chapter.

A natural consequence of Paul's definitions of these terms in the allegorical equation is that Hagar becomes a symbol of the covenant at Mount Sinai. At this point in his interpretation, however, the basis for Paul's definitions becomes more problematic. How can Paul make the "Hagar = Mount Sinai" and "Sinai = present Jerusalem" equations in the face of the fundamental Jewish conviction that the Mosaic law was given to the descendants of Isaac at Mount Sinai and had nothing to do with Hagar?

The most satisfactory explanation of Paul's allegorical equations is simply stated in verse 25: *because she is in slavery with her children.* In Paul's allegorization of the text, slavery is the common feature that links Hagar (the slave woman), the covenant given at Mount Sinai, and the present Jerusalem. Paul has already attributed this feature of slavery to the Mosaic law (3:22-24; 4:1-10) and to a certain faction of "false brothers" at Jerusalem (2:4). His allegorization therefore must be seen as a counterattack on that Jewish-Christian faction within the church at Jerusalem which had tried to rob Gentile believers of their freedom by requiring them to be circumcised (2:3-6) and which was now attempting to do the same thing at Galatia. This actual experience of "false brothers" in the church gave rise to Paul's allegorical treatment of the text and is the key to its interpretation.

Paul's basic typological interpretation is supplemented by an allegorical treatment in order to relate the people in the story to the specific issues in the Galatian church and so to counterattack the false teachers' use of the same text.

Now that we have taken time to get an overview of this complex passage, we can turn to verse-by-verse exposition.

After his introductory question (v. 21), Paul sets forth the historical contrast between the two sons of Abraham (vv. 22-23); he develops this contrast by means of allegorical comparisons (vv. 24-26) and then adds a scriptural confirmation (v. 27). In verses 28-30 Paul addresses his readers directly and spells out the personal consequences of his interpretation for their lives. Finally, Paul underscores the main point again in his conclusion (v. 31).

Historical Contrast (4:22-23) The contrast between Abraham's two sons is established in terms of their social status (v. 22) and the manner of their birth (v. 23). Ishmael's mother, Hagar, was Abraham's slave; Isaac's mother, Sarah, was Abraham's wife, a free woman. Since the social status of the mothers determined the social status of their sons, Ishmael was a slave and Isaac was free. Furthermore, there was nothing supernatural about Ishmael's birth: it happened *in the ordinary way,* as a natural result of the sexual union of Abraham and Hagar. NIV's *in the ordinary way* is a good paraphrase of "according to the flesh." In this context *flesh* is not used as a negative, judgmental term; it simply indicates that Ishmael's birth was not caused by anything except the normal biological processes of conception and birth. On the other hand, Isaac *was born as the result of a promise.* The only way that Abraham's sexual union with his aged, barren wife Sarah could have resulted in conception and birth was by the supernatural fulfillment of the promise of God.

So far Paul has simply summarized the biblical narrative of Abraham's two sons. But what a dramatic contrast his simple summary sets forth: slavery by natural birth and freedom by supernatural birth! It does not take much imagination to see how this contrast could be effectively used to illustrate and apply the truth already given in this letter. If you have only experienced natural birth, you are by nature a slave. But if you have experienced supernatural birth by the fulfillment of God's promise in your life, you are by God's grace set free. Before Paul develops these personal implications, however, he sets up a series of allegorical comparisons.

Allegorical Comparisons (4:24-26) Since contemporary Jewish exegesis of the Hagar-Sarah story would have supported the position of the false teachers in Galatia, it was necessary for Paul to redefine the terms of the story so that he could draw out its real meaning as he saw it. The purpose of his allegorical comparisons is to establish the identification of the false teachers with Hagar and Ishmael (vv. 24-25) and the identification of the Galatian believers with Sarah and Isaac (vv. 26-28).

The identification of the false teachers with Hagar and Ishmael is developed in four steps. The first step identifies Hagar with the covenant from Mount Sinai and the children of Hagar with the children of the Sinaitic covenant: *the women represent two covenants. One covenant is from Mount Sinai and bears children who are to be slaves: This is Hagar* (v. 24). This comparison is based on the common understanding that the children of slave women are slaves. If Hagar represents the covenant from Mount Sinai, then the children of that covenant are destined to be slaves, since the children of Hagar, the slave woman, were destined to be slaves. Paul has already argued that those who adhere to the Sinaitic covenant are enslaved by it (3:19—4:10). His allegorical comparison here builds on that argument and leads to the identification of the rival teachers with Hagar's children, so that he can appeal to the Galatian believers in the words of Genesis 21:10 to resist the influence of those teachers.

The second step in this identification process undergirds the Hagar-Sinaitic covenant comparison. Such a comparison contradicts the common Jewish understanding that the Sinaitic covenant was given to the descendants of Isaac and was therefore not related to Hagar and her descendants. So now Paul sets forth a Hagar-Mount Sinai equation to support his Hagar-Sinaitic covenant equation: *Now Hagar stands for Mount Sinai in Arabia* (v. 25). Paul appears to be connecting Hagar with Mount Sinai on the basis of her name and the geographical location of Mount Sinai. In what way the name Hagar can be connected with Mount Sinai is extremely difficult to understand. There may have been some Jewish way of equating the numerical value of the words *Hagar* and *Sinai* or the sound of the Hebrew name Hagar may have been similar to the sound of a word associated with Mount Sinai. It is easier to understand how Hagar could be connected with Mount Sinai on a geographical basis, since Mount Sinai is *in Arabia,* the land inhabited by the Arabians, the descendants of Hagar and Ishmael.

The third step in Paul's identification of the children of Hagar as the false teachers in Galatia is his assertion that Mount Sinai *corresponds to the present city of Jerusalem* (v. 25). Paul's addition of Jerusalem to his allegorical equations makes sense only if the false teachers themselves were closely identified with the Jerusalem church. In other words, Paul mentions Jerusalem to increase the number of contact points between the false teachers who were associated with Jerusalem and the descendants of Hagar. Perhaps Paul's declaration in the next verse—*but the Jerusalem that is above is free, and she is our mother*—was his response to one of the slogans of the false teachers: "We come from the mother church in Jerusalem" (Lincoln 1981:17).

The fourth step supports the "Mount Sinai = Jerusalem" equation by drawing attention to the common characteristic of slavery of both the children of the Sinaitic covenant and the children of Jerusalem: *because*

4:25 The use of the neuter article *(to)* with the female name Hagar indicates that Paul's concern is the name itself (so Betz 1979:244). Perhaps Paul's identification of Hagar with Mount Sinai was accomplished by the use of a Jewish method of interpretation called *gematria,* which analyzes the numerical value of words (King 1983:369), or Paul equated the name Hagar with the Arabic word for rock *(hadjar),* which was associated with Sinai (Burton 1921:259; Hanson 1959:81), or he was connecting the name of Hagar with el Hegra,

she is in slavery with her children. Jerusalem was the proud capital city for all the recipients of the covenant given at Mount Sinai. And the center of life in Jerusalem was the study and teaching of that covenant. The goal of life in Jerusalem was to regulate all of life by the law given at Mount Sinai. Since the Sinaitic covenant enslaved all who relied upon it and tried to regulate their lives by it (see 3:19—4:11), it followed that Mount Sinai and Jerusalem could be equated on the basis of this common characteristic of slavery. Furthermore, since the false teachers were characterized by their emphasis on the demands of the Sinaitic covenant and their appeal to the authority of the Jerusalem church, it follows that they were themselves in slavery and could therefore be identified as the children of Hagar, the slave woman.

Paul's allegorical comparisons are not easy to follow. They have raised a host of unresolved problems for interpreters. But we need to remember that whatever rationale Paul used for his equations of Hagar with Mount Sinai and the present Jerusalem, the goal of these comparisons was the identification of the false teachers with Ishmael as the children of slavery because of their emphasis on the Sinaitic covenant. Once this identification was established, Paul could then appeal to the Galatians in the words of the law itself to *get rid of the slave woman and her son.*

The identification of the Galatian believers with the children of Sarah begins with a contrast between the present Jerusalem, whose children are in slavery, and the Jerusalem above, which is free. *She is our mother,* Paul declares (v. 26). This contrast mixes two pairs of opposites: present-future, below-above. In Jewish prophecy the Jerusalem above was the consummation of all of God's promises for his people. In the heavenly new Jerusalem the people of God would experience the perfect rule of God in peace and harmony with him, one another and all of the new creation. But Paul does not put the heavenly Jerusalem in the future. His use of present tense indicates that the Galatian believers are already

a location two hundred miles north of Midian (Davies 1972:152-63). All of these suggestions are problematic.

4:26 The image of a future, heavenly Jerusalem is common in Jewish prophecy; see Isaiah 2; 54:10-14; 60—62; Ezekiel 40—48; Zechariah 12—14; see also the discussion in Lincoln 1981:18-25.

citizens of the heavenly Jerusalem. Since they are already experiencing the Spirit of God, they are already enjoying the fulfillment of the promises of God. This means that they have already entered the heavenly Jerusalem. They can shout with joy, *She is our mother!*

This contrast is a dramatic way to show how foolish it would be to follow the demands of the false teachers. They were commending themselves as representatives of Jerusalem and teachers of the law of Moses. But there was no good reason for those who were experiencing the freedom of life as citizens of the heavenly Jerusalem to be bound by slavery to the law, which was characteristic of the present, earthly Jerusalem.

The Jewish pride in Jerusalem is an understandable human affection. We often take special pride in the city of our origin. I'm quite happy to identify myself as a "Chicago boy," since I was born in Chicago. Chicago is one of the great cities of the world, I think. But like Christian in John Bunyan's *Pilgrim's Progress,* we look forward to the city of our destination, the heavenly Jerusalem. And even now, as Paul insists here, we can rejoice that we are citizens of the heavenly Jerusalem by faith in Christ. One of the greatest reasons for taking delight in our citizenship in the heavenly Jerusalem is that people from every race, nation, language group and social class belong to that city. Whereas identification with the city of our origin sets us apart from people from other cities, identification with our city of destination unites us with people from every city.

Scriptural Confirmation (4:27) Paul confirms his identification of his converts as the children of the Jerusalem above with a quotation from Isaiah 54:1. This prophecy assures Israel during her *barren* time of the Babylonian captivity that she will one day have more children than ever before. The Jews took it as a prophecy not only of the restoration of Israel but also of the time when multitudes of Gentiles would turn to God and claim Israel as their mother by becoming full members of the Jewish nation. Paul sees the fulfillment of the prophecy in the birth and growth

---

4:27 Isaiah saw the multiplication of the children of Jerusalem as the ingathering of the nations (44:5; 45:22; 49:6; 56:6-7; 66:18-21) and as the work of the Spirit of God (44:3-5). In light of the practice of the early church to interpret Isaiah 40—66 christologically, it is not surprising that Paul appropriates this prophecy for the Galatian churches. From the "voice" of Isaiah 40:3 (see Mk 1:3; Jn 1:23) to the "new heavens and a new earth" of Isaiah 65:17 (see 2 Pet 3:13; Rev 21:1), Isaiah 40—66 was one of the most quoted sources of the

of the church. The multiplication of the children of Sarah and the heavenly Jerusalem was a tangible reality for Paul as he witnessed the faith of Gentiles and their reception of the Spirit. Moreover, they were not *born in the ordinary way* but *as the result of a promise* (v. 23)—this promise from Isaiah! As Paul saw this ancient promise of God fulfilled in his own mission to the Gentiles, he must have also fulfilled the commands of the prophecy: *Be glad . . . break forth and cry aloud!* What a wonderful surprise it was for him to see God fulfilling his word in this way as he preached the gospel to Gentiles.

Personal Consequences (4:28-30) After his use of Scripture to confirm what has actually happened in his mission, Paul draws out the personal consequences for the Galatian believers: *Now you, brothers, like Isaac, are children of promise* (v. 28). Just as Isaac was *born as the result of a promise,* so the Gentile believers were born as a result of the fulfillment of God's promise to Abraham (3:8) and his promise through the prophet Isaiah (4:27). So the link between the Galatians and Isaac is established.

That link is confirmed by the Galatians' experience of persecution. The Jewish Christian teachers have been harassing them with their requirements and demands. That is exactly what happened in the story of Ishmael and Isaac: *At that time the son born in the ordinary way persecuted the son born by the power of the Spirit. It is the same now* (v. 29). Genesis says that Ishmael mocked Isaac (Gen 21:9). Interpreting this text in the light of his own experience, Paul saw Ishmael's treatment of Isaac as derisive and abusive.

One personal consequence of being like Isaac is being mocked and persecuted by "false brothers" like Ishmael. Paul experienced fierce opposition from "false brothers" who tried to destroy him and his work. As it was *at that time . . . it is the same now* (v. 29). His story has been repeated many times throughout the history of the church. Often the most painful opposition comes not from those who are totally unrelated

New Testament writers.

4:29 The Hebrew text of Genesis 21:9 simply says Sarah saw Hagar's son "playing." The LXX added the words "with her son Isaac." But Jewish tradition interpreted this text as a record of Ishmael's hostile aggression against Isaac (see Bruce 1982:223-24 and Baasland 1984:135).

to the church, but from those who have positions of power within the church but lack the true power of the Spirit. We can see this illustrated in the time of the Protestant Reformation, when the powers of the Church of Rome ruthlessly persecuted the Reformers.

Now Paul is ready to apply the law directly to the Galatian crisis: *But what does the Scripture say? "Get rid of the slave woman and her son"* (v. 30). Paul has really turned everything upside down. To those who want to be under the law he gives a command that must be interpreted within his framework of definitions to mean that they should expel the law teachers: Obey the law by getting rid of the law teachers! Excommunicate them!

The command for expulsion also carries with it an exclusion from inheritance: *For the slave woman's son will never share in the inheritance with the free woman's son* (v. 30). This has sometimes been taken as an absolute exclusion of all Jews, or at least of all unbelieving Jews. But Paul has a more specific target in mind. He is concerned about the subversive influence of those who have been teaching another gospel (1:6-9), those who have been bewitching his converts with their demand for law observance (3:1), those who are zealous to win the Galatians to themselves and to alienate them from Paul (4:17). It is these people who are forfeiting their inheritance by depending on the law rather than on the promise fulfilled in Christ (3:18).

The clear implication of this exclusion of the law teachers from the inheritance is that those who depend on the promises of God fulfilled in Christ will receive the inheritance. They are the true children of Abraham and Sarah; they are the Isaacs.

The consequence of being an Isaac is not only persecution, it is also inheritance. The pain of rejection by "false brothers" is more than offset by the joy of acceptance as children and heirs of promises made and kept by God. Already all who have faith in Christ enjoy the inheritance: they have received their citizenship in the heavenly Jerusalem. The proof of that citizenship is the presence of the Spirit in their lives: they have been

---

4:30 Burton takes this passage as an attack on "all the adherents of legalistic Judaism" (Burton 1921:262, 267), but Longenecker is certainly right to warn against such a misinterpretation: "The directive of v 30 is not a broadside against all Jews or Judaism in general. . . . Rather, here in v 30 Paul calls for the expulsion of the Judaizers who had come into

born by the power of the Spirit (v. 29).

Conclusion (4:31) The conclusion of the entire Hagar-Sarah allegory emphasizes once again the identification of believers in Christ: *Therefore, brothers, we are not children of the slave woman, but of the free woman.* The freedom-slavery and Spirit-flesh antitheses which Paul has constructed in his allegory serve as the framework for his ethical instructions in the rest of the letter. The children of the free woman, who were *born by the power of the Spirit* (v. 29) must learn to express their freedom by walking in the Spirit. They must not submit to slavery under the law or gratify the desires of the flesh.

Identity is the basis of behavior: a clear understanding of who we are in Christ guides our conduct in the Spirit.

□ Authoritative Appeal (5:1-12)

In our day we highly esteem the value of religious tolerance. We want to guard against destructive conflict between religious fanatics and against totalitarian control of our society by one religion. We want to protect the freedom of all members of our society to hold their own religious convictions and to practice their faith without fear of attack or coercion from those of other religions.

Our religious tolerance may cause us to be offended by the sharp antitheses Paul draws between true and false religion in this section. But if we listen carefully to Paul's argument, we will find that he is defending the freedom of his readers from the coercive tactics of those who were forcing them to conform to a particular religious tradition. What we really find here is the basis for preserving true religious freedom. Paul's authoritative appeal is not an example of authoritarian religious tyranny, but just the opposite: it is a charter for genuine spiritual freedom.

In Galatians 5:1-12 Paul calls for his readers to protect their freedom (5:1-6). Then he exposes the false teachers who are robbing them of their freedom (5:7-12).

---

the Galatian congregations from the outside" (1990:217). See also Siker: "Paul is addressing in Galatians an intramural dispute between rival groups of Christians. He does not address the issue of non-Christian Judaism" (1991:48).

Protecting Freedom (5:1-6) *It is for freedom that Christ has set us free!*
This declaration of our freedom is both a statement of an accomplished
fact and a goal to pursue. Freedom is ours because of the accomplishment of Christ: *Christ has set us free!* Paul does not appeal to his readers
to fight to be free. Our Christian freedom is not the result of our long
march. We have not liberated ourselves by our efforts. We are not able
to do so. But now that freedom has been given to us by Christ, that
freedom is our goal and our responsibility.

Imagine a prisoner who is suddenly surprised to find out that he has
been pardoned and set free. He did nothing to accomplish this. He was
not even aware that it had happened. But there he stands outside the
prison walls, a free man. Now it is his responsibility to live as a free man.

Charles Wesley captures the Christian experience of this liberation in
one of his great hymns:

Long my imprisoned spirit lay
Fast bound in sin and nature's night;
Thine eye diffused a quickening ray,
I woke, the dungeon flamed with light.
My chains fell off, my heart was free;
I rose, went forth, and followed thee.

Our imprisonment has been a major theme in Paul's letter to the Galatians: "The Scripture declares that the whole world is a prisoner of sin"
(3:22). "We were held prisoners by the law, locked up" (3:23). "We were
in slavery under the basic principles of the world" (4:3). So there is no
doubt about the nature of our slavery. We were condemned prisoners
under the judgment of the law of God, doomed to live under the severe
restrictions of the law but with no hope of earning our freedom by our
obedience to the law, since all the law could do was to point out our
transgressions (3:19). This imprisonment under the law separated Jews
from Gentiles (2:14; 3:23); the law isolated its prisoners in different cell
blocks according to their ethnic origins.

Our release from prison and our release from slavery run as parallel

Notes: 5:1 Deissmann discovered that in Paul's day the phrase *for freedom* was used in
formal procedures to express the purpose of the ceremony to set slaves free from their
former masters and from anyone else who would seek to force them back into slavery
(1909:324-28; see also Longenecker 1964:173-74; Barrett 1985:55). This social context of the

themes in the letter: Jesus Christ "gave himself for our sins to rescue us from the present evil age" (1:4). "Christ redeemed us from the curse of the law" (3:13). "God sent his Son . . . to redeem those under law" (4:4-5). "Therefore, brothers, we are not children of the slave woman, but of the free woman" (4:31). So the nature of our freedom is clear. We have been delivered from the judgment of the law of God, and we no longer live under its disciplinary regulations. In the imagery of the preceding story of Hagar and Sarah, we are not children of the slave woman, who stands for the Mosaic commandments; we are children of the free woman, who stands for the promise. Our lives are not imprisoned by the dread terror of breaking the commandments: "You shall . . . ; you shall not . . . !" Our lives are lived in the joyful freedom of knowing that in Christ God has fulfilled his promises: "I will bless you!" This freedom from imprisonment under the law has led to a new community in which the divisions between race and class and gender are removed (3:28).

The liberating, redemptive act of Christ that sets us free from slavery and imprisonment under the law has also been a major theme of this letter. It was by his death on the cross when he took the curse of the law for us (3:13) that Christ has set us free. For when we believe that message of Christ crucified, we receive the Spirit (3:1-2) and participate in the benefits of the cross ourselves: we then view ourselves to have been crucified with Christ, set free from the curses and demands of the law, but now able by the indwelling life of Christ to live for God (2:19-20). Now that we are set free from living like slaves under the law, we can all live together in one family as the beloved children of God who by the indwelling Spirit call God "*Abba,* Father" (4:4-7).

Set Free for Freedom (5:1) All these major themes of slavery, freedom and the liberating work of Christ are now summed up in the ringing affirmation of 5:1: *It is for freedom that Christ has set us free.*

That indicative is followed by an imperative, *Stand firm, then.* This may sound like a dull lesson in grammar, but it is actually central in Pauline ethics. What we must do (the imperative) is always based upon

---

phrase *for freedom* is reflected in Paul's argument that participation in the crucifixion of Christ sets believers free not only from bondage to sin but also from social pressures: Christ set Gentiles free *for freedom* from those who "force Gentiles to follow Jewish customs" (2:14).

what God has already done (the indicative). Or to put it another way, what God has done gives us the opportunity and power to do what we must do. This indicative-imperative structure is seen here in verse 1 and also in verses 13 and 25. So it provides the structure for the whole chapter: God's gift of freedom must be defended (v. 1); God's gift of freedom must not be abused but must be used to serve (v. 13); God's gift of life by the Spirit must be expressed through the Spirit (v. 25).

In Paul's letters he often exhorts his readers to *stand firm:* "stand firm in the faith" (1 Cor 16:13); "stand firm in one spirit" (Phil 1:27); "stand firm in the Lord" (Phil 4:1). Here he appeals to them to stand firm in the freedom Christ has given to them. Paul illustrated in his autobiography how he stood firm in his freedom against "false brothers" who "infiltrated our ranks to spy on the freedom we have in Christ Jesus and to make us slaves" (2:4). He did not give in to their pressure to make Titus, a Gentile convert, a Jew by circumcision. Now similar false teachers have infiltrated the ranks of the Galatian churches with the same demand. They have been putting the Galatian converts under intense social pressure to become Jews by being circumcised. *Stand firm,* Paul says. *Do let yourselves be burdened again by a yoke of slavery* (v. 1).

In Paul's day one could often see oxen harnessed by a yoke to a heavily laden cart, straining to pull their burden uphill while being goaded with sharp sticks. Paul uses the word *yoke,* as it was often used by his contemporaries, to refer to the yoke of the law. We can see from his statement in verse 3 that the crushing weight of this yoke is the obligation to obey the whole law. A similar use of *yoke* can be seen in Peter's speech at the Jerusalem council, as reported in Acts 15:10: "Why do you try to test God by putting on the necks of the [Gentile] disciples a yoke that neither we nor our fathers have been able to bear?" The yoke of the law is a yoke of slavery, because it places us under the burden of commandments we cannot keep and under curses that we deserve for our disobedience. But God sent his Son to lift this heavy yoke from our shoulders and to take it upon himself: he was "born under law" (4:4) and kept all its demands for us; he died under the curse of the law for us (3:13). Since he has set us free from this yoke of slavery, we must not take it on ourselves again. In contrast to the yoke of slavery under the law, his yoke is easy and his burden is light (Mt 11:30).

In order to strengthen his readers' resolve to defend their freedom in Christ and resist the false teachers' efforts to put them under the yoke of slavery to the law, Paul sets forth the terrible negative consequences of submitting to this yoke of slavery in verses 2-4. Then in contrast to this negative picture, he sets out a positive description of maintaining our freedom in Christ in verses 5-6.

Negative Consequences (5:2-4) Paul's list of the negative results of getting circumcised and *trying to be justified by law* is prefaced by strong reminders that he is speaking with authority: *Mark my words! I, Paul, tell you* (v. 2). *Again I declare to every man* (v. 3). There must be no doubt about his warnings. They come from Paul, "an apostle—sent not from men nor by man, but by Jesus Christ and God the Father" (1:1).

His warnings are given to those who are getting circumcised. The present tense indicates that the process has just begun. Paul wants to stop the slash of the knife. This is the first explicit reference in the letter to this fact that the Galatians are being circumcised. Since the surgical procedure of circumcision has no theological significance to us today, it is difficult to understand why Paul is so upset about it.

In Paul's day circumcision was the mark of belonging to the Jewish nation. For a Gentile to get circumcised in the Greco-Roman world, where circumcision was repugnant, indicated that inclusion within the Jewish nation had become a very high priority for him. But why would inclusion in the Jewish nation become so extremely important to Gentiles? Paul understood their motive as *trying to be justified by law*. In other words, they thought they could gain God's approval only by belonging to the Jewish nation. This meant they did not consider faith in Christ to be a satisfactory basis for God's approval. They were being convinced that faith in Christ had to be supplemented with identification with the Jewish people through circumcision and law observance.

Paul lists four inevitable, negative consequences of adding such a supplement to faith in Christ. First, *Christ will be of no value to you at all* (v. 2). If you start to trust in circumcision to gain God's blessing, then you have stopped trusting in Christ. If you do not trust in Christ, then Christ is of no value to you. When you put your trust in your own position or performance for God's blessing, you are indicating that who you are and what you have done has more value that who Christ is and what he has done. You have turned your back on Christ.

Second, the consequence of getting circumcision is the obligation *to obey the whole law* (v. 3). Evidently the Galatians thought that by observing a few important laws they could identify themselves as full members of the Jewish nation and thus secure God's blessing for themselves. But Paul now informs them that the law is a vast, interdependent network of legal codes. Getting circumcised indicates that you are relying on keeping the law for God to bless you. If you are relying on the law, then you are obligated to keep the whole law. You cannot be selective. You have embarked on an impossible mission. Once you have decided to base your relationship with God on your performance, you will not be graded on a curve. You must get 100 percent all the time.

The third and fourth consequences of following the demands of the false teachers are given in verse 4: *You . . . have been alienated from Christ; you have fallen away from grace.* No doubt the rival teachers had assured them that keeping the law was not abandoning their faith in Christ; it was the way to "attain your goal" (3:3)—perfection—in Christian life. But Paul says that those who regulate their lives by the law are removed from the reign of Christ over their lives. If you trust in your own efforts to keep the law, then you are no longer trusting in God's grace. Circumcision or Christ, law or grace: these are exclusive alternatives. You cannot have it both ways. You must choose.

The danger of apostasy, falling away from grace, must have been very real, or Paul would not have used such strong language. If we use the doctrine of eternal security to deny the possibility of falling from grace, we are ignoring Paul's warnings. People who ignore warnings are in great danger. Just observe the person who sees the warning sign of a sharp curve and a fifteen-mile-per-hour speed limit but keeps driving at seventy miles per hour.

Positive Description (5:5-6) Having painted a negative picture of what will happen if freedom in Christ is given up for the yoke of slavery, Paul describes in verses 5-6 how freedom in Christ is maintained. Both verses focus on faith. Faith in Christ is the only way to protect our

---

5:3 No doubt the obligation *to obey the whole law* would have been accepted in principle by the false teachers, but it appears that in practice they required only the acceptance of circumcision and the observance of certain Jewish festivals, since these were the two min-

freedom in Christ. Paul spells out in very concise terms what this life of faith is like. His terms echo what he has already taught at some length in the preceding chapters; they also introduce the central themes of the rest of the letter.

First, the life of faith is life by the Spirit: *by faith we eagerly await through the Spirit* (v. 5). By faith in the gospel we received the Spirit (3:2). We now "live by the Spirit" (5:16), "are led by the Spirit" (5:18) and "keep in step with the Spirit" (5:25). The presence of the Spirit marks us the children of God (4:6), and the power of the Spirit produces in us the character of God (5:22-23). The control of the Spirit in our lives makes the yoke of the law unnecessary (5:18).

Second, the life of faith is a life of confident expectation of righteousness: *by faith we eagerly await through the Spirit the righteousness for which we hope* (v. 5). Paul's focus here is the future righteousness which is ours when God completes his work in us by his Spirit. By depending on the Spirit, we can expect to reap the harvest of eternal life in the future (see 6:8). In the past, when we put our faith in Christ at the beginning of our Christian life, God credited righteousness to us (3:6-9). In the present, by the power of the Spirit, God produces righteousness in us (5:13-25). Or to put it in more theological language, our righteousness—credited to us by justification, produced in us by sanctification and perfected in us by glorification—is always a gift received from God by faith.

Third, in this life of faith what matters is union with Christ, not union with the Jews or Gentiles or any other racial or social group: *For in Christ Jesus neither circumcision nor uncircumcision has any value* (v. 6). The world's divisions between Jew and Greek, slave and free, male and female have been obliterated in our union with one another in Christ (3:28).

Fourth, our life of faith is a life of loving one another: *The only thing that counts is faith expressing itself through love* (v. 6). Freedom from the law does not leave our life without moral direction. Faith in Christ gives us not only moral direction but also the moral dynamic to fulfill

---

imum requirements for claiming the title and benefits of Abraham's children (so Jewett 1970:207; Sanders 1983:29: "Paul's opponents may have adopted a policy of gradualism, requiring first some of the major commandments [circumcision, food, days]").

the true intent of all the law by serving one another (vv. 13-14). The evidence of true faith will be genuine love, for true faith in Christ is inevitably expressed through love.

These four concise descriptions of the life of faith enable us to see how faith in Christ is the only way to maintain our freedom in Christ. In his ethical appeal (5:13—6:10) Paul fills in the implications and applications of these brief statements. But first he exposes the false teachers for who they really are in order to rid the church of their destructive influence.

Exposing the False Teachers (5:7-12) In his exposure of these false teachers, Paul gives us six identifying marks that can guide us to discern the presence of "wolves in sheep's clothing" in our midst today.

First, false teachers distract Christians from obeying the truth of the gospel (v. 7). Paul compliments the Galatian believers for *running a good race.* Running a race was one of Paul's favorite images for living the Christian life. Here this image portrays how well they were *obeying the truth.* The gospel set the course for their life, and they were running well in that course. The reality of their belief in the truth about Christ was demonstrated by their obedience to Christ. But then they were distracted, tripped and so hindered from running this race. Paul asks them, *Who cut in on you and kept you from obeying the truth?* The question is rhetorical. Paul knows the answer. But by asking the question this way he exposes the false teachers' negative effect on the life of the believers. The picture is of a runner who distracts another runner, blocks his way, cuts in on him and trips him. Everyone would have been very angry with a runner who did such a thing. He would have broken the clear rules against cutting in or tripping in the foot races of the Greek festivals. He would be immediately disqualified and excluded from the festival.

The false teachers are hindering the Christians from obeying the truth of the gospel with all their talk about joining the Jewish people and keeping the law. All those who get the church off on a tangent, away from the clear direction given by the central truth of the gospel, are like these false teachers. They should be disqualified and excluded from the churches.

Second, false teachers replace the call of God with their own deceptive persuasiveness (v. 8). *That kind of persuasion does not come from the one who calls you,* Paul informs his readers. When Paul had preached the gospel, the Galatians heard the voice of God calling them through Paul (1:6). But when the false teachers teach, all that can be heard is flattery, boastfulness and empty rhetoric. They are skillful orators. No doubt they claim to be giving God's message backed by Scripture. But all one can hear through their strident voices is a harsh repetition of the demands of the law. What a contrast to "the one who called you by the grace of Christ" (1:6) and the God who "called me by his grace" (1:15). Their message is all about the works of the law, not about God's work of grace in Christ. So obviously their persuasion does not come from God, who always calls by his grace.

Third, false teachers gain control over the whole church (v. 9). Just as *a little yeast works through the whole batch of dough,* so the negative influence of a few false teachers has penetrated the whole church and is quickly coming to control the direction of the church. False teachers are like that; they seek to dominate every situation in the life of the church.

Fourth, false teachers cause confusion and discouragement (v. 10). When the Galatians were converted, they related to God with the joyful confidence of children, calling him "*Abba,* Father" through the Spirit. But their confidence in God's grace has been badly shaken by the false teachers, who threaten them with the judgment of God if they do not keep the law of God. They are confused and discouraged. So Paul reassures the Galatians of his confidence in the Lord regarding them: *I am confident in the Lord that you will take no other view.* And then he turns the tables on the false teachers by putting them under the judgment of God: *The one who is throwing you into confusion will pay the penalty, whoever he may be.*

Fifth, false teachers spread false reports about spiritual leaders. We may infer that verse 11 is Paul's response to a false report that had been given about him. Since the immediate context focuses on the corrupting influence of the false teachers, it seems reasonable to suppose that they claimed Paul's support for their campaign to circumcise the Gentile believers. We don't know on what basis they would have done this.

Perhaps if this letter was written after Paul circumcised Timothy, as recorded in Acts 16:3, they may have appealed to that incident. Or maybe they pointed to Paul's own willingness to continue his Jewish way of life even after his conversion (see 1 Cor 9:20). Whatever their basis may have been, they gave a false report about Paul to strengthen their own position.

Paul had, of course, preached circumcision before his conversion. He had been "extremely zealous for the traditions" of Judaism (1:14). But after his conversion he preached the cross of Christ as the only way of salvation. True, he continued to support Jewish Christian adherence to the traditional Jewish way of life. But he consistently resisted anyone who tried to "force Gentiles to follow Jewish customs" (2:14). That was a key point of his autobiography (1:13—2:21). Paul proves that the report that he is still preaching circumcision is false by pointing to the fact that he is being persecuted (5:11). Both non-Christian Jews and many Christian Jews fiercely opposed him precisely because he did not require circumcision. His refusal to require circumcision clearly implied that it was not necessary to belong to the Jewish nation to belong to the covenant people of God. By denying the exclusive claim of the Jewish people to be the only true people of God, Paul seemed to deny the reason for the Jewish people's very existence. No wonder, then, that they persecuted him from one country to another. If Paul had preached circumcision, then he would not have been persecuted by the Jews. By preaching circumcision, he would have been communicating that it was necessary to belong to the Jewish nation because the salvation of God was available only to those within this nation.

Paul says in verse 11 that if he has communicated that salvation is only in the Jewish nation by preaching circumcision, *the offense of the cross has been abolished.* For then the message that salvation is only through the cross of Christ would have been denied. The offense of the cross is that it denies a "most favored nation" status, a "superior race" category,

---

5:11 Other explanations of the false report that Paul was *still preaching circumcision* are (1) the opponents had in mind Paul's preconversion zeal for circumcision (Schoeps 1961:219), (2) the opponents actually thought that Paul still required physical circumcision, since they were unaware of Paul's recent disclosure of his law-free gospel (Howard 1979:10, 29, 44), and (3) the opponents defined Paul's preaching against fleshly passions and desires

as the reason for God's blessing. For the blessing of God comes only through the cross, where the judgment of God upon all was removed by Christ's death (see 3:13-14). The message of Christ crucified is offensive not only to Jews but also to the pride of all who want to claim some personal merit as the basis of God's approval.

Sixth, false teachers emphasize sensational rituals. Verse 12 sounds terribly harsh and crude, but we must interpret it in its historical and cultural context. It would indeed have been a sensational ceremony if all the male members of the Galatian churches had been circumcised by the false teachers. But then, Paul says, somewhat sarcastically, if they really want to put on a sensational show, *I wish they would go the whole way and emasculate themselves!* He is probably referring here to a barbaric ritual that actually took place in his day in Galatian pagan temples. The priests of Cybele, the mother goddess of the earth, castrated themselves with ritual pincers and placed their testicles in a box. (Such a box is now on display in the Fitzwilliam Museum in Cambridge, England.) The false teachers were leading the Galatian Christians to think that the ritual of circumcision was a sacred act that would bring them into fellowship with God. But Paul has already said that "in Christ Jesus neither circumcision nor uncircumcision has any value" (v. 6). Now he puts the ritual of circumcision in the same category as the ritual castration of the Galli, the priests of the mother-goddess of the earth, Cybele; it had no more significance to the Gentile Christians than any of the other barbaric, bloody rituals practiced in the ancient world.

So Paul has totally discredited the value of circumcision and the motives of the false teachers who want to impose it upon the churches in Galatia. They only "want to make a good impression outwardly" (6:12); they want to boast in their sensational ceremony (see 6:13). Since their motive is to put on an impressive ritual show, they might as well learn a few lessons from the pagan priests, who really know how to put on a good show when it comes to using a knife on the human body!

---

in terms of ethical circumcision and then presented their demand for bodily circumcision as the logical and necessary completion of Paul's message (Borgen 1982:37-46). It is difficult to determine the basis for their false report.

5:12 The engraving on the box used in ritual castration is described in detail by Gill (1991:80-81).

It is never pleasant to expose the deceptive, destructive tactics of the "false brothers." But it is necessary to do so in order to protect the freedom of fellow Christians. Of course circumcision is not an issue today. But we are constantly faced with a choice between different religious options. They are not all the same; they are not all spokes on a wheel leading to the same hub. Some religious options lead to slavery and imprisonment. Only by obedience to the truth of the gospel of Christ can we protect the freedom that is ours in Christ.

□ Ethical Appeal (5:13—6:10)

Paul begins his ethical appeal with a second declaration of freedom: *You, my brothers, were called to be free* (v. 13). This declaration echoes the central points of his first declaration in chapter 5 ("It is for freedom that Christ has set us free"). Both declarations focus on the initiative of God: Christ's action set us free! God's call set us free! When the whole human race was hopelessly locked up under law, imprisoned by sin, "God sent his Son" into human history to set us free. When we were enslaved, "God sent the Spirit of his Son into our hearts" to set us free. Our freedom is not the result of our decisions or our actions. God acted in history on the cross and through the resurrection to set us free. God acted in our hearts by his Spirit to set us free. The gracious initiative of God is underscored by Paul's repetition.

Both declarations of freedom also emphasize that freedom is the purpose of God's action in Christ. The NIV translation brings this out in verse 1 but not in verse 13. Paul puts the purpose of God's action right at the beginning of both sentences: "For freedom . . . ! To freedom you were called, brothers!" What is the purpose of your Christian life? Freedom in Christ! Paul blasts out these trumpet calls of freedom to Christians who are in danger of putting themselves under a heavy yoke of slavery. Their immediate goal is circumcision—painful discipline under the law. Their larger purpose would then be, as Paul informs them in verse 3, the obligation to obey the whole law. Their total preoccupation would be to learn the Jewish traditions and keep the Jewish customs. Paul knows

Notes: 5:13—6:10 I highly recommend John Barclay's excellent study of this entire section. He surveys the alternative interpretations of this section and argues convincingly for his view that "the problem that lies behind these chapters is not libertinism but moral

very well from his own experience (1:14) that that road does not lead to freedom. So he repeats his declaration of freedom to emphasize the new purpose of their life in Christ: they are called to freedom from slavery under the law.

So far we have seen two similarities between these two declarations of freedom in verse 1 and verse 13. Now we need to observe a great contrast. After the first declaration Paul gives a command to protect freedom by refusing to accept the "yoke of slavery." After the second declaration Paul gives a command not to use freedom *to indulge your sinful nature* but *to serve one another in love*. In other words, we are first told not to lose our freedom by turning back to slavery; then we told to use our freedom by entering into slavery.

No doubt Paul sets up this apparent contradiction as a kind of warning signal. Paul clearly sees the danger that his teaching about freedom from slavery under the law might be interpreted to mean freedom to do whatever our selfish desires lead us to do. A more literal translation of the second phrase of verse 13 than we have in the NIV is "only do not use your freedom as an opportunity for the flesh." The Greek word I have translated as "opportunity" was originally a military term for "the starting point of a military offensive" or "a base of operations." It was commonly used to mean "occasion" or "opportunity." An abuse of Christian freedom from slavery under the law could be a base of operations for the flesh, an opportunity for the "flesh" to launch a terribly destructive attack against us.

Paul uses the term *flesh* eight times in 5:13—6:10 to refer to that aspect of our being that is opposed to the Spirit of God (5:16-17) and that produces all that is evil and destructive in our human experience (5:19-20). The NIV translation of *flesh* as *sinful nature* is a helpful, interpretive translation. Human nature apart from God's intervening grace is both a captive of sin and the source of "passions and desires" (5:24) that lead to sin. No doubt one reason the Galatian Christians were attracted to the law is that they viewed the law as the only way to restrain and control the passions and desires of the flesh. They saw the law as a needed

confusion together with a loss of confidence in Paul's prescription for ethics. It is precisely because of the Galatians' attraction to the law that Paul has to demonstrate the sufficiency and practical value of his proposal for ethics—'walking in the Spirit' " (1988: 218).

disciplinarian to keep them from being destroyed by their own sinful desires.

The law's restraining power over sinful desires is a common subject in Jewish literature and must certainly have been a theme in the campaign of the false teachers who were trying to bring the Gentile Christians under the law. We can imagine them saying, "How can you ever hope to win the battle against your evil desires? There is only one way. Come under the yoke of the law. The law was given to guard, protect and keep you from evil. Live under it as your master and guide." But now in contrast to this message of the false teachers, Paul says that he has "died to the law" (2:19), that "we are no longer under the supervision of the law" (3:25) and that we should not let ourselves "be burdened again by a yoke of slavery," by which he means the law (5:1). "Does this mean that we are free to follow the desires of our sinful nature?" the Galatians may have wondered. Paul, who was always sensitive to the questions in the minds of his readers, counters their misunderstanding with a strong prohibition: *Do not use your freedom to indulge the sinful nature* (v. 13).

I have interpreted this section of Paul's letter as his response to the possible misunderstanding of his gospel in contrast to the message of the law teachers. Others have interpreted this section as Paul's response to a "libertine group" in the church that advocated doing away with all restraints upon the flesh. In other words, they think Paul was fighting on two fronts: against the law teachers on one side and against the libertines on the other side. A somewhat different version of this "two-front" interpretation suggests that the Galatian converts were torn in two directions: by the message of the law teachers from the outside and by the libertine tendencies of their own Hellenistic culture. According to this interpretation, Paul wrote 1:6—5:12 against the threat of legalism (you are free from slavery under the law) and he wrote 5:13—6:10 against the threat of libertinism (you are not free to indulge your sinful nature).

But it seems better to interpret 5:13—6:10 as a continuation of Paul's argument against the law teachers for two reasons: First, Paul focuses on these law teachers immediately before (5:1-12) and after (6:11-14) this section. Second, this section constantly refers to the law (5:14, 18, 23;

6:2). So Paul is not aiming in a new direction in this section. It is still a response to people who wanted to live under the yoke of the law. They were hoping to be able to overcome their moral problems by concentrating on keeping the law. Paul seeks to convince them that the law has no power to restrain the flesh. On the contrary, those who try to overcome the sinful nature (the flesh) by observing the law become more deeply enslaved to the sinful nature (the flesh). Certainly Christian freedom from the law does not mean giving into the sinful nature. It means serving one another in love. And this is only possible by walking in the Spirit. That is the essence of Paul's ethical appeal. His appeal defines freedom as freedom to love (5:13-15), freedom by the Spirit (5:16-18), freedom from evil (5:19-21), freedom for moral transformation (5:22-26) and freedom to fulfill responsibilities (6:1-10).

Freedom to Love (5:13-15) Christian freedom is the freedom to *serve one another in love* (v. 13). The slavery of love is contrasted to two other kinds of slavery. First, the immediate context puts this command to serve in love in direct contrast to indulging the sinful nature. Our sinful nature causes us to be slaves to our own selfish desires, but love expresses itself in service to the needs of others. Second, the command to serve in love is contrasted to slavery under the law. Christians are not to be under the law, enslaved to it, but they are commanded to be under others as slaves to them. Christian obligation is not subjection to the law (v. 3) but subjection to one another in love.

These two other kinds of slavery always threaten to rob us of our freedom to serve others in love. If I am enslaved to the law, I am more interested in keeping the commandments to establish my own merit than in loving others. Even if I serve others out of obligation to observe the law, I do it for myself rather than for them. If I am enslaved to my own sinful nature, I am absorbed in my selfish interests rather than the needs of others. Even if I serve others, I do it to fulfill my own desires. So slavery to the law and slavery to the flesh cause us to use people to meet our goals rather than to serve people in love. Only when we are free from slavery to the law and slavery to the flesh will we be free to serve one another in love.

We have already learned two things about the meaning of love in this letter: first, love was expressed by Christ's giving of himself for us (2:20); second, love is the expression of true faith (5:6). Now we learn that love is expressed by serving one another. When the object of our faith is Christ, who loved us, we are motivated and empowered to express his kind of love to others.

When such love is expressed, the whole law has been fulfilled. *The entire law is summed up in a single command: "Love your neighbor as yourself"* (v. 14). Paul's reference to law at this point cannot possibly mean that he is putting Christians under obligation to keep the law. If he meant that, he would be contradicting all that he has been saying so far in the letter about dying to the law and being set free from the law. Just a few verses later Paul emphasizes freedom from the law again: *If you are led by the Spirit, you are not under law* (v. 18). Paul's reference to law in verse 14 is not prescriptive but descriptive. He is not prescribing the requirements of the law in order to regulate Christian living. He is describing the result of Christian faith expressed in loving service to others. The result of Christians' loving service to others is that all the prescriptions and prohibitions of the law are fulfilled, since they can all be summed up in one command: Love your neighbor as yourself. Paul does not quote the law to motivate love; he quotes the law to show that love, motivated and empowered by faith (v. 6) and the Spirit (v. 22), fulfills the demands of the law.

The moral standards of the law are not discarded or violated by Christians who are free from the law. For "the law is holy, and the commandment is holy, righteous and good" (Rom 7:12). Freedom from the law is not license to break the law and pursue every selfish desire. No, freedom from bondage to the law is experienced by those who believe in Christ and are led by his Spirit. They use their freedom to serve one another in love. And in that loving service the high moral standards of the law are fully realized in their lives. Though the law is holy and good, since it is God's revelation of his moral standards for our lives, the law provides no power to overcome sin.

5:14 Westerholm points out the important difference in Paul's thought between "doing the law," which is not the way of faith (3:12) and living by the Spirit so that the "whole law is fulfilled" (NIV: *the entire law is summed up*): "For Paul it is important to say that Christians 'fulfill' the whole law, and thus to claim that their conduct (and theirs alone) fully

To run and work the law commands,

Yet gives me neither feet nor hands.

Only the power of the Spirit at work in us can enable us to overcome sin and fulfill God's moral design for our lives through loving service to others.

The Galatian readers of this letter wanted to be under the law (4:21) as a way to attain spiritual perfection (3:3). But their preoccupation with keeping the law did not lead them to spiritual perfection. On the contrary, their bondage to the law produced a competitive, angry, judgmental spirit. Paul warns them of the results of their bondage to the law: *If you keep on biting and devouring each other, watch out or you will be destroyed by each other* (v. 15). These words are often taken as a description of the libertine tendencies of the Galatians, who are destroying each other by indulging the passions of their sinful nature. But note the similarities between this description and Paul's description of himself before his conversion. When he was competing against his fellow Jews to advance beyond them in his zealous devotion to the traditions of Judaism (1:14), he was persecuting and trying to destroy the church (1:13). Paul knew from his own experience that zealous devotion to keep the law can accompany and even intensify destructive attitudes toward the church. When he saw the Galatian believers biting each other in their criticism and chewing each other up in their negative reports, he was reminded of his own attacks on the church during the time in his life when he was most zealous to keep the law. When churches define their purpose in terms of law observance, they need to watch out or they will be destroyed by a competitive, critical, judgmental spirit.

The tragic irony of the Galatians' situation was that the more they came under bondage to keep the law, the more they violated the basic moral standard of the law: *love your neighbor as yourself.* Paradoxical as it may seem, that standard is only fulfilled in the lives of those who resist slavery under the law (v. 1) and serve as slaves in love to others (v. 13). Freedom in Christ is freedom to love.

---

satisfies the real purport of the law in its entirety while allowing the ambiguity of the term to blunt the force of the objection that certain individual requirements (with which, Paul would maintain, Christian behavior was never meant to conform) have not been 'done' " (1988:205).

Freedom by the Spirit (5:16-18) The attempt of the Galatian believers to attain spiritual perfection by keeping the law had ended in failure. Their churches were torn apart by conflict: they were "biting and devouring each other" (v. 15). Obviously their devotion to the law had not enabled them to be devoted to each other in love. And since they did not love each other, they were breaking the law. Where could they find the motivation and power to resolve their conflicts and renew their love for each other? Many Christians are asking the same question today. They are members of Bible-teaching churches torn apart by conflict. What went wrong? How can they be so devoted and yet so divided? How can they be empowered to really love each other?

Paul's answer is the Spirit of God. *So I say, live by the Spirit* (v. 16). The command *live by the Spirit* is the central concept in Paul's ethical appeal. Since the Christian life begins with the Spirit (3:3; 4:6, 29), the only way to continue the Christian life is by the power of the Spirit. The Spirit is not only the source of Christian life but also the only power to sustain Christian life. Actually, "walk by the Spirit" would be a more literal translation of Paul's command in verse 16. The command to walk in a certain way speaks of choosing a way of life—or we might say a "lifestyle," as long as we realize that what Paul has in mind is more than a matter of outward style. His command speaks of a way of living in which all aspects of life are directed and transformed by the Spirit.

The Galatian believers began their Christian life by receiving the Spirit (3:2-3), but they soon turned to the law to direct their lives. They probably felt that observance of the law was the way of life that would establish their identity and guide their behavior as the people of God. By turning to observance of law as their way of life, however, they were denying the Spirit's sufficiency to identify them as the people of God and to direct their conduct. Paul's references to the Spirit in chapters 3 and 4 assure his readers that their experience of the Spirit has clearly established their identity as the true children of Abraham and as the children of God. In this section (5:13—6:10) his references to the Spirit express

---

5:17 Ridderbos interprets the phrase *you do not do what you want* in the traditional way as a reference to the moral defeat caused by the conflict between the flesh and the Spirit: "Because of it the believers, too, do not do what they want to do by virtue of the new man in them" (1953:204). But as Barclay points out, "This interpretation would not only put 5:17

his confidence that the Spirit is more than adequate to direct their moral behavior. The Spirit is the best guarantee of Christian identity and the only sure guide for Christian behavior. The Spirit is the only source of power to love in a way that fulfills the whole law.

Paul's confidence in the directive power of the Spirit is emphatically asserted in the promise that follows his command: *Live by the Spirit, and you will not gratify the desires of the sinful nature* (v. 16). Paul's use of a double negative in the Greek could be expressed in English by saying, "You will absolutely not gratify the desires of your sinful nature." The fulfillment of this promise depends on the implementation of the command.

Walking is excellent exercise, my doctor says! Walking by the Spirit demands active determination to follow the direction of the Spirit in the power of the Spirit. Those who follow the Spirit's direction in the Spirit's power will not carry out the evil intentions of their sinful nature. Walking by the Spirit excludes the destructive influence of the sinful nature. Walking by the Spirit can transform people who are "biting and devouring each other" into people who are serving each other in love.

In verse 17 Paul explains the basis of his confidence in the Spirit. He describes the war between the flesh and the Spirit and the result of that war. The Spirit and the sinful nature are two hostile forces opposed to each other: *the sinful nature desires what is contrary to the Spirit, and the Spirit what is contrary to the sinful nature. They are in conflict with each other.* So walking by the Spirit (v. 16) means fighting in a war between the Spirit and the sinful nature (v. 17). The connection between verse 16 and verse 17 indicates that those who *live by the Spirit* are not neutral in this war. They are committed to fight on the side of the Spirit against the desires of the sinful nature.

This inner spiritual warfare is the nature of the Christian life; it is the experience of all those who *live by the Spirit.* The conflict Paul is describing here is not the moral conflict that everyone feels at some time, nor the conflict of a wayward Christian who is no longer committed to Christ.

in sharp contrast to the confidence of 5:16 but it would also wholly undermine Paul's purpose in this passage; if he is admitting here that the flesh continually defeats the Spirit's wishes, Paul is hardly providing a good reason to 'walk in the Spirit' " (1988:113).

This is the conflict of a thoroughly committed Christian who is choosing each day to "walk by the Spirit." Each day the Christian who chooses to walk by the Spirit is engaged in a fierce battle between the Spirit and the sinful nature. It is important to stress this point, because many Christians feel ashamed to admit that they are experiencing such a conflict. They feel that mature Christians should somehow be above this kind of struggle. They imagine that the great saints were surely too spiritual to feel the desires of the flesh. But Paul flatly contradicts such images of superspirituality. His perspective is expressed by an old hymn:

And none, O Lord, have perfect rest,

For none are wholly free from sin;

And they who fain would serve Thee best

Are conscious most of wrong within.

But while Paul honestly portrays the reality of incessant moral warfare in the life of a Spirit-led Christian, he is not painting a picture of defeat. If you have sworn your allegiance to the Spirit in this war between the Spirit and your sinful nature, you "do not use your freedom to indulge the sinful nature" (v. 13), nor will you *gratify the desires of the sinful nature* (v. 16). The result of this fierce conflict is that *you do not do what you want* (v. 17), but what the Spirit desires you to do.

Some interpreters have taken the phrase *you do not do what you want* as an admission of defeat: the sinful nature defeats the Spirit-given desires of the believer, or at best the conflict ends in a stalemate between the flesh and the Spirit. But such an interpretation fails to see that Paul sets forth verse 17 as the explanation of his confident promise in verse 16 of the Spirit's victory over the sinful nature for those who live by the Spirit. If the Spirit's direction is continually defeated by the sinful nature, then there is no good reason to live by the Spirit or to have confidence in the Spirit's directive power.

The common interpretation of verse 17 as an admission of defeat in the conflict is influenced by Paul's admission of defeat in Romans 7:14-25 and the frequent experience of defeat in Christian experience. But there are significant differences between Romans 7:14-25 and this passage in Galatians 5, not least of which is that there is no mention of the Spirit in the Romans 7:14-25 passage. Furthermore, our common experience of moral failure should not determine our understanding of Paul's explanation of life in the Spirit. In this context Paul is presenting a reason for confidence in the Spirit's power to guide Christian behavior. His confidence is based on the fact that Christians who walk by the Spirit are involved in a war that determines the direction of every choice and every action. Their Christian freedom does not mean that they are left without moral direction to do whatever they want. They do not do what they want. They march under the Spirit's orders, to fulfill the directions of the Spirit.

In my elementary school we stood at the beginning of every day with our hands over our hearts to pledge allegiance to the flag of the United States of America "and to the republic for which it stands, one nation under God, indivisible, with liberty and justice for all." Mrs. Crane, our principal, often reminded us that some had upheld their pledge of allegiance at the cost of their own lives so that we could experience liberty and justice. And she challenged us to dedicate our own lives to keeping our pledge of allegiance in order to preserve true liberty and justice for all. In the war for true Christian freedom, victory is possible only for those who continually renew their allegiance to the Spirit in the unremitting war against the sinful nature. Then they do not do whatever they want, but only what the Spirit directs them to do.

Those who are living by the guiding power of the Spirit in their lives and are fighting each day against the influence of the sinful nature do not need to be supervised and restrained by the law. So Paul says, *If you are led by the Spirit, you are not under law* (v. 18). Life in the Spirit was pictured in verse 16 as an active determination: "Walk by the Spirit!" Walking demands active determination to get up out of the soft armchair and endurance to keep going at a steady pace. But now Paul speaks of life in the Spirit as passive submission: *if you are* led *by the Spirit.* The verb suggests pressure and control. A donkey and her colt were led by the disciples to Jesus (Mt 21:2). Soldiers arrested Jesus and led him away (Lk 22:54). Soldiers arrested Paul and led him away (Acts 21:34; 23:10). Paul has already described the control of the law in similar terms: "we were held prisoners by the law, locked up" (3:23); "the law was put in charge to lead us" (3:24), "subject to guardians and trustees" (4:2). But while the law exercised control, it could not give life or transform character (3:21). The law controlled by locking up all under sin (3:22). Now

Paul depicts an alternative kind of control: the control of the Spirit. Life begins with the Spirit (3:3); children of promise are born by the power of the Spirit (4:29). The Spirit produces a transformation of character (5:22-23). The one who submits to the control of the Spirit is not under the control of the law.

If the Spirit is leading you to forgive your sister who wronged you instead of being resentful toward her, you are under the control of the Spirit rather than under the restriction of the command "You shall not kill." When your conduct is guided and empowered by the Spirit, your conduct will fulfill the law, so you will not be under the condemnation or supervision of the law.

Life by the Spirit involves active obedience to the direction of the Spirit (v. 16), constant warfare against the desires of the sinful nature by the power of the Spirit (v. 17) and complete submission to the control of the Spirit (v. 18). Such a life will be an experience of freedom from the control of the sinful nature and the control of the law.

Freedom from Evil (5:19-21) So far Paul has talked in general terms about life in the Spirit. He has assured his readers that the Spirit will enable them to resist the desires of their sinful nature. What the law cannot do for them, God will do by the work of his Spirit in them. But he realizes that the Galatians are attracted to the law because it gives them specific moral guidelines that they can apply to their practical problems. After all, the Jewish law teachers were renowned for their ability to develop applications of the law for every conceivable situation. There seems to be a sense of moral security in such well-defined codes of conduct. In comparison, Paul's command to "live by the Spirit" seems to leave everything up in the air. How can they know they are not gratifying the desires of their sinful nature if the behavior of the sinful nature is not defined? How can they know what life in the Spirit is like if it is not defined?

There seems to be a common tendency to develop a "computer manual" approach to the Christian life. People want a very specific list of

---

5:19 The Hellenistic catalogs of vices and virtues which made the *acts of the sinful nature*

steps to follow. "Let's be practical," they say. "Tell me exactly what to do and what not to do, and then I will feel safe; I'll know how to act." But this approach to the Christian life is in danger of repeating the Galatian error. It is an attempt to live under law rather than under the direction of the Spirit.

But is there any objective basis for evaluating when we are following the direction of the Spirit and when we are gratifying the desires of the flesh? Paul obviously thinks so. Having described in general terms the Spirit's victory over the sinful nature, he does define their specific characteristics in a list of the *acts of the sinful nature* (vv. 19-21) and a list of the *fruit of the Spirit* (vv. 22-23). These specific lists of vices and virtues are not offered as a new set of specific codes to replace the law codes. Rather, they provide an objective basis for evaluation, so we can determine whether we are living to gratify the desires of the sinful nature or living by the Spirit.

The acts of the sinful nature are obvious, Paul says (v. 19). His point may be that while the "desires of the sinful nature" (vv. 16-17) are hidden, the acts produced by those desires are public, plain for all to see. So an evaluation of our outward behavior makes it easy to see if we are gratifying the hidden desires of our sinful nature. But since some of the *acts* listed also refer to inward attitudes of the heart (for example, *hatred, selfish ambition* and *envy*), the word *obvious* is probably not drawing a contrast between hidden attitudes and public acts. Instead Paul seems to be emphasizing that the Galatians do not need the Mosaic law to define the nature of evil. Since he has just told them that they are not under the supervision of the law (v. 18), it would be strange if he now turned to the law for moral instruction. In fact, he does not do that; he does not describe *the acts of the sinful nature* as transgressions of law. His list of vices is similar to many lists in the ethical teaching of the Greeks and Romans of his day. Pagan philosophers often published lists of vices and virtues. So when Paul says that the acts of the sinful nature are obvious, he means that all of us already know what is evil when we see it.

His list gives a representative sampling of commonly recognized vices.

obvious in Paul's day are described at some length by Longenecker (1990:249-63; see also Betz 1979:281-83).

At the end of the list he says *and the like* to indicate that his list is not meant to be comprehensive; it is merely typical of the things that were widely viewed to be contrary to high moral standards. The huge difference between Paul and his contemporary pagan philosophers is not the content of the list of vices but the context: Paul gives the list in a context that offers the way to freedom from these vices; the pagan moralists were not able to offer any such solution to the rampant immorality of their day.

Although the list of acts of the sinful nature can be systematized under several headings, there is little discernible order in the list. In fact, "the seemingly chaotic arrangement of these terms is reflective of the chaotic nature of evil" (Betz 1979:283). The chaos caused by theses vices is contrasted to the wholeness and unity of the *fruit of the Spirit.* We must be careful, however, not to think that the contrast between *acts* and *fruit* is a contrast between active and passive, our effort and supernaturally produced growth. We have already seen that life in the Spirit is both active (walking) and passive (being led). And though love and goodness are fruit of the Spirit, Paul urges the believers to work at loving and doing good (5:6, 13-14; 6:4-5, 9-10).

Paul's use of the word *acts* (literally "works") connects this list to his frequent reference in this letter to the "works of the law." They are not one and the same, of course. But the tragic irony of the situation is that while the Galatian believers are trying so hard to do the "works of the law," they are actually producing "works of the flesh" (NIV: *acts of the sinful nature*). This is another way of saying again that the law has no power (as the Spirit does) to overcome the destructive influence of the sinful nature.

Paul's list of fifteen *acts of the sinful nature* can be divided into four categories: (1) illicit sex, (2) religious heresy, (3) social conflict and (4) drunkenness.

1. Illicit sex. Paul mentions three kinds of illicit sex: *sexual immorality, impurity and debauchery.* The first is a general term that encompasses all kinds of immoral sexual relationships. The next two terms refer to sexual perversions. The art and literature of Paul's day provide ample evidence for the widespread practice of sexual immorality. When we read that "the sexual life of the Graeco-Roman world in NT times was a lawless chaos" (Barclay 1962:24), we only need to observe the chaos in our own world to understand the conditions in Paul's day. In fact, a good case could be made that in the two millennia since the Roman Empire, our generation comes closer than any previous one to the blatant prevalence of sexual perversions that was characteristic then. And a study of the fall of the Roman Empire suggests that any society that tolerates the unchecked promotion of such perversions will inevitably fall apart from the rottenness within.

2. Religious heresy. From Paul's teaching on *idolatry* in his other letters we learn that idolatry is not merely worshiping the image of a god but also participating in the temple feasts (1 Cor 10:7, 14) and even being greedy for possessions (Col 3:5). *Witchcraft* is a translation of a Greek word from which our English word *pharmacy* is derived. The Greek word could have the positive meaning of dispensing drugs, but its more common meaning was the use of drugs in sorcery and witchcraft and to poison people.

False religion is the worship of other gods (whether images in temples or in shopping malls) and dependence on other powers (whether the power of drugs or of occult practices). The forms of false religion in Paul's day differ from the forms of our day, but we can still see its pervasive influence today.

3. Social conflict. Paul's major emphasis in this list is on those acts of the sinful nature which cause social conflict. He lists eight such acts: *hatred, discord, jealousy, fits of rage, selfish ambition, dissensions, factions and envy.* Since the NIV translation provides a clear and accurate rendering of each term, there is little need for expanded discussion of their meanings. Some terms are roughly synonymous, such as *jealousy* and *envy.* It seems that Paul added more terms under this category of social conflict because this was the area of greatest need in the Galatian churches. The attitudes and actions that destroy personal relationships were the most evident manifestation of the sinful nature in those churches. We can see reflections of this problem of social conflicts in verses 15 and 26 as well: Christians were "biting and devouring each other" and "provoking and envying each other." The Galatian churches were divided into bitterly antagonistic factions. The rest of the letter indicates that these conflicts were caused by the false teachers' campaign to enforce the observance of the law in the churches. The curse on "all who rely upon observing the law" (3:10) was already being experienced in the tragic breakdown of relationships between Christians. While they concentrated on performing "works of the law," their lives were characterized by the "works of the flesh," especially these eight in the area of social conflict.

Often the "desires of the sinful nature" and the *acts of the sinful nature* are equated only with sexual immorality. Paul's list starts with that category. And that was undoubtedly a real problem in the Galatian churches. All churches seem to be plagued to some degree with sexual immorality. But it is likely that Paul began there because he knew that most of the church would quickly condemn those who were guilty of sexual immorality and yet consider themselves "safe," since they had performed the "works of the law" by getting circumcised (5:2) and observing special days (4:10). Paul then turns to these "lawkeeping" Christians and gives them a long list of flagrant acts of the sinful nature which they had committed. This is something like the story of the woman caught in adultery (Jn 8:1-11). The teachers of the law were ready to stone her. But Jesus said that only those without sin could stone her. Then he began to write on the ground. What he wrote we don't know. But those teachers of the law were convicted of their own sin and left her.

When Paul confronts law teachers who are ready to stone lawbreakers, he writes out a list of acts and attitudes that are generated by the desires of their sinful nature. They can find no safety in their selective observance of the law. They too are enslaved to sin. Only Christ can set them free; only the Spirit can keep them free.

4. Drunkenness. Paul concludes his list with two terms that refer to the wild drinking parties held in honor of pagan gods, particularly the god Bacchus. *Drunkenness* and *orgies* were part of pagan culture; they still are. And the church has never been immune to these *acts of the sinful nature.*

Paul begins and ends his list with the most obvious expressions of the sinful nature. The list is weighted, however, in the direction of the major

5:21 Teaching about the kingdom of God was part of Paul's early message to the churches in Galatia, according to Acts 14:22: "We must go through many hardships to enter the kingdom of God." See also 1 Corinthians 6:9 and 15:50 for Paul's teaching on the obstacles

problem of divisions caused by ambitious, angry people. Their preoccupation with keeping the law may have blinded them to their own sinful
nature. Intent on establishing a secure place for themselves in the kingdom of God, they were actually destroying the people of God. Paul gives
them a very severe warning: *I warn you, as I did before, that those who
live like this will not inherit the kingdom of God* (v. 21). Those who are
so concerned to secure their own place that they deny any place for
others will lose their own place in the end.

It may come as a shock that Paul is announcing judgment on the basis
of works. But there can be no doubt that that is exactly what he is doing.
Those who practice the works of the flesh are denied entrance to the
kingdom of God. How can Paul, who so vehemently defends justification
by faith in Christ, not by works of the law (2:16), now turn around and
declare that judgment will be on the basis of works? Is this a glaring
contradiction in his theology? Some have thought so. But some reflection
on the flow of Paul's argument will show the consistency of his thought.
The evidence that the Galatian believers had really been justified by faith
was the presence of the Spirit in their lives. They had received the Spirit
simply by believing the gospel, not by observing the law—just as righteousness had been reckoned to Abraham on the basis of his faith (3:1-
6). Those who receive the Spirit experience a moral transformation by
the directive power of the Spirit (5:16-18). If there was no evidence of
moral transformation, then there was no basis for claiming the presence
of the Spirit, and hence there was no basis for claiming justification by
faith. And if they had not experienced justification by faith, then of course
they would not inherit the kingdom of God.

To put it in traditional theological language, sanctification is not the
basis of justification but the inevitable result of justification. Those whom
God declares righteous on the basis of their faith in Christ's work for
them, God also makes righteous by the work of his Spirit within them.
Those whose lives are characterized only by the expressions of the sinful
nature demonstrate that they have not been born by the power of the
Spirit. *Those who live like this will not inherit the kingdom of God* (v. 21).

to an inheritance of "the kingdom of God." In Romans 14:17 Paul defines the kingdom of
God as a kingdom of "righteousness, peace and joy in the Holy Spirit."

It is clear that Paul does not consider freedom in Christ to be freedom from moral obligation. On the contrary, "Christ has set us free" to "live by the Spirit." All who live by the Spirit and are led by the Spirit reap a great harvest of moral transformation: *the fruit of the Spirit.*

Freedom for Moral Transformation (5:22-26) *The fruit of the Spirit* is the moral character developed by the power of the Spirit. The nine character qualities are a unity, a perfectly formed Christlike character. Paul has expressed his desire to see Christ formed in the Galatian believers (4:19). Now he describes what they will be like when that formation is complete. These character qualities are not a new list of laws or moral codes that must be kept; they are the result of living and being led by the Spirit.

Paul's image of the fruit of the Spirit is probably drawn from the imagery of the Old Testament and the teaching of Jesus. The promise of the Spirit and the promise of moral fruitfulness in God's people are connected in the Old Testament:

Until a spirit from on high is poured out on us,
and the wilderness becomes a fruitful field,
and the fruitful field is deemed a forest.
Then justice will dwell in the wilderness,
and righteousness abide in the fruitful field.
The effect of righteousness will be peace,
and the result of righteousness, quietness and trust forever.
(Is 32:15-17 NRSV; see also Joel 2:18-32)

Jesus also taught that the genuineness of his followers would be demonstrated by good fruit from their lives (Mt 7:16-20; Lk 13:6-9), and he promised that the presence of the Spirit and communion with him would produce the fruit of love and obedience (Jn 14—16). These promises of righteousness by the Spirit are the background for Paul's description of the believers' eager expectation of righteousness (5:5); now in verses 22-23 he focuses on the believers' expression of righteousness, which fulfills God's promises for his people.

Paul's list of moral qualities produced by the Spirit provides assurance that those who "live by the Spirit" will actually fulfill God's requirements for his people. There is no need to worry that following Paul's ethical appeal to live by the Spirit will lead to moral license and sin. Just the opposite will be the case. The Spirit will produce those moral qualities that God requires.

The first place in the list, the place of emphasis, is given to *love*. Love is the focus of the entire ethical appeal: "serve one another in love" (v. 13). Love fulfills the law (v. 14); love is the expression of faith (v. 6). Love is demonstrated in a tangible way in the sacrificial love of Christ (2:20) and the service of Christians (5:13). All the other moral qualities in the list define and flow from love.

Joy is the result of healthy relationships. When relationships fall apart because of broken commitments, there is a loss of joy (see 4:15). When there is conflict and bitterness, as there was in the Galatian churches, there is no joy. But the first result of true love in relationships is the renewal of joy.

Peace is also the result of relationships built by loving service. Instead of "hatred, discord, . . . dissensions, factions" there is harmony and order in relationships.

Patience is the opposite of "fits of rage" or short temper. It is the quality of staying with people even when constantly wronged and irritated by them.

Kindness and *goodness* are joined with *patience* to teach that a sweet disposition and doing good toward people (see v. 10) is the way to stay with them in love.

Faithfulness is the quality of keeping commitments in relationships. The Galatians had proved to be fickle in their attitude toward Paul (4:13-16). Only the Spirit can produce the quality of loyalty no matter the cost.

Gentleness is the opposite of "selfish ambition." Gentle people are not "conceited, provoking and envying each other" (v. 26). Gentleness is an expression of humility, considering the needs and hurts of others before one's personal goals.

Self-control is the opposite of self-indulgence. Those who are Spirit-led will not indulge the sinful nature (v. 13). They are not characterized by "sexual immorality, . . . drunkenness, orgies." They do not use other people to gratify their own appetites. They have the strength to say no to themselves, to the desires of their sinful nature.

In Paul's ethical appeal this list of qualities paints a picture of relationships that are built and nourished by the presence of the Spirit. No wonder Paul says, *Against such things there is no law.* Here again we see that Paul is directing his comments to people who want to be under the supervision of law. Paul assures them that if they are led by the Spirit, they are not under law (v. 18) because the Spirit produces all the qualities that fulfill the requirements of the law (vv. 14, 23). There is no rule in the Mosaic lawbook which can be cited against such character qualities. The Spirit-led life is not a life against the law; it is a life that fulfills the law. The way to the fulfillment of the law is not to live under the law like slaves, but to live by the Spirit as children of God.

Paul concludes his two lists of *the acts of the sinful nature* and *the fruit of the Spirit* with a summary statement about putting to death the sinful nature (v. 24) and living by the Spirit (v. 25). The death of the sinful nature opens the way for the life of the Spirit. This movement from death to life is parallel to 2:19-20 and 6:14-15, where death is also followed by new life.

The remarkable feature of Paul's statement about the crucifixion of the sinful nature in verse 24 is the use of the active voice: *Those who belong to Christ Jesus have crucified the sinful nature with its passions and desires.* Galatians 2:19 and 6:14 say that Christians have been crucified with Christ, but 5:24 says that they themselves have acted to put to death their sinful nature. Believers are responsible to crucify their sinful nature. Since Roman crucifixion was a merciless, painful means of execution, Paul's statement describes an absolute and irreversible renunciation of evil. The past tense may point to the time of baptism, when the Christian publicly identified with Christ. A common liturgy of baptism expresses it this way:

Do you turn to Christ?

I turn to Christ.

Do you repent of your sins?

I repent of my sins.

Do you renounce evil?

I renounce evil.

If this repentance and renunciation of evil is as decisive as crucifixion, it means that Christians have said an absolute, unconditional no to all of their sinful desires and passions. Renunciation of evil is not only a baptismal vow, it is a practical everyday discipline. When my sinful nature subtly suggests paging through a pornographic magazine, I shout a defiant no to my sinful nature. When I hear a juicy bit of gossip and start to repeat it, I close my mouth and say "no way" to my sinful desire. When another Christian criticizes me unfairly and my flesh screams for revenge, I say "absolutely not" to my sinful passion.

The fact of warfare against the sinful nature, described in verse 17, indicates that the sinful nature is never fully eradicated in this life and therefore this no must be continually renewed. But the fact of the execution of the sinful nature described in verse 24 shows that goal of the war against the sinful nature is not a negotiated peace but final execution.

Both the continuous war against the sinful nature and the absolute execution of the sinful nature must be kept in mind if we are to have the full picture. The perfectionists who talk as if the sinful nature has been or can be totally conquered in this life have lost sight of the need to fight the war every day. The pessimists who are halfhearted in battling the flesh because they never expect victory have lost sight of the victory that is ours through active identification with Christ on the cross.

The active execution of the sinful nature is followed by an active expression of new life in the Spirit: *Since we live by the Spirit, let us keep in step with the Spirit* (v. 25). Paul's combination of an indicative *(we live)* with an imperative *(let us keep in step)* is parallel to the same combination of indicative and imperative in verses 1 and 13. The indicative describes God's gift to us: freedom in Christ and life in the Spirit. The imperative expresses our responsibility: to protect our freedom from slavery under the law, to use our freedom to serve one another in love and to keep in step with the Spirit. *Keep in step* is a military command to make a straight line or to march in ordered rows. The Spirit sets the line and the pace for us to follow. Keeping in step with the Spirit takes active concentration and discipline of the whole person. We constantly see many alternative paths to follow; we reject them to follow the Spirit. We constantly hear other drummers who want to quicken or slow down our pace; we tune them out to listen only to the Spirit.

What does this mean in practice? Paul gives a general but practical application to the Galatian churches: *Let us not become conceited, provoking and envying each other* (v. 26). This verse and verse 15 clearly indicate that the community life of the Galatian churches had been torn apart by pride, which caused provoking and envying. In their concentration on keeping the law, the Galatian believers had become very competitive in their spiritual life, attempting to outdo each other. To *provoke* means to challenge to a contest. Some were so sure of their spiritual superiority that they wanted to prove it in a contest. Others felt spiritually inferior and resented those who made them feel that way. Both attitudes were caused by pride that could not tolerate rivals.

C. S. Lewis says that the devil laughs when he sees us overcome by pride: "He is perfectly content to see you becoming chaste and brave and self-controlled provided, all the time, he is setting up in you the Dictatorship of Pride—just as he would be quite content to see your chilblains cured if he was allowed, in return, to give you cancer. For Pride is spiritual cancer: it eats up the very possibility of love, or contentment, or even common sense" (Lewis 1943:45).

The only treatment for the cancer of pride is radical surgery: we must crucify the pride of sinful nature and be led by the Spirit, who alone has the power to overthrow the dictatorship of pride.

Freedom to Fulfill Responsibilities (6:1-10) "So where do we go from here? What practical steps can we take to resolve this crisis?" The couple asking these questions had taken a long time just to understand the crisis they were facing in their marriage. But now that they had gained some insights into the reasons for their conflict, they were ready to work to put things right.

So far Paul has led the Galatian believers to understand the historical and theological background for the crisis in their churches and given them general principles about life in the Spirit. Now he spells out specific responsibilities for those who are led by the Spirit so that they can rebuild their broken relationships.

6:1 The NRSV translation "if anyone is detected in a transgression" (NIV: *if someone is caught in a sin*) takes the phrase to mean that someone has been detected by others in the church ("caught in the act of a real transgression," so Betz 1979:296). But probably the

The responsibilities of those *who are spiritual* (v. 1) are directly related to the problem of division in the Galatian churches. We have already noted that when Paul describes the problem in the churches, he speaks of "biting and devouring each other" (5:15) and "provoking and envying each other" (5:26). The false teachers' campaign to force all the Gentile believers to become Jews would have divided the churches into hostile groups: the Jewish Christians who zealously campaigned for the necessity of circumcision and observance of the Mosaic law, the Gentile believers who zealously pursued the goal of living like Jews, and the Gentile believers who were not willing or able to live by the Mosaic law. Paul's list of responsibilities in this section shows how those who are truly led by the Spirit can bring healing and unity in their divided churches. The responsibilities include both the believers' corporate responsibilities to one another and the individual believer's personal accountability before God. Our public care for one another must be matched by integrity in our private walk before God. Note how corporate responsibilities and individual accountability are woven together in this section:

1. corporate: *restore him gently*

2. individual: *watch yourself*

3. corporate: *carry each other's burdens*

4. individual: *each one should test his own actions . . . each one should carry his own load*

5. corporate: *share all good things with his instructor*

6. individual: *do not be deceived . . . a man reaps what he sows*

7. corporate: *do good to all people, especially to those who belong to the family of believers*

Restoring Sinners, Examining Yourself (6:1) The first responsibility of those who are spiritual is the restoration of one who has sinned. Paul's conditional clause, *if someone is caught in a sin,* is framed in such a way as to point to the high probability that members of the church will sin. Sin in the church is not a hypothetical possibility, it is a reality. Paul and his readers both knew of believers in the church who had been

---

phrase "in a transgression" should be taken as the agent of entrapment: someone is overtaken, suddenly seized, by moral wrongdoing (so Longenecker 1990:273).

trapped by sin. The kind of sin in view here is not specified by Paul. It could be any one of the "acts of the sinful nature" (5:19-21). Paul is more concerned about the manner in which sinners in the church are treated than in the sin itself.

Moral failure in the church should not be a surprise, nor should it be considered fatal to the life of the church. What is important is the church's response when such failure occurs. The church may respond with harsh condemnation under the law. That response will crush the sinner and divide the church. That seems to have been what was happening in the churches in Galatia. The zealots for the law were merciless to sinners. But Paul wants to show that the occasion of sin is the opportunity for Spirit-led people to display the fruit of the Spirit in order to bring healing to the sinner and unity in the church.

In order to bring healing to the sinner, we must have a compassionate view of the one who has sinned. Paul does not define the kind of sin, but he does describe the consequence of sin. He views the sinner as one who *is caught in a sin.* When a person sins, other people are hurt; other people are victims of that sin. But we must remember that sinners themselves are also in some sense victims of sin. Abusers have also been abused. They have been overtaken, ambushed and seized by sin. Paul is not excusing the sinner of personal responsibility. But he is recognizing the terrible captivating force of sin. Just as Jesus said, "Everyone who sins is a slave to sin" (Jn 8:34), so now Paul says that the one who sins is trapped by sin. When we view moral offenders as those who are enslaved and entrapped, we have a compassionate attitude toward them. We will want to help them break the bondage of sin over their life.

Paul appeals to those *who are spiritual* to help the one who is caught in a sin. The *spiritual* are not some elite leadership group of spiritual giants. All the way through the letter Paul has been emphasizing that all of his converts in Galatia have received the Spirit (3:2-5, 14; 4:6, 29; 5:5, 16-18, 22-23, 25). All of those whom he addresses in 6:1 as *brothers* (by which Paul also means to include sisters, according to 3:28) are *spiritual,* since all who are the children of God have received the Spirit of God, according to 4:6. In other words, Paul is calling on all who have believed the true gospel and received the Spirit to be actively engaged in the ministry of restoration. One way to "keep in step with the Spirit" (5:25) is to restore one who has been trapped in sin.

Paul's directive to the spiritual is to *restore* the sinner. The verb *restore* could be used in physical or material contexts to signify resetting a broken bone or mending a torn net (see Mt 4:21; Mk 1:19). In spiritual contexts it meant perfecting in spiritual maturity and equipping for service (2 Cor 13:11; Eph 4:12; 1 Thess 3:10; Heb 13:21). In 1 Corinthians 1:10 Paul uses the same verb to express his desire that the divided church in Corinth "be perfectly united." The church had been broken and torn by divisions; it needed to be reset as a physician would reset broken bones and mended as a fisherman would repair torn nets. Here in Galatians 6:1 the verb *restore* calls for spiritual therapy so that a broken member of the body can once again work properly and perform its vital functions for the benefit of the whole body.

As long as any member of the body is broken, the whole body suffers. If the broken member of the body is amputated, the whole body suffers the loss. What is needed is restoration. The goal is the recovery of Christian brothers and sisters who have sinned so that the whole body will be healthy and productive again.

The exact methods of restoration are not described by Paul. They will vary according to the individual circumstances. But Paul does specify the manner of restoration: *restore him gently.* Literally, he says, restore "in a spirit of gentleness." "Gentleness" is one aspect of the fruit of the Spirit (5:23). Gentleness is not weakness; it is great strength under control. When gentle Christians see someone caught in a sin, they do not react with violent emotions or with arrogance. Even when sinful actions are scandalous and harmful, the emotions of the gentle person are under control, and the will of the gentle person is devoted to loving the sinner all the way to total recovery. Only the Holy Spirit can empower a person to respond in such a "spirit of gentleness."

Gentleness is not only consideration of the needs of others but also humility in recognition of one's own needs before God. So Paul moves from his command for restoration in the plural form, addressed to all, to a command for self-examination in the singular form, addressed to each individual. Corporate responsibility must be undergirded by the personal integrity of each individual before God. *But watch yourself,* Paul commands. Close observation of the inner life is necessary because everyone is vulnerable to temptation: *you also may be tempted.*

Awareness of my own vulnerability to moral failure not only puts me on guard against temptation but also enables me to respond with a spirit of gentleness to someone trapped in sin. The specific temptation in view here seems to be the temptation to react with arrogance and anger to the sin of the offender. Both 5:26 and 6:3-4 speak directly to this temptation. It is understandable that the Galatians' desire to live under the law (4:21) had produced moral watchdogs who were pouncing on sinners, "biting and devouring each other" (5:15). Their sins of conceit (5:26) and their "fits of rage" (5:20) were just as serious as the sin of the offender whom they were so harshly condemning.

In contrast, those who are led by the Spirit are aware that they are "only sinners saved by grace." All their responses to other sinners are guided by the personal insight of their own weakness and their total dependence on the redemptive love of God.

Carrying Burdens (6:2) Paul turns again to the corporate responsibility of all Spirit-led Christians: *Carry each other's burdens.* To "serve one another in love" (5:13) means to bear each other's burdens. After all, bearing burdens is the work of servants. The term *burdens* may refer to all kinds of physical, emotional, mental, moral or spiritual burdens: for example, financial burdens, the consequences of cancer or the results of divorce. The list of burdens crushing fellow Christians could be extended indefinitely. And no doubt the command to carry each other's burdens covers every conceivable kind of burden and calls for us to be sensitive enough to perceive even the unseen burdens that our brothers and sisters try to hide.

But in the context the command seems to be directed primarily to the burdens of sin referred to in 6:1. Sin always has a kind of domino effect in a person's life. The consequences of one moral failure can be multiplied almost indefinitely. For example, the sin of fornication, sexual union before marriage, may seem natural in the heat of passion. But then the young woman finds out that she is pregnant. And the burdens caused by a moment of sin start to multiply. My wife spends time each week with such young women. Without condoning the sin, she walks with

---

6:2 For recent discussion of *the law of Christ* see Longenecker 1964:183-90; Hays

these friends through their emotional turmoil and constantly reassures
them that she does not reject them and God does not reject them. She
tries to lead them to understand what got them into trouble in the first
place and how they can walk in moral freedom. She demonstrates her
loving acceptance not only through her warm, affectionate attitude toward them but also by getting involved in their lives. She helps them in
many ways to get ready for the birth of their children. She is often called
upon to be a mediator between them and their angry, upset families.
When the call comes in the middle of the night that her friend is in labor,
she goes to the hospital to encourage and comfort. In many ways she
bears their burdens.

When we carry each other's burdens in this way, we will *fulfill the law
of Christ* (v. 2). Paul's reference to the law of Christ here establishes a
striking contrast between fulfilling the law of Christ and keeping the law
of Moses. Keeping the law of Moses was the preoccupation of the law
teachers and all who followed their message in the Galatian churches.
But their focus was on how the observance of the Mosaic law separated
God's people, the Jewish nation, from "Gentile sinners" (2:15). Circumcision, purity and dietary laws, and sabbath and festival regulations were
boundary markers established by the law of Moses to preserve the
unique identity of the Jewish people. Maintaining the ethnic identity of
the Jewish people by observing these boundaries was viewed as a fulfillment of the purpose of the law of Moses. All who lived within these
boundaries would certainly enjoy the blessing of God; all who lived
outside of these boundaries by neglecting to observe them were under
God's curse. The law teachers insisted that the Gentile believers had to
live within these boundaries to be reckoned among the people of God.
Their zeal for the law made them intolerant of all nonconformists to
these standards.

Paul knew from his own experience in Judaism before his encounter
with Christ how destructive such zeal for the law could be (1:13-14). His
conflict with "false brothers" in the Jerusalem church (2:4-5) and with
Peter in the church at Antioch confirmed how quickly zeal for the law
could divide the church by classifying Gentile believers as "Gentile

1987:268-90; Barclay 1988:126-35; Garlington 1991:173-76.

sinners" and excluding them from the people of God. And now the zealous teachers of the law are inciting Christians in the Galatian churches to bite, devour, provoke and envy each other. Ironically, their preoccupation with keeping the Mosaic law resulted in breaking the central commandment to "love your neighbor as yourself."

In contrast to this attitude, Paul says that the law of Christ is fulfilled when his people carry the burdens of sinners! Serving sinners in the church, not separating sinners from the church, is the way to fulfill the law of Christ. There are two striking parallels between this reference to the law of Christ in 6:2 and the quotation of the love commandment from the law of Moses in 5:13-14. First, both "laws" are prefaced by parallel references to mutual service: "serve one another in love" and *carry each other's burdens.* Second, in both places Paul uses the term *fulfill* to describe what happens when mutual service is performed: "the entire law is summed up" (literally, "fulfilled") and *you will fulfill the law of Christ.*

These parallels in 5:13-14 and 6:2 indicate that despite the great contrast between keeping the law of Moses and fulfilling the law of Christ, there is also a close connection between Moses' law and Christ's law. Some have thought that this close connection indicates that the law of Moses and the law of Christ are one and the same. Others suggest that only the command to love, apart from any other external principles, is the law of Christ. Still others say that the love commandment defined and clarified by Christ's words and example is the law of Christ. The simple equation of the first interpretation does not work, since at least some aspects of the Mosaic law (such as dietary laws [2:14], sabbath/festival regulations [4:10] and circumcision [5:1-3]) are clearly not applicable to the Gentile churches. The second interpretation is too reductionistic, since both Jesus and Paul do define and apply the command to love in terms of external principles. The third interpretation is not entirely adequate either, because Paul does not simply substitute one code of precepts, the Mosaic law, with a new collection of rules based on Jesus' words and illustrated by Jesus' works. He does not simply replace the Mosaic law with a Messianic law. What such an interpretation misses is the centrality of the cross and the Spirit in Paul's ethical teaching.

The law of Christ is not so much the law taught by Christ, though of course he did teach and apply the love commandment. But when he taught the love commandment, he directed attention to himself: "Love each other as I have loved you" (Jn 15:12). The law of Christ is the love commandment fulfilled, confirmed and heightened in the life, death and resurrection of Christ. He loved sinners and gave himself for them (Gal 2:20); on the cross he bore the terrible burden of the law's curse against them (3:13); he set them free from the burden of the yoke of slavery under the law (5:1). Hence all who are united with Christ and are led by the Spirit will also fulfill the high standard of love established by the life, death and resurrection of Christ: like him, they will love sinners and carry their burdens. Serving one another in love in this way expresses Christ's love and so fulfills Christ's law.

And here is a delightful surprise: those who have received the Spirit and have been set free from the Mosaic law actually fulfill the requirements of the Mosaic law (see Rom 8:4) summed up in the single command "Love your neighbor as yourself"! Christlike, Spirit-empowered love fulfills the law.

Evaluating Your Work (6:3-5) Paul turns back again to the need for personal evaluation. Self-evaluation is necessary since there is always the danger of self-deception (v. 3). Personal evaluation must be made on the basis of a careful examination of one's own work, not on the basis of comparison with others (v. 4). Personal evaluation should clarify one's God-given mission in life (v. 5).

The warning against self-deception (v. 3) enlarges upon the warning against conceit (5:26) and temptation (6:1). The most serious spiritual danger of all is the self-delusion of pride: someone who *thinks he is something when he is nothing*. In the immediate context, Paul's rebuke must be aimed at those who thought so highly of their own status that they were unwilling to take the role of servants to carry the burdens of others. The Jewish Christian law teachers were so impressed with the importance of their mission of imposing the Mosaic law on Gentile believers that they had no time or interest to bear the sin-burdens of "Gentile sinners" who had come to Christ. The Gentile Christians were so intent on coming under the yoke of the law to establish their status as full members of the favored Jewish people that they did not lift a finger to help carry the burdens of their fellow Christians.

These zealots' pride in the law kept them from serving one another in love. And so, thinking themselves to be something, they were in fact nothing. For as Paul says in another letter, "if I . . . have not love, I am nothing" (1 Cor 13:2). Instead of loving one another, these zealots for the law were provoking one another (5:26). Their arrogance caused them to react in angry condemnation toward those who sinned, rather than to help restore sinners by carrying their burdens. No wonder then that Paul interweaves this warning against the self-delusion of pride with his call to service. Only those who are freed from delusions of their own importance will be able to serve others in love.

The only way to prevent self-deception is to examine the value of one's own work: *each one should test his own actions* (v. 4). The term Paul uses for *test* means to examine for the purpose of determining true worth. As the jeweler examines a precious stone under a magnifying glass in very bright light to determine its worth, so each Christian should scrutinize his or her actions to determine their true worth before God. The standard used for this evaluation is the law of Christ: the love of Christ expressed in his life and death and produced by his Spirit in all who believe in him. Paul has said that "the only thing that counts is faith expressing itself through love" (5:6). In other words, to examine one's work is to evaluate whether one's faith in Christ is expressing itself in Christlike actions of love.

If a Christian's careful examination of his life indicates that at least to some extent the love of Christ is being expressed through his actions, *then he can take pride in himself, without comparing himself to some-body else* (v. 4). At first reading these words seem to contradict what Paul has just said. If he has just warned against the self-deception of pride (v. 3), how can he now say that a Christian *can take pride in himself* (v. 4)? The NIV translation is a paraphrase of words that could be translated more literally as "then he will have a reason for boasting in himself and not by comparison with someone else." What Paul is doing here is contrasting two kinds of boasting. These two kinds of boasting are clar-ified a few verses later where Paul says, "They want you to be circum-cised that they may boast about your flesh. May I never boast except in the cross of our Lord Jesus Christ" (vv. 13-14). The law teachers were boasting on the basis of comparisons between the circumcised and the uncircumcised. They were the circumcised, the faithful people of God; the uncircumcised Gentile sinners were despised and excluded. But such boasting on the basis of a comparison of national differences or religious practices was all passé. "For in Christ Jesus neither circumcision nor uncircumcision has any value" (5:6). Paul vows never to boast in his own standing as a pedigreed member of the Jewish nation or in his zealous devotion to the Jewish traditions. But Paul the Christian continues to boast: he boasts in the cross of Christ (v. 14). That is his boast in 2:20, "I have been crucified with Christ and I no longer live, but Christ lives in me. The life I live in the body, I live by faith in the Son of God, who loved me and gave himself for me." Paul boasted in the cross because the cross was the ultimate display of the love of God for sinners. When we are united with Christ in his death and resurrection, that love of God for sinners can be expressed through us by the power of the Spirit. And that is the reason for Christians to boast!

It is important to stress that the boasting of Christians is not in the "flesh" (v. 13)—racial superiority and religious practices. Such boasting is like that of the Pharisee who said, "God, I thank you that I am not like other men—robbers, evildoers, adulterers—or even like this tax collector. I fast twice a week and give a tenth of all I get" (Lk 18:11-12). Notice how his boasting is based on the kind of comparison with others which Paul expressly forbids in 6:4. The boasting of Christians is paradoxical: it is a boasting in something considered shameful by the standards of the world. That the Messiah should suffer on a Roman cross was shameful. But by his cross "Christ redeemed us from the curse of the law by becoming a curse for us" (3:13). That Christians should serve each other by carrying each other's burdens was also considered shameful from the perspective of the world's values. But when the self-sacrificing love of Christ is seen in the actions of Christians, there is reason for boasting. Christians should celebrate that they can love because of their experience of the cross of Christ and the power of the Spirit.

When we engage in this kind of self-evaluation, we are renewed in our commitment to our own God-given mission: *for each one should carry his own load* (v. 5). Each of us has been called by God to carry our own load. There is no contradiction here with verse 2, which calls for Christians to carry each other's burdens. In fact, Paul uses two different Greek words to make a clear distinction between the *burden (baros)* and the *load (phortion)*. Though these two words are basically synonymous in other contexts, the change of nouns in this context indicates a change of reference. Verse 2 refers to the need to come to the aid of others who cannot carry the crushing burden of the consequences of their sin. Verse 5 refers to work given to us by our Master, before whom we will have to give an account of how we used the opportunities and talents he gave us to serve him. It is because we desire to fulfill our God-given mission in life that we learn how to carry the burdens of others. In other words, as Christians examine their actions to see if they reflect the love of Christ, they are at the same time led by that self-evaluation to consider how to serve others in love.

My father is a Christian businessman who constantly seeks to use his business as a way to serve others in love. All my life I have heard him pray and seen him work for opportunities to be a witness for Christ to his business associates and his customers by the way he serves them. He and his partners call their business ServiceMaster, which means "servants of the Master" and "masters of service." For me he will always be one of the best examples of one who serves the Master by serving others. In Paul's words, he carries his own load by carrying the burdens of others.

Supporting Teachers of the Word (6:6) Paul's challenge to fulfill one's God-given mission in life (carry one's own load) is now balanced by a recognition that some who are fulfilling their God-given mission in the church by teaching the Word need special support from the whole church. *Anyone who receives instruction in the word must share all good things with his instructor* (v. 6). Here we see an extremely practical application of the fruit of the Spirit. The love empowered by the Spirit is expressed in "goodness." In practice, that means sharing *good things* with our teachers.

This simple instruction to support teachers opens a window for us to see some important aspects of the life of the early church. First, we learn that formal instruction in the word was going on in the churches of Galatia. The title *catechist* is derived from the Greek word translated *instructor,* and the title *catechumen* is derived from the Greek word translated *anyone who receives instruction.* In other words, the early church had a catechism: formal instruction in basic Christian theology.

In our day there is often a negative reaction to any attempt to communicate doctrine or theology in the church. Of course academic speculation unrelated to the problems of everyday life is unprofitable. But Christian growth is dependent on sound biblical teaching. Paul saw the need for instruction in Christian theology and sought to encourage it by this practical guideline.

Second, Paul's guideline to support teachers indicates that Christian teaching was a full-time occupation that precluded the opportunity to earn money in some other profession. We know that Paul did at times support himself by his tentmaking. But he considered himself to be an exception to the rule. He thought that teachers in the church should work hard at their job of teaching and be well paid for it (1 Cor 9:14; 1 Tim 5:17). Sometimes full-time Christian teachers are made to feel inferior because they do not have a "real job." But why should those who work hard at teaching the Word of God feel that they are doing something less important than others who sell computer chips, unless the value of work is measured by the amount of money earned? That is surely a questionable measuring stick to use for determining the ultimate value of work. Paul places great value on the work of teaching the Word. It is the basis for strong churches and healthy Christians.

Third, we learn that when teachers faithfully give the Word to the churches and the churches give back good things, there is unity in the church. The command *must share* is a translation of an often-repeated Greek word: *koinōnia,* "fellowship" or "partnership." Undoubtedly Paul was concerned to encourage this kind of partnership in the Word because he knew that this letter alone could not bring about a complete resolution of the crisis in the Galatian churches. If the churches were to be united and strong again, there had to be a full-time teaching ministry in the church. Gifted teachers needed to devote themselves to an accurate interpretation and application of the "truth of the gospel." In order for them to do that, they needed to receive enthusiastic, generous support for their work of teaching. The same is true today.

Reaping What You Sow (6:7-8) The responsibilities listed so far present two opposite ways of life: the way of the Spirit and the way of the sinful nature. The absolute contrast between these alternatives has been developed throughout Paul's ethical appeal. Now it is the hour of decision. Now his readers must consider very carefully the consequences of choosing one way or the other. They cannot drift; they cannot remain neutral; they must decide whether they are going to walk by the Spirit or gratify the desires of their sinful nature. Since each individual must decide for himself or herself which way to live, Paul puts his challenge in a singular form.

Paul introduces his call for decision with a solemn warning based on an agricultural principle: *Do not be deceived: God cannot be mocked. A man reaps what he sows* (v. 7). When people think and act as if they will not reap what they have sown, or as if they will reap something different from what they have sown, they are deceiving themselves and mocking God. But since the inexorable law of reaping what is sown has always been proved true, the proverbial statement of warning *God cannot be mocked* is also true: no one can mock God and get away with it.

Yet there is a common tendency to think that there is one exception to this universal principle: "Though it proves true for everyone else, it is not true for me. I will not have to reap a harvest from the seeds I sow. I can sow whatever seed I want and still expect a good harvest." This common line of thought only proves the words of the prophet Jeremiah, "The heart is deceitful above all things and beyond cure" (Jer 17:9). Our capacity for self-deception is frightening. It is amazing how blind otherwise brilliant people can be to their own spiritual direction in life. In fact, the more brilliant people are, the more skilled they are at developing rationalizations to deceive themselves and to hide from God. The story of Adam and Eve's hiding from God behind their skimpy clothes and even skimpier excuses is our common human experience. Paul's warning needs to be heard, and to be heard often, to warn us against our most brilliant self-delusions.

Paul then applies the agricultural principle of reaping what is sown: *The one who sows to please his sinful nature, from that nature will reap destruction; the one who sows to please the Spirit, from the Spirit will reap eternal life* (v. 8). Here we are faced with a decision, a decision that determines our destiny. We are not victims of fate, bad luck or even predestination. Our destiny is determined by our decision: shall we sow to the sinful nature or to the Spirit? The old proverb is true: "Sow a thought, reap an act; sow an act, reap a habit; sow a habit, reap a character; sow a character, reap a destiny."

Those who are sowing to please the sinful nature are destroying relationships with others: they are biting, devouring, provoking and envying others (5:15, 26). In their arrogance they are seeking to pressure everyone to conform to the same ethnic customs and traditions. Churches are being torn apart and destroyed by ethnic rivalries and social competition. Sowing to please the sinful nature will always result in a harvest of destruction, a destruction of relationships with others and with God.

Sowing to please the Spirit means "serving one another in love" (5:13), restoring one who has been caught in sin (6:1), carrying the burdens of others (6:2), giving generously to those who teach in the church (6:6) and doing good to all (6:9). Sometimes sowing to the Spirit has been defined in terms of private, personal holiness, as if it were something done in a closet by oneself. But sowing to the Spirit in the context of Paul's teaching here involves building love relationships with others. Sowing to the Spirit cannot be done in isolation or separation from others. Carrying the burdens of others requires in-depth participation in their pain and sorrow. As we see in verse 9, sowing to the Spirit means *doing good* to others. If sowing to the sinful nature means selfish indulgence, then sowing to the Spirit means selfless service. The harvest of sowing to the Spirit is *eternal life*. The meaning of *eternal life* must be understood within the "already-not yet" structure of Paul's thought in this letter. From Paul's perspective, Christians have already been delivered from the present evil age (1:4) and are already in the new creation (6:15). But the battle between the Spirit and the sinful nature is not yet over (5:17). In Christ we already have new relationships with God and with one another: we now relate not as slaves but as children who call God Father (4:6-7); and we relate to one another not as people divided by racial, social and gender barriers but as people united in Christ (3:28). But since the battle between the Spirit and the sinful nature continues, we do not yet experience total harmony in these relationships. Those who continue to grow in these relationships by the power of the Spirit will ultimately experience the fullness of eternal life—perfect harmony in relationship with God and others.

Doing Good (6:9-10) Growth in our relationships does not happen

automatically; growth takes effort. Hard work is required if broken relationships are to be rebuilt. In these two verses Paul simply encourages
Christians to keep on working at building their relationships: *Let us not
become weary in doing good* (v. 9). To say that Paul's emphasis on faith
means that he was against works is obviously an inaccurate interpretation. Although he warned against relying on the works of the law as the
basis of blessing (3:10-14), he clearly taught that true faith expresses
itself through love (5:6) and in the hard work of serving one another
(5:13) and carrying each other's burdens (6:2).

One of the greatest obstacles to rebuilding broken relationships is
simply fatigue. We can easily lose heart and run out of strength when
we come up against the same problems over and over again as we deal
with others. Even Paul sounds discouraged when he talks about his
efforts to rebuild his relationship with the Galatian believers: "I fear for
you, that somehow I have wasted my efforts on you" (4:11). Paul recognized that fatigue and discouragement might cause Christians to throw
in the servant's towel and quit. So he presents two incentives to keep
us from giving up when we grow weary of serving others in love. First,
he assures us of a reward for doing good: *at the proper time we will reap
a harvest if we do not give up* (v. 9). Sometimes the harvest is experienced in this life. When we sow acts of love, we reap a harvest of love
in return. When we give generously and sacrificially to the needs of
others, we reap a harvest of gratitude as those needs are met. When we
sow the seed of God's Word in needy lives, we experience the joy of
response. But we must remember that reaping a harvest almost never
happens on the same day as sowing the seed. We may not even see a
harvest in this life from what we have sown. Nevertheless, we must never
give up, because we know that *at the proper time* our Master will return
and reward those who have been faithful servants.

Second, Paul motivates perseverance in service to one another by
reminding us that we are part of a great family: *Therefore, as we have
opportunity, let us do good to all people, especially to those who belong
to the family of believers* (v. 10). Although there are no limits placed on

---

6:10 A literal translation of the phrase *the family of believers* (NIV) is given by NASB: "the
household of the faith." The household metaphor is also used in Ephesians 2:19—
"members of God's household"—and speaks eloquently of the unity of all Christians as one

the scope of our service to *all people,* our priority is certainly to serve *the family of believers.* Here Paul picks up a central theme of his letter. All believers are children of Abraham by faith in Christ, the seed of Abraham (3.6-29). All believers enjoy the full rights of the children of God (4:4-7). All believers are the true children of the free woman; the heavenly Jerusalem is our mother (4:21-31). These great truths about the family of believers should motivate us to keep on doing good to our brothers and sisters in Christ. We belong to one another in one family, since we belong to Christ.

☐ Summary and Benedictions (6:11-18)

Careful studies of thousands of letters written in Paul's day have led to the discovery that most of the letters exhibit two styles of handwriting: a refined style of a trained secretary in the body of the letter and a more casual style of the author in the conclusion. It appears that it was common practice for letters to be written by dictation to secretaries. The author would personally write only a few lines at the end of the letter. Usually these concluding lines in the author's own hand summarized the cardinal points of the letter. Evidently the author's summary of the main points served not only to verify that he had actually made those points in his dictation to his secretary but also to underline the points he wanted his readers to remember. For this reason the conclusion of a letter often provided important interpretive clues to the entire letter.

We see this common practice of letterwriting in Paul's letter to the Galatians. At verse 11 he indicates that he has taken up the pen to conclude the letter: *See what large letters I use as I write to you with my own hand!* Since most of the members of the Galatian churches would not be able to see that there was a change in script when his letter was read to the churches, it was necessary for Paul to draw attention to the fact that he had picked up the pen and was writing the conclusion. Some have suggested that he wrote with *large letters* because he had poor eyesight or because he had a clumsy workman's hand. Such conjectures have little evidence to support them. It makes more sense to suppose

---

family in one household.

6:11 Bahr (1968:27-41) shows the similarities between Paul's subscriptions and those found in common Greek letters of his day.

that Paul wrote his conclusion in large letters because he wanted to emphasize to the Galatian congregations the importance of the main points of the letter in his concluding summary. In our day we might draw attention through boldface type or double underlining of the main points.

The main points to which Paul draws attention in his conclusion are points of contrast between himself and the false teachers who have misled the Galatian churches. To clarify these points of contrast, Paul first summarizes the position of the false teachers, the way of the world (vv. 12-13), and then restates his own position, the way of the cross (vv. 14-15). He concludes with a peace benediction (v. 16), a final statement of his authority (v. 17) and a grace benediction (v. 18).

The Position of the False Teachers—the Way of the World (6:12-13) Paul's character sketch of the false teachers in these two verses is the clearest picture we have of them in the entire letter. From his perspective, Paul detects three motives behind their mission to the Galatian churches. First, he says they are motivated by an obsession with outward uniformity: *Those who want to make a good impression outwardly are trying to compel you to be circumcised* (v. 12). Their emphasis on circumcision proved that they were concerned only about making everybody look the same *outwardly* (literally "in the flesh").

Although many Gentiles in Paul's day viewed circumcision as a barbarous custom, and most today would view it as merely an optional medical procedure, for the Jews it was the mark of belonging to the covenant people of God. Before we react too harshly to their preoccupation with such a personal mark "in the flesh," perhaps we should see how often outward uniformity in such things as mode of baptism, type of clothes and even hairstyle has become a major concern in our contemporary churches. Some teachers in our churches have also been so totally preoccupied by the "circumcision" or "cutting away" of certain external practices (smoking, drinking and dancing) that they seem relatively unconcerned with inward change. Since we can keep impressive statistics about outward conformity, we tend to focus on it: so many people came to church, so many people were baptized, so many people were well dressed and clean-cut, so many people voted for the right politician. What an impressive church! But all of this *good impression outwardly* may conceal proud, unrepentant hearts.

The second motive Paul detects in the false teachers is their concern for their own personal safety: *The only reason they do this is to avoid being persecuted for the cross of Christ* (v. 12). If Jewish Christians associated with Gentile Christians simply on the basis of their common belief that the cross of Christ is the only way of salvation, then they would be condemned by zealous Jews for negating the central Jewish teaching that only faithful, law-abiding Jews were included in the covenant of salvation. But if the Jewish Christians led Gentile Christians to live as faithful Jews should live by getting circumcised and observing sabbath regulations and dietary laws, then their zealous Jewish friends would compliment rather than condemn them for their association with Gentiles. For then it would be obvious that what really mattered to them was not their belief in a crucified Messiah, but identification with the Jewish nation.

Paul pierces through the hypocrisy of the false teachers to disclose a third motive driving their circumcision campaign. They were motivated by pride in their national identity: *Not even those who are circumcised obey the law, yet they want you to be circumcised that they may boast about your flesh* (v. 13). They were not really interested in the moral transformation of the Galatian Christians; they were not teaching circumcision and the law so that Galatian churches would attain new heights of spirituality. Their own inconsistency in following the law demonstrated that devotion to the law was not their basic motivation. What they were really interested in was being able to boast to fellow Jews that they were good Jews. "Look at all the Gentiles we have circumcised and brought into the Jewish nation," they boasted. They sought to earn credit with the Jews by proselytizing the Gentile Christians and forcing them to live like Jews. So what was most important to them was not encouraging the spiritual growth of others but maintaining their own national identity as zealous Jews. Because they were driven by their nationalistic pride, they were breaking the central command of the law: "Love your neighbor as yourself."

The Position of Paul—the Way of the Cross (6:14-15) In contrast to the prideful boasting of the false teachers, Paul quickly reaffirms his own commitment to the cross of Christ (v. 14) and the new creation in Christ (v. 15).

All prideful boasting is excluded by the cross of Christ, because identification with Christ in his death on the cross results in the death of all reasons for such boasting: *May I never boast except in the cross of our Lord Jesus Christ, through which the world has been crucified to me, and I to the world.* The world is characterized by prideful boasting about national identity, social status and religious practices. When I live in the world, my life will inevitably be characterized by such boasting. But when I die, the way of the world will no longer govern my life. My belief in the cross of Christ includes not only the realization that he died for me to rescue me from judgment under the law of God, but also the constant awareness that I must reckon myself to have died with him. My participation in Christ's death means that I no longer have any reason for boasting in myself, since the old self characterized by the values of the world is dead. This absolute renunciation of all prideful boasting because of total identification with the crucified Messiah is the aspiration of every true believer.

Belief in Christ leads not only to death but also to life: *Neither circumcision nor uncircumcision means anything; what counts is a new creation.* The reality of life in this new creation has been a theme of the entire letter. We have a new relationship with God: we are no longer slaves; we are his children and are free to address him by the Spirit as Father, *Abba* (4:6). We have a new relationship with one another: we are no longer imprisoned and divided by racial, social or gender barriers; we are now free and one in Christ (3:28).

The gospel is the rule for Paul's life; it determines both the spiritual and the social dimensions of his life. No longer does he relate to God or to others on the basis of his Jewish identity, but on the basis of his union with Christ in his death and resurrection.

The Benediction of Peace (6:16) Paul closes his letter with a benediction: *Peace and mercy to all who follow this rule, even to the Israel*

6:16 The relationship between *all who follow this rule* and *the Israel of God* is the subject of debate. It is grammatically possible to interpret this statement as a sharp distinction between the Gentile churches in Galatia and the Israel of God, or as an equation between the Gentile churches and the Israel of God. Those who argue for the former position interpret *Israel of God* as a reference to Jewish Christians (Schrenk 1949:94), to Jewish Christians who agree with the rule of verse 15 (Betz 1979:323), to the nation Israel (Davies 1977:10), to pious Israel within the Jewish nation (Burton 1921:358) or to those within Israel

of God (v. 16). Throughout the entire letter Paul has appealed to the gospel as the *rule* to follow in our relationship with God and with one another. *All who follow this rule* of the gospel will certainly experience peace and mercy in their relationship with God and in their relationships with others. For the gospel gives peace with God on the basis of his mercy. And all who have experienced the gospel work for peace with others by expressing the same compassion that they have received from God through Christ.

Some have interpreted Paul's reference here to *the Israel of God* as a reference to the national entity, the Jewish people. In other words, they interpret Paul as pronouncing a benediction both on those who believe in and live by the gospel and on the Jewish people. This interpretation is often defended on the basis of Paul's clear expression of compassion and hope for Israel in Romans 9—11. In that context Paul uses the title "Israel" to mean the Jewish people and promises God's blessing for Israel. But in the context of his letter to the Galatian believers, it appears that Paul is using *Israel of God* as a title for the Galatian believers. By giving this title to the Galatian Christians, he is able to summarize his major arguments that they are indeed the true children of Abraham (3:6-29), the children of the free woman, just as Isaac was (4:21-31). The false teachers were claiming that only those who followed the law belonged to Israel. Now Paul proclaims that all those who follow the gospel are the true *Israel of God.*

The Authority of Paul (6:17) After the benediction on all believers, Paul adds a warning directed against those who have been causing trouble in the churches. Paul takes their attack on the churches personally and gives the basis of his authority for stopping their attack: *Finally, let no one cause me trouble, for I bear on my body the marks of Jesus* (v. 17). The marks on Paul's body were the scars caused by his sufferings as an apostle of Christ. These marks demonstrated his unswerving loyalty

who will receive the good news of Christ, the mercy of God (Richardson 1969:82). Longenecker succinctly states the case for the latter interpretation: "In a letter where Paul is concerned to treat as indifferent the distinctions that separate Jewish and Gentile Christians and to argue for the equality of Gentile believers with Jewish believers, it is difficult to see him at the very end of that letter pronouncing a benediction that would serve to separate groups within his churches" (1990:298).

to the gospel of Christ. While the false teachers were preoccupied with the mark left by the ritual of circumcision, Paul drew attention to the marks left by the reality of serving Christ. Such a proof of devotion to Christ should silence all critics.

The Benediction of Grace (6:18) The final benediction sums up the message of the letter: *The grace of our Lord Jesus Christ be with your spirit, brothers.* The grace of Jesus Christ experienced in the spirit makes all believers true brothers and sisters in the family of God.

6:17 In Paul's day the term used for *marks (stigma)* referred to marks made in the branding of slaves or the tattooing of devotees of religious cults. The scars on Paul's body caused by the many beatings he received for faithfully preaching the gospel demonstrated that he belonged to Jesus, his Master and Lord; those scars were the *marks of Jesus* (see Bauer 1979:768).

Bibliography

Baasland, Ernst
   1984   "Persecution: A Neglected Feature in the Letter to the
                 Galatians." *Studia Theologica* 38:135-50.
Bahr, Gordon J.
   1968   "The Subscriptions in the Pauline Letters." *Journal of
                 Biblical Literature* 87:27-41.
Bammel, Ernst
   1960   "Gottes *ΔIAΘHKH* (Gal. III.15-17) und das jüdische
                 Rechtsdenken." *New Testament Studies* 6:313-19.
Barclay, John M. G.
   1987   "Mirror Reading a Polemical Letter: Galatians as a Test
                 Case." *Journal for the Study of the New Testament* 31:73-93.
   1988   *Obeying the Truth: A Study of Paul's Ethics in Galatians.*
                 Edinburgh: T & T Clark.
Barclay, William
   1962   *Flesh and Spirit: An Examination of Galatians 5:19-23.*
                 London: SCM.
   1976   *The Letters to the Galatians and Ephesians.* Rev. ed.
                 Edinburgh: St. Andrews Press.
Barr, James
   1966   *Old and New in Interpretation.* London: SCM.

Barrett, C. K.
   1982   *Essays on Paul.* London: SPCK.
   1985   *Freedom and Obligation: A Study of the Epistle to the
                 Galatians.* London: SPCK.
Barth, Markus
   1968   "Jews and Gentiles: The Social Character of Justification in
                 Paul." *Journal of Ecumenical Studies* 5:241-67.

Bassler, Jouette M.
1982   *Divine Impartiality: Paul and a Theological Axiom.* Society
of Biblical Literature Dissertation Series 59. Chico, Calif.:
Scholars Press.

Bauer, Walter
1979   *Greek-English Lexicon of the New Testament and Other
Early Christian Literature.* Translation and adaptation of
W. Bauer's 4th ed. by W. F. Arndt and F. W. Gingrich. 2nd
ed. revised by F. W. Gingrich and F. W. Danker. Chicago:
University of Chicago Press.

Behm, J.
1964   "διαθήκη." In *Theological Dictionary of the New Testament,*
2:104-34. Edited by G. Kittel and G. Friedrich. 10 vols.
Grand Rapids, Mich.: Eerdmans.

Belleville, Linda L.
1986   " 'Under Law': Structural Analysis and the Pauline Concept
of Law in Galatians 3.21—4.11." *Journal for the Study of the
New Testament* 26:53-78.

Bertram, G.
1964   "ἔργον." In *Theological Dictionary of the New Testament,*
2:635-52. Edited by G. Kittel and G. Friedrich. 10 vols.
Grand Rapids, Mich.: Eerdmans.

Betz, Hans Dieter
1979   *Galatians: A Commentary on Paul's Letter to the Churches
in Galatia.* Hermeneia. Philadelphia: Fortress.
1992   "Epistle to the Galatians." In *Anchor Bible Dictionary,* 2:872-
75. Edited by D. Freedman. 6 vols. New York: Doubleday.

Blass, F., and
A. Debrunner
1961   *A Greek Grammar of the New Testament and Other Early
Christian Literature.* 9th ed. Translated and edited by
R. Funk. Chicago: University of Chicago Press.

Borgen, Peder
1982   "Paul Preaches Circumcision and Pleases Men." In *Paul and
Paulinism: Essays in Honour of C. K. Barrett.* Edited by
M. D. Hooker and S. G. Wilson. London: SPCK.

Brinsmead,
Bernard H.
1982   *Galatians as Dialogical Response to Opponents.* Society of
Biblical Literature Dissertation Series 65. Chico, Calif.:
Scholars Press.

Bruce, F. F.
1982   *The Epistle to the Galatians.* New International Greek
Testament Commentary. Grand Rapids, Mich.: Eerdmans.

Buck, Charles H.
1951   "The Date of Galatians." *Journal of Biblical Literature*
                70:113-22.

Burton, Ernest
   De Witt
1921   *A Critical and Exegetical Commentary on the Epistle to the
                Galatians.* International Critical Commentary. Edinburgh: T
                & T Clark.

Byrne, Brendan
1979   *Sons of God—Seed of Abraham: A Study of the Idea of the
                Sonship of God of All Christians Against the Jewish
                Background.* Analecta Biblica 83. Rome: Pontifical Biblical
                Institute.

Callan,
   Terrance D., Jr.
1980   "Pauline Midrash: The Exegetical Background of Gal 3:19b."
                Journal of Biblical Literature 99:549-67.

Carson, D. A.
1986   "Pauline Inconsistency: Reflections on 1 Corinthians 9.19-23
                and Galatians 2.11-14." *Churchman* 100:6-45.

Cole, R. Alan
1989   *The Epistle of Paul to the Galatians.* Rev. ed. Tyndale New
                Testament Commentaries. Grand Rapids, Mich.: Eerdmans;
                Leicester, England: Inter-Varsity Press.

Cosgrove,
   Charles H.
1989   *The Cross and the Spirit: A Study in the Argument and
                Theology of Galatians.* Macon, Ga.: Mercer University Press.

Cousar, Charles B.
1982   *Galatians.* Interpretation. Atlanta: John Knox.

Cullmann, Oscar
1953   *Peter: Disciple, Apostle, Martyr.* Translated by F. V. Filson.
                London: SCM.

Dahl, Nils A.
1977   *Studies in Paul.* Minneapolis: Augsburg.

Davies, G. I.
1972   "Hagar, el-Hegra and the Location of Mount Sinai." *Vetus
                Testamentum* 22:152-63.

Davies, W. D.
1977   "Paul and the People of Israel." *New Testament Studies*
                24:4-39.
1984   *Jewish and Pauline Studies.* London: SPCK.

Deissmann, A.
1978   *Light from the Ancient Near East.* Reprint ed.; orig. 1909.
                     Grand Rapids, Mich.: Baker Book House.
Delling, G.
1964   "βασκαίνω." In *Theological Dictionary of the New Testa-
                     ment,* 1:594-95. Edited by G. Kittel and G. Friedrich. 10 vols.
                     Grand Rapids, Mich.: Eerdmans.
1971   "στοιχεῖον." In *Theological Dictionary of the New Testa-
                     ment,* 7:670-87. Edited by G. Kittel and G. Friedrich. 10 vols.
                     Grand Rapids, Mich.: Eerdmans.
Donaldson,
Terence L.
1986   "The 'Curse of the Law' and the Inclusion of the Gentiles:
                     Galatians 3.13-14." *New Testament Studies* 32:94-112.
1989   "Zealot and Convert: The Origin of Paul's Christ-Torah
                     Antithesis." *Catholic Biblical Quarterly* 51:655-82.
Donfried, Karl P.
1992   "Chronology: New Testament." In *Anchor Bible Dictionary,*
                     1:1016-22. Edited by D. Freedman. 6 vols. New York:
                     Doubleday.
Drane, John W.
1975   *Paul, Libertine or Legalist? A Study in the Theology of the
                     Major Pauline Epistles.* London: SPCK.
Duncan, George S.
1934   *The Epistle of Paul to the Galatians.* New York: Harper.

Dunn, James D. G.
1990   *Jesus, Paul and the Law: Studies in Mark and Galatians.*
                     Louisville, Ky.: Westminster/John Knox.
1993a   *The Epistle to the Galatians.* Black's New Testament
                     Commentary. Peabody, Mass.: Hendrickson.
1993b   *The Theology of Paul's Letter to the Galatians.* Cambridge,
                     U.K.: Cambridge University Press.
Ebeling, Gerhard
1985   *The Truth of the Gospel: An Exposition of Galatians.*
                     Translated by D. Green. Philadelphia: Fortress.
Ellis, E. Earle
1957   *Paul's Use of the Old Testament.* London: Oliver and Boyd.

Fitzmyer, J. A.
1978   "Crucifixion in Ancient Palestine, Qumran Literature and the
                     NT." *Catholic Biblical Quarterly* 40:493-513.

Fuller, Daniel P.
1980   *Gospel and Law: Contrast or Continuum?* Grand Rapids, Mich.: Eerdmans.

Fung, Ronald Y. K.
1988   *The Epistle to the Galatians.* New International Commentary on the New Testament. Grand Rapids, Mich.: Eerdmans.

Gaventa, Beverly R.
1986   "Galatians 1 and 2: Autobiography as Paradigm." *Novum Testamentum* 28:309-26.

Gill, David W. J.
1991   "Behind the Classical Façade: Local Religions of the Roman Empire." In *One God, One Lord in a World of Religious Pluralism,* pp. 72-87. Edited by A. Clarke and B. Winter. Cambridge, U.K.: Tyndale House.

Guthrie, Donald
1973   *Galatians.* New Century Bible Commentary. London: Marshall, Morgan & Scott.

Hall, Robert G.
1987   "The Rhetorical Outline for Galatians: A Reconsideration." *Journal of Biblical Literature* 106:277-87.

Hansen, G. Walter
1989a   *Abraham in Galatians—Epistolary and Rhetorical Contexts.* Journal for the Study of the New Testament Supplement Series 29. Sheffield, U.K.: Sheffield Academic Press.
1989b   "Paul's Three-Dimensional Application of Genesis 15:6 in Galatians." *Trinity Theological Journal* 1:59-77.
1990   "The Basis of Authority (Galatians 1 and 2)." *Trinity Theological Journal* 2:42-54.

Hanson,
Robert P. C.
1959   *Allegory and Event.* London: SCM.

Hays, Richard B.
1983   *The Faith of Jesus Christ: An Investigation of the Narrative Substructure of Galatians 3:1—4:11.* Society of Biblical Literature Dissertation Series 56. Chico, Calif.: Scholars Press.
1987   "Christology and Ethics in Galatians: The Law of Christ." *Catholic Biblical Quarterly* 49:268-90.
1989   *Echoes of Scripture in the Letters of Paul.* New Haven: Yale University Press.

Hemer, Colin
1990   *The Book of Acts in the Setting of Hellenistic History.* Edited by C. Gempf. Winona Lake, Ind.: Eisenbrauns.

Hendriksen, W.
1969   *The Epistle to the Galatians.* New Testament Commentary.
                Grand Rapids, Mich.: Baker Book House.
Holmberg, Bengt
1978   *Paul and Power.* Philadelphia: Fortress.

Howard, George
1979   *Paul—Crisis in Galatia: A Study in Early Christian Theology.*
                Society for New Testament Studies Monograph Series 35.
                Cambridge, U.K.: Cambridge University Press.
Jewett, Robert
1971   "The Agitators and the Galatian Congregation." *New
                Testament Studies* 17:198-212.
Kennedy, George A.
1984   *New Testament Interpretation Through Rhetorical Criticism.*
                Chapel Hill: University of North Carolina Press.
Kilpatrick, G. D.
1959   "Galatians 1.18 ἱστορῆσαι Κηφᾶν." In *New Testament
                Essays: Studies in Memory of T. W. Manson.* Edited by A. J.
                B. Higgins. Manchester, U.K.: Manchester University Press.
1983   "Peter, Jerusalem and Galatians 1:13—2:14." *Novum
                Testamentum* 25:318-26.
Kim, Seyoon
1982   *The Origin of Paul's Gospel.* Grand Rapids, Mich.: Eerdmans.

King, D. H.
1983   "Paul and the Tannaim: A Study in Galatians." *Westminster
                Theological Journal* 45:340-70.
Knox, John
1950   *Chapters in a Life of Paul.* Nashville: Abingdon.

Koptak, P. E.   "Rhetorical Identification in Paul's Autobiographical
1990   Narrative: Galatians 1.13—2.14." *Journal for the Study of the
                     New Testament* 40:97-115.
Lambrecht, Jan
1978   "The Line of Thought in Gal 2.14b-21." *New Testament
                Studies* 24:485-95.
1991   "Transgressor by Nullifying God's Grace: A Study of Gal
                2,18-21." *Biblica* 72:217-36.
Lewis, C. S.
1943   *Christian Behavior.* London: Centenary.

Lightfoot, J. B.
1957   *Saint Paul's Epistle to the Galatians.* Reprint ed.; orig. 1865.
               Grand Rapids, Mich.: Zondervan.

Lincoln, Andrew T.
1981   *Paradise Now and Not Yet.* Society for New Testament Stud-
               ies Monograph Series 47. Cambridge, U.K.: Cambridge Uni-
               versity Press; Grand Rapids, Mich.: Baker (1992).

Longenecker,
Richard N.
1964   *Paul, Apostle of Liberty.* New York: Harper & Row.
1975   *Biblical Exegesis in the Apostolic Period.* Grand Rapids,
               Mich.: Eerdmans.
1982   "The Pedagogical Nature of the Law in Galatians 3.19—4.7."
               Journal of the Evangelical Theological Society 25:53-61.
1984   *New Testament Social Ethics for Today.* Grand Rapids,
               Mich.: Eerdmans.
1990   *Galatians.* Word Biblical Commentary 41. Dallas: Word.

Luhrmann, Dieter
1992   *Galatians: A Continental Commentary.* Translated by O. C.
               Dean Jr. Minneapolis: Fortress.

Lull, David J.
1980   *The Spirit in Galatia: Paul's Interpretation of Pneuma as
               Divine Power.* Society of Biblical Literature Dissertation Se-
               ries 49. Chico, Calif.: Scholars Press.
1986   " 'The Law Was Our Pedagogue': A Study in Galatians 3.19-
               25." *Journal of Biblical Literature* 105:481-98.

Luther, Martin
1979   *A Commentary on St. Paul's Epistle to the Galatians.* Reprint
               ed. Grand Rapids, Mich.: Baker Book House.

Lyall, F.
1969   "Roman Law in the Writings of Paul—Adoption." *Journal of
               Biblical Literature* 88:458-66.

Lyons, George
1985   *Pauline Autobiography: Toward a New Understanding.*
               Society of Biblical Literature Dissertation Series 73. Atlanta:
               Scholars Press.

Martyn, J. Louis
1983   "A Law-Observant Mission to Gentiles: The Background of
               Galatians." *Michigan Quarterly Review* 22:221-35.
1985   "Apocalyptic Antinomies in Paul's Letter to the Galatians."
               New Testament Studies 31:412-20.

Matera, Frank J.
1992   *Galatians.* Sacra Pagina Series 9. Collegeville, Minn.: The
              Liturgical Press

Michaelis, W.
1967   "πάσχω." In *Theological Dictionary of the New Testament,*
              5:904-39. Edited by G. Kittel and G. Friedrich. 10 vols.
              Grand Rapids, Mich.: Eerdmans.

Mitchell, Stephen
1992   "Galatia." In *Anchor Bible Dictionary,* 2:870-72. Edited by
              D. Freedman. 6 vols. New York: Doubleday.

Moo, Douglas J.
1983   " 'Law,' 'Works of the Law' and Legalism in Paul."
              Westminster Theological Journal 45:73-100.

Neyrey, Jerome H.
1988   "Bewitched in Galatia: Paul and Cultural Anthropology."
              Catholic Biblical Quarterly 50:72-100.

O'Donovan, Oliver
1986   *Resurrection and Moral Order: An Outline for Evangelical
              Ethics.* Grand Rapids, Mich.: Eerdmans; Leicester, England:
              Inter-Varsity Press.

Räisänen, Heikki
1985   "Galatians 2.16 and Paul's Break with Judaism." *New
              Testament Studies* 31:543-53.

Ramsay, W. M.
1962   *St. Paul the Traveller and the Roman Citizen.* Reprint ed.;
              orig. 1897. Grand Rapids, Mich.: Baker Book House.

Rengstorf, K.
1964   "ἀπόστολος." In *Theological Dictionary of the New
              Testament,* 1:413-47. Edited by G. Kittel and G. Friedrich. 10
              vols. Grand Rapids, Mich.: Eerdmans.

Richardson, Peter
1969   *Israel in the Apostolic Church.* Society for New Testament
              Studies Monograph Series 10. Cambridge, U.K.: Cambridge
              University Press.
1980   "Pauline Inconsistency: 1 Corinthians 9:19-23 and Galatians
              2:11-14." *New Testament Studies* 26:347-62.

Ridderbos,
  Herman N.
1953   *The Epistle of Paul to the Churches of Galatia.* Translated by
              H. Zylstra. New International Commentary on the New
              Testament. Grand Rapids, Mich.: Eerdmans.
1975   *Paul: An Outline of His Theology.* Translated by J. R. De
              Witt. Grand Rapids, Mich.: Eerdmans.

Sampley, J. P.
1977 " 'Before God, I Do Not Lie' (Gal. 1.20): Paul's Self-Defense in the Light of Roman Legal Praxis." *New Testament Studies* 23:477-82.

Sanders, E. P.
1977 *Paul and Palestinian Judaism.* Philadelphia: Fortress.
1983 *Paul, the Law and the Jewish People.* Philadelphia: Fortress.

Schoeps, H. J.
1961 *Paul: The Theology of the Apostle in the Light of Jewish Religious History.* Translated by H. Knight. Philadelphia: Westminster Press.

Schreiner,
Thomas R.
1984 "Is Perfect Obedience to the Law Possible? A Re-examination of Galatians 3:10." *Journal of the Evangelical Theological Society* 27:151-60.

Schrenk, G.
1949 "Was bedeutet 'Israel Gottes'?" *Judaica* 5:81-94.
1964 "δικαιόω." In *Theological Dictionary of the New Testament,* 2:211-25. Edited by G. Kittel and G. Friedrich. 10 vols. Grand Rapids, Mich.: Eerdmans.

Schütz, John H.
1975 *Paul and the Anatomy of Apostolic Authority.* Society for New Testament Studies Monograph Series 26. Cambridge, U.K.: Cambridge University Press.

Schweizer, E.
1972 "υἱοθεσία." In *Theological Dictionary of the New Testament.* Edited by G. Kittel and G. Friedrich. 10 vols. Grand Rapids, Mich.: Eerdmans. 8:398.

Siker, Jeffery S.
1991 *Disinheriting the Jews: Abraham in Early Christian Controversy.* Louisville, Ky.: Westminster/John Knox.

Smail, Thomas A.
1980 *The Forgotten Father.* London: Hodder and Stoughton.

Smit, J.
1989 "The Letter of Paul to the Galatians: A Deliberative Speech." *New Testament Studies* 35:1-26.

Stendahl, Krister
1976 *Paul Among Jews and Gentiles.* Philadelphia: Fortress.

Stott, John R. W.
1968   *The Message of Galatians.* Downers Grove, Ill.; Leicester,
               England: InterVarsity Press.
Taylor, George M.
1966   "The Function of πίστις Χριστοῦ in Galatians." *Journal of
               Biblical Literature* 85:58-76.
Watson, Francis
1986   *Paul, Judaism and the Gentiles.* Society for New Testament
               Studies Monograph Series 56. Cambridge, U.K.: Cambridge
               University Press.
Wenham, David
1985   "Paul's Use of the Jesus Tradition: Three Samples." In *The
               Jesus Tradition Outside the Gospels.* Edited by David
               Wenham. Gospel Perspectives 5. Sheffield, U.K.: JSOT Press.
Westerholm,
Stephen
1988   *Israel's Law and the Church's Faith.* Grand Rapids, Mich.:
               Eerdmans.
Williams, Sam K.
1987   "Justification and the Spirit in Galatians." *Journal for the
               Study of the New Testament* 29:91-100.
1988   "Promise in Galatians: A Reading of Paul's Reading of
               Scripture." *Journal of Biblical Literature* 107:709-20.
Wrede, William
1907   *Paul.* Translated by E. Lummis. London: Green.

Wright, N. T.
1991   *The Climax of the Covenant: Christ and the Law in Pauline
               Theology.* Edinburgh: T & T Clark.
Young, N. H.
1987   "*Paidagōgos:* The Social Setting of a Pauline Metaphor."
               Novum Testamentum 29:150-76.
Ziesler, John A.
1972   *The Meaning of Righteousness in Paul: A Linguistic and
               Theological Inquiry.* Society for New Testament Studies
               Monograph Series 20. Cambridge, U.K.: Cambridge Univer-
               sity Press.